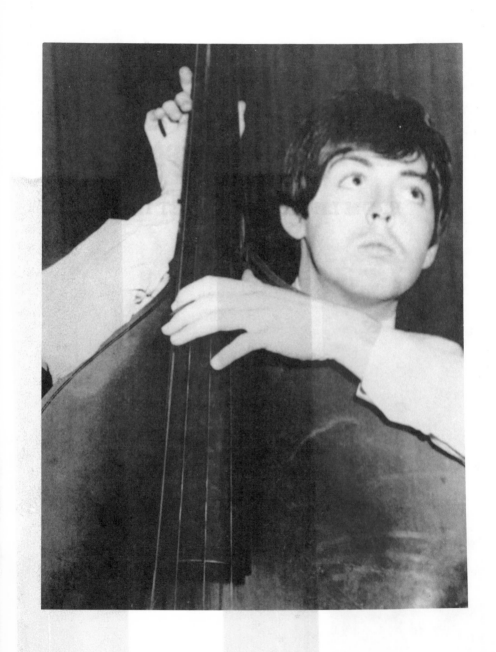

PAUL McCARTNEY:
FROM LIVERPOOL TO LET IT BE

BY
HOWARD A. DEWITT

Introduction by
Mike Lefebvre

HORIZON BOOKS
PO BOX 3083
FREMONT, CA. 94539
1992

PUBLISHED BY: HORIZON BOOKS
    P.O. BOX 3083
    FREMONT, CALIFORNIA 94539
    PHONE: (510)-657-6439

ISBN NO. 0-938840-04-5

LIBRARY OF CONGRESS CATALOG
CARD NUMBER: 92-74360
FIRST PRINTING, NOVEMBER, 1992

Book design, layout, photo assistance and computer advice by Jim McCue
Photo consultation and picture layout by Lee Cotten
Consulting Editors: Mike Lefebvre, Neal F. Skok and Bruce Wilson
Cover Design by Mick Gray
Printed in the U.S.A. on recycled paper.
BOOK TITLE COURTESY OF MARK LAPIDOS

TABLE OF CONTENTS

Paul McCartney

INTRODUCTION
BY
MIKE LEFEBVRE

The Beatles are dead. Some say it happened on December of 1980. Others prefer blaming it on John's dragon lady. Most will agree that it was McCartney versus Lennon, Harrison, and Starkey in 1970. The truth of the matter is the Liverpool musicians had too much too soon and realized that they had achieved all they could as a group.

1968 is a classic example that found all four struggling with their own identity and creativity. Their album, **The Beatles**, aka the **White Album**, may not of been the first time they had a need to do their "own thing." However, it was an impetus for the clock to quickly wind down, but with an added punch.

John had his own ideas. Paul saw fit to continue with little help from John. George was setting his niche as songwriter with, "Savoy Truffle" and "Piggies." He would not only prove his worth to the world, but most importantly to himself. And Ringo? Ringo was bored. He felt he wasn't needed. His tune, "Don't Pass Me By" had more truth to it than just the title. His calling as an actor and media personality was just around the corner. All four were headed for a divorce.

Paul, like the others, saw what was going down. Unlike the others, he stepped in as before, to take charge; and as before, take the criticism that was thrown back his way. Paul wanted the band to stay together. To do this, he felt the need to exercise the control he felt was needed, but Paul couldn't understand the other's resentment.

Earlier on, Paul always saw that The Beatles needed direction. From the time he plucked away playing Little Richard tunes for John at their first meeting, his suggestions took the boys through the streets of Liverpool and into the satellites via the "Our World" broadcast with Lennon's "All You Need Is Love." Paul was always there as the spokesperson, whether it was introducing the playlist at concerts, telling management how things should be run, or "running" the other three when all they wanted was to be alone. Paul simply had be in the forefront. Great for fans, but not for all around him. Anything good he did at Apple, didn't usually set well with the others. Everyone just wanted Paul to stick to his own job, a member of the band.

Paul McCartney: From Liverpool To Let It Be explores what author Howard A. DeWitt feels were the influences in Paul's life. Early on, we learn things about McCartney that tells the readers what he is made of and how his chemistry added that perfect ingredient for the most famous band of all time. This biography could of centralized itself around any one of the

Beatles. Since Paul had taken reign during the most crucial time in the Band's history, it is only fitting to see how Paul rode shotgun in handling a newly formed company (Apple), how Paul handled himself for that matter through the psychedelic drug culture, and most importantly, how Paul "managed" his fellow three band members with perfectionist nature.

Paul didn't break up the Beatles. The Beatles broke themselves up. They showed up, did their thing, and left a legacy for us to remember among the screams and applause for generations to come.

PREFACE: FROM LIVERPOOL TO LET IT BE

In 1968 Paul McCartney assumed control of the Beatles' musical and business reins. With an album entitled **The Beatles (The White Album)**, Paul emerged as the key influence upon the group. In 1970 when the group broke up there was little mention of McCartney's prominence in the Beatles' business and music affairs. The popular press and electronic media were too busy examining McCartney's private life to notice his ascendancy.

By concentrating upon 1968 it is possible to see not only McCartney's dominance, but some of the reasons why the Beatles eventually broke up. Because of Paul's long standing song writing and musical partnership with John Lennon, the myth of a harmonious songcrafting relationship has dominated most Beatle books. We now know that the working conditions surrounding the Lennon and McCartney partnership were not ideal ones. They fought incessantly. Outside pressures caused petty differences. The bureaucratic structure created by their manager, Brian Epstein, led to a disorganized and decentralized business empire. One that was never straightened out during Epstein's lifetime.

The Beatles had problems, but generally Paul and his mates were usually on good terms. Because of stardom, however, it was a rocky relationship. During the 1960s the Beatles revolutionized the rock and roll world. They became international celebrities and the press scrutinized their lives. To biographers, however, McCartney has been the most enigmatic Beatle.

Paul is very conscious of his public image. For years the media trashed his life, invaded his privacy and attacked his character. So journalists find it difficult to penetrate his protective shell. A case in point of McCartney's careful control of the press occurred when Brian Epstein's biographer complained that McCartney had little to say about his old manager. Ray Coleman's, **The Man Who Made The Beatles: An Intimate Biography of Brian Epstein**, published in 1989, mentions McCartney only seventeen times. Coleman argues that McCartney was "the most combative" Beatle.

Other McCartney biographies by Chet Flippo, Chris Salewicz and Chris Welch present new research, and incorporate the latest findings in the history of rock and roll music. Yet, these books are unable to reveal the "real Paul McCartney." These books have another common deficiency, they fail to examine the Beatles' business career and the fate of the Apple Corporation.

Paul McCartney's life is so fascinating that biographers have approached it from every nook and cranny. This book scrutinizes the musical direction and business skill that McCartney brought to the Beatles. In doing so it is necessary to analyze his family, personal relationships, as well as the books, music, art and other cultural artifacts that shaped his life. By concentrating upon the year 1968, Paul's role in the Beatles affairs during the period of the **White Album** is analyzed in relationship to the group's career.

The Beatles were so upset with McCartney during the production of the **White Album** that they began to talk openly to the press. In 1969 George Harrison, in an interview with Canadian journalist Ritchie Yorke, suggested that the Beatles' "peak for playing was in Hamburg." Anyone who has listened to the Hamburg Tapes would wonder what Harrison meant. An enraged Harrison was taking a nasty swipe at McCartney. McCartney was in charge and Harrison disliked his old mate. John and Ringo were often upset when the press called Paul the "cute Beatle."

There were also petty hatreds that developed over McCartney's ability to manipulate the press. His songwriting success with Lennon created envy. He was called "too pop" by some and "too commercial" by others. Yet, the Beatles meteoric American record sales in 1964 depended equally upon McCartney's songwriting input. Yet much of the credit went to John Lennon. Not only did Lennon dominate press accounts of the Beatles' success, but he relegated McCartney to a secondary position. The press unwittingly intensified the differences that drove Paul and John apart.

Clive Epstein told me in a series of interviews in 1983 that Brian admired McCartney musically but he couldn't understand his preoccupation with business matters. "My brother listened to Paul, but I don't think he heeded his advice," Clive Epstein remarked. Consequently, the real McCartney has eluded biographers. Fame forced Paul to retreat. During his last two years with the Beatles, he built a wall around his career. It was not until the 1970s and 1980s that McCartney warmed up to the press. Then it was in an atmosphere that he controlled in form and context.

The new McCartney was evident during the Wings period when he arrived in Los Angeles for a concert. An interview was scheduled with Joe Benson of KLOS and when the LA disc jockey arrived he found McCartney in complete control. "I've never seen anyone who had a better grasp of this business," Benson remembered. "I was comfortable and didn't find him to be the uncooperative ogre that the press described."

Although John Lennon, George Harrison and Ringo Starr contributed enormously to the Beatles' success, McCartney evolved into the Beatle who kept the music and business flowing in a pop, commercial direction. From the standpoint of continued show business monetary success, Paul deserves a great deal of credit. Largely because it was difficult for Paul to step in to guide the Beatles' affairs. After all John founded the band. It was presumptuous for Paul to even consider taking over the Beatles. He did so reluctantly in 1968 when the others left the kingdom to follow their own interests.

The group that McCartney once referred to in an early Liverpool radio interview as "John's band" was turning out music by the mid-1960s that was more and more the product of McCartney's musical mind. It isn't that John Lennon wasn't important, the simple fact is that he grew tired of the Beatles. Lennon continued to contribute excellent music but he was preoccupied with other ventures. Once Lennon turned to other interests McCartney took over the musical reins by default.

The reasons for McCartney's emergence as the Beatles' leader are complex and varied ones. From his earliest Beatle days, he was a singularly talented, charismatic and independent singer-songwriter. Contrary to popular myth, McCartney didn't need Lennon to write songs. But Paul did create a strong working relationship with John and this was beneficial in the songcrafting process. From their first meeting Lennon and McCartney had a solid respect for each other. John was a slow, cumbersome songwriter and found it difficult to make decisions. Whereas Paul was a songstylist who wrote in an obsessive-compulsive manner. By crafting songs with John, Paul developed a musical vision that merged with his bandmates to produce some of the finest rock tunes of the 1960s. "I don't think Paul McCartney's music would have had the bite to it had it not been for John Lennon," Bob Wooler remarked. "It was John's musical and lyrical changes which made Paul's songs smoke." Wooler's comment is reflected by nearly everyone close to the Beatles. "I don't think John could have written so well without Paul," Clive Epstein remarked. "I saw Paul as the main contributor in most Lennon-McCartney songs," Joe Flannery remarked. The sense of discipline in Paul's life and the need to write songs led to a leather satchel full of potential hit records.

During the early years as John's loyal friend, Paul graciously deferred to Lennon---the "Chief Beatle." It was out of loyalty to John, the band's founder, that McCartney didn't interfere with the groups early direction. Clearly, Paul saw new vistas. His was a pop, musical hall vision which clashed immediately with Lennon's ideas about roots rock and roll music. While roots rock was important to Paul, he had a broader vision.

To understand the rise of McCartney as the Beatles' leader, it is necessary to examine the relationship between John and Paul as well as the background that McCartney grew up in during World War II and its aftermath. The personality that Paul developed in his early life had a strong impact upon his later years.

PROLOGUE: CLIVE EPSTEIN AND PAUL MCCARTNEY FROM LIVERPOOL TO LET IT BE

Liverpool is a dank, dirty seaport city. To the casual observer it appears as a metropolis in a state of terminal decay. The streets are deserted early in the evening and there is an air of gloom. This initial Liverpool picture, however, is a deceptive one. Beneath the high unemployment rate, the frenetic popularity of soccer, the prevalence of rock and roll bands and the large number of pubs and small restaurants there is a veritable paradise.

Local citizens pride themselves on a relaxed life. They view the hustle and bustle of Londoners with disdain. Since the 1920s Liverpool has been a boom and bust city with economic cycles that at time spew forth prosperity and then there is a massive depression. As a result, the local character is an adjustable one. The Manchester ship canal often surpasses Liverpool economically. London has a stranglehold on goods and Birmingham's industrial concerns have hurt the economy. Despite these difficulties there is a strong sense of local nationalism.

One reason for Liverpool's pride is the birth of the Mersey beat. In the early 1960s this rock and roll sound burst upon the English and eventually the American rock music world. No group was more representative of the Mersey sound than the Beatles. Although they were only one of many local bands, the Beatles paved the way for English rock and roll in a world market. This didn't surprise Liverpudlians. They knew that a special sound began to form in the late 1950s.

In this atmosphere there were a number of people who were an integral part of the Beatles' early success. Most significant among these early individuals is Allan Williams. Now something of a joke in Liverpool, Williams is commonly referred to as "the man who gave away the Beatles." He was their first manager, but the band quickly signed with Brian Epstein. Yet, it is important to remember Williams. He is typical of local citizens in a blue collar city that thrives on drink.

Williams was one of my most revealing interviews. I met him during an afternoon drinking session at a private club. Liverpool pubs are closed in the afternoon and Bob Wooler had graciously taken me to meet Williams. I wasn't quite prepared for what happened. I entered the club in my best double breasted blue blazer complete with a Brooks Brothers tie.

"Nice to meet you Allan," I intoned.

"You asshole," Williams hollered the day that I met him. "I think all you blimy Americans are crazy."

I drank my beer and wondered what Hunter Thompson would do. In fact, I wondered where Charles Manson was when I really needed him. Then Allan Williams became another person. I felt like I was in the middle of a bad dream.

Williams smiled bought me a drink and offered to sell me Beatle memorabilia. Bob Wooler chimed in: "Be careful, he sells fake goods." Wooler chuckled and walked to the bar for another drink. I wasn't sure what to do. Finally, I left the bar with Williams and went to his house.

In Williams' garage I found Beatle items from a local variety store that were manufactured in 1982. So much for Allan Williams' contribution to Beatle history. For every charlatan like Williams there are many open and honest people. It was not long before I met more than two dozen local Liverpudlians who wove tales of the Beatles. They described Liverpool as a city which thrives on the average, the mundane and maintains a predictable pace of life. "I would say that Liverpool is boring," Bob Wooler, the Cavern compere remarked. "That's why we all live here." To many of the young people Liverpool is boring, out of the English mainstream and too confining. This is one reason that rock bands flourish and the young men play music in order to move to London and eventually America.

During my lengthy stay in Liverpool I was continually reminded about the Beatles' past. I was on a sabbatical leave from my position as a Professor of History at Ohlone College in California, and I didn't want the dean to think that I wasn't working. So I wandered off to see every sight in town.

As I walked to my room at the Aachen Hotel I gazed at the Empire Theater on Lime Street. An older man walked up and started talking to me. It was Charlie Lennon, John's Uncle, and he wove spellbinding tales of local Beatle lore. I imagined what it must have been like for the Quarry Men on June 9, 1957 to audition for Carroll Levis's television show. I remembered that Paul McCartney talked to touring performers like Lonnie Donegan at the Empire Theater and these conversations helped to strengthen McCartney's resolve to pursue a musical career. Then on October 28, 1962 The Beatles played the Empire for their growing legion of fans.

A brisk walk took me to the Adelphi Hotel where I had a drink in the bar and talked with the locals. The Adelphi is the Grand Duchess of Liverpool hotels. Across the street at Lewis's Store on Ranalegh Street I chuckled at the thought of the Beatles playing at a November 28, 1962 dance for the staff. Paul McCartney worked driving one of the store's delivery vans. History is everywhere in Liverpool.

It is in the pubs that the best historical sources are discovered. So I hopped a taxi to Ye Crack on Rice Street. This was the local pub that John Lennon walked down an alley to after his classes at the nearby Liverpool College of Art. The patrons in Ye

Crack thought that I was nuts but they humored me with tales of the Beatles. Then I took another cab to the Grapes Pub on Mathews Street. This was affectionately called "the Beatles Pub" because of its proximity to the Cavern. After drinking a few more rounds with the locals I went home to bed. The tales of the Beatles' exploits swirled in my head. It was obvious that I had material for more than one book.

The next day I began my research in earnest. I took a cab to the Cavern on Mathews Street and Bob Wooler walked me through the cool basement cellar which brought the Beatles toward their earliest fame. Bob laughed as he described these days. He showed me the three separate sections where the audience sat and we walked through what he called the backstage area. Over a lengthy lunch, Wooler talked about how things changed when the Beatles left Liverpool. He lamented the Beatles' move to London. He was asked to go along, but he stayed in Liverpool. "I think the Apple experiment was the beginning of the end for the boys," Wooler remarked. "But then you're not doing a book about Apple are you?" I told him that I wasn't. Yet, he had planted a seed. I wondered why no one had really discussed Apple. I asked Wooler about Apple Records and he told me to see Clive Epstein. After some small talk, Wooler went to the telephone and arranged a meeting with Brian's brother.

In May, 1983, as I was sitting in Liverpool's Holiday Inn waiting for my appointment with Clive Epstein, I reflected on the conversation with Bob Wooler. He had planted a seed; one which led me directly to the Apple experiment. As I was thinking about Apple the waitress walked up and asked what I would like to drink. An Anchor Steam beer was out of the question. Since I wasn't in San Francisco I ordered a Watneys and sat back in my big comfortable chair. A week earlier I had lugged my suitcase to the Aachen Hotel.

After seeing the locals shrines to the Beatles, I was beginning the research for my book, **The Beatles: Untold Tales**. The research led me to a number of helpful people. Joe Flannery and Bob Wooler put me in touch with Clive Epstein whom I hoped to feature in my book, but things didn't work out that way. Clive didn't want an in-depth profile. To my surprise what followed was one of the most interesting interviews of my career. Very little of the interview centered around the Epstein's rather it was a Paul McCartney interview.

As Clive Epstein walked into the pub at the Holiday Inn, the waitress and a few patrons looked at him with obvious admiration. He smiled, walked to my table, shook my hand and sat down. Clive was slightly overweight and appeared ill at ease. He had dark hair, a foreboding look and a precise manner of speaking. I immediately developed a dislike for Clive. I found him stuffy, arrogant and condescending.

After some small talk he set down a number of rules.

There were parts of the conversation that I could not use in my book. These reminiscences related to drugs, sex and business problems. After a three hour conversation, I found Clive to be a warm, caring individual in matters relating to his brother, the Beatles and the historical record. When we concluded our conversation he invited me to the house for dinner. I declined. The interview hadn't touched on the topics that I was researching for **The Beatles: Untold Tales**. Out of respect to Clive I included a short, if incomplete, chapter on him in my book.

What resulted from the Holiday Inn session with Clive Epstein was a penetrating analysis of the Beatles business problems. During our conversation he referred to the Apple years as "a psychedelic hangover." I never forgot these words. They haunted me for years, and this book resulted from Epstein's sage observations. **Paul McCartney: From Liverpool To Let It Be** is the product of my initial conversations with Epstein.

During our lengthy meeting he talked about Paul McCartney's early life, the Beatles formative years and the "Apple fiasco." What stunned me about Clive's observations was his lack of knowledge about rock and roll music. He also had no interest in it. His primary concern was with marketing the Beatles. During our talks he cried out psychologically about his brother's life. When Clive mentioned his brother it was with phrases such as "the trouble that we had with Brian."

After a number of drinks Clive loosened up and began to talk about Brian's death. He ranted and raved about the Peter Brown book, **The Love You Make: An Insider's Story of The Beatles**.

"Peter Brown used my brother," Clive remarked. "He put together a string of half truths, innuendoes and outright lies. Peter made a lot of money with this tripe. Brian hired him and made him an important person. This book is Brown's thanks." Clive looked out toward the middle of the room and nervously signaled for another drink.

I stirred nervously in my chair. "What types of things have bothered you the most about Brian and the Beatles?" I asked.

He scratched his nose, took a sip of his drink, looked at the waitress and searched for an answer. "I think that the journalists have concentrated too heavily upon Brian's personal life," Clive reflected. "They aren't concerned with the facts. My brother, for example, didn't get on with Paul very well. No one has written about that." Clive stopped. He looked at me pensively. "But you haven't come for that story, have you?"

I didn't know what to say. Finally, I mustered up something. "Tell me about Paul McCartney and Apple."

"Find out for yourself," Clive chuckled. "There is a story there and a good one." He stopped. "Let me tell you my thoughts on the business end." For the next hour Clive talked about Apple Records, London night life (of which he sampled very little), the individual Beatles and Paul. The germs of another book resulted from this conversation. Before we shook hands and I left, Clive gave me Horst Fascher's phone number in Hamburg. This proved to be an important asset. But there were other sights to see in Liverpool. I spent the next week reliving the old Beatle days.

During my spare time I drank beer with Charlie Lennon. John's Uncle is a marvelous old gentleman who revels in his association with his famous kin. Uncle Charlie spent hours regaling me with tales of the old days. He suggested that the Beatle story had as much to do with Hamburg as Liverpool. "You look in that German city, it will tell you a lot," Lennon remarked.

The six weeks that I spent in Liverpool produced gossip, humor, hard facts and a wealth of stories. Now I was off to Hamburg for a new round of interviews. It had been more than two decades since the Beatles played on the famed Reeperbahn at the Indra, Top Ten and Star Club. Yet, surprisingly, many people close to the Beatles remained in this German seaport city. The untold tales of Beatle intrigue continued, and I discovered a new cast of characters.

The contrast between Hamburg and Liverpool is a stark one. The German city is wide open, vulgar, boisterous and wildly sexual. Drugs, alcohol and the pleasures of the skin are everywhere. The loud Germans can hardly contain their boisterous behavior and the presence of a full time cabaret atmosphere makes Hamburg a mecca for the young.

Horst Fascher, the Beatles bodyguard, still lives in Hamburg. He is a well to do tennis shoe importer and continues to promote rock music. With a stable and loving family, he is a wealthy man who is no longer the picture of the stern boxer who once killed a man in the ring with his fists.

He remembers the Beatles with a personal fondness and above his couch in the living room of his home is a huge drawing of Paul McCartney. As I conducted the interview in Fascher's house, Paul was looking over my shoulder. After three hours of interviews I had the material for **The Beatles: Untold Tales**. Casually, I asked Horst about the Apple years. Like the others he talked about the manner in which the Apple experiment splintered the Beatles. He suggested I talk to Tony Sheridan.

We walked out front, got into Fascher's car and drove to see Sheridan. The next night I had dinner with Tony and we talked at length about the Beatles. The dinner with Sheridan was the highpoint of my Hamburg trip. We drank copious amounts of wine and ate spaghetti until the wee hours of the morning. After reliving the days on the Reeperbahn, Sheridan gave his opinions on the Apple experiment. "I think that McCartney used the business side of the Beatles to get rid of his mates," Sheridan remarked. "It's a story someone should tell."

Once again I was confronted by the Apple years. I thanked Tony for his time and left for the Blockhutte. This is a small country western bar where the bar maid, Corey, still serves drinks to the locals. She was one of McCartney's early Hamburg girl friends. After three beers Corey and I were great friends. She talked at length in her broken English about Paul and we laughed at the tales of the early days. She had never heard of Apple Records. I was relieved but perplexed.

Back in London I began looking over the Apple business sites. No one in London seemed to care about the Apple experiment. I called a number of people close to the Beatles and they wanted to talk about themselves. So I took pictures, saw the sights and took the train to the Colindale Library. For two weeks I scanned the files of **Disc**, **Melody Maker** and the **New Musical Express**. While working at the Colindale library I met a former Apple employee, and we went to dinner. It was over dinner that I heard the first inside tales of the Apple years. With my notebooks filled I was ready to head back to America. That was seven years ago. I hope that the material in this book sheds some light on the Beatles' problems in the late 1960s.

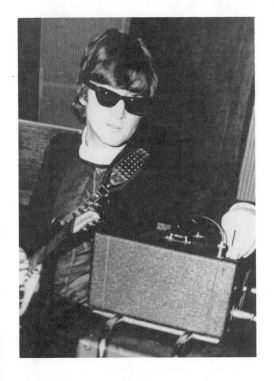

Above: Paul plays violin bass.

Left: John Lennon relaxing in the studio.

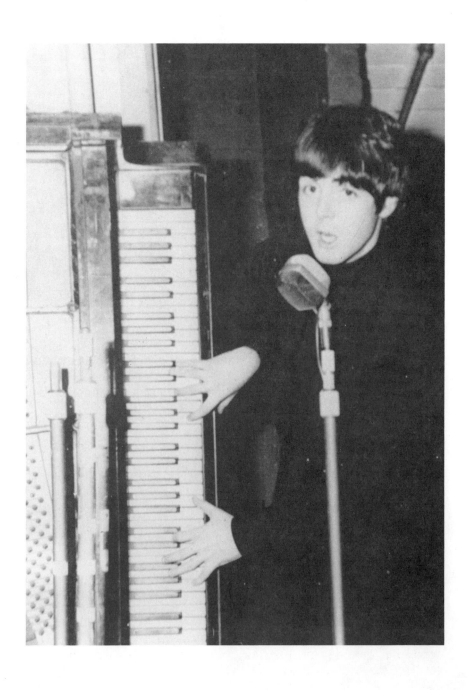

1: PAUL'S YOUTH IN LIVERPOOL: A MUSICAL GENIUS NURTURED, 1942-1959

When Paul McCartney was born on June 18, 1942, his father Jim "Mac" McCartney was on duty as a "fire watcher" or one of the thousands of Englishmen who looked out for German planes during the nightly bombings of Liverpool. All the lights in Liverpool shut down as England blacked out. The men stood around and talked of better days. This was a condition required by World War II. It was a lesson that Jim Mac never forgot; he preached that out of adversity came triumph. When he talked about his family Jim Mac often mentioned that it was created during difficult times.

Jim's wife, the former Mary Patricia Mohin, was a young Irish Catholic girl with many skills. She had a talent for "things medical." At least this is how Charlie Lennon remembered Mary. "Long before John met Paul I heard about Mary's healing powers," Charlie remarked. "She was special to many people." This was one of many references to Mary's fame as a healer. "I think Mary McCartney was something of a folk hero to young women about to give birth," Bob Wooler remembered.

Paul's mother had a spirit and perseverance she passed on to her eldest son. Mary Patricia Mohin was born on September 29, 1909, at 2 Third Avenue, Fazakerly, Liverpool. Her mother, Mary Teresa Danher Mohin, died while giving birth and young Mary Patricia soon found herself with a stepmother. Things were strained for years between Owen Mohin's daughter and her new mother. At the tender age of thirteen, Mary left home and searched for a suitable profession.

She gravitated to nursing at fourteen and secured a junior position at Alder Key Hospital. Her skill with patients prompted Liverpool's Walton Hospital to offer her specialized employment. There was a radiance and intellectual brilliance to Mary Mohin that attracted the young men. She was not interested, because of her difficult early years. She devoted herself to nursing and became something of a skilled amateur historian. This love for local history was passed on to her son.

Liverpool itself influenced young Paul, shaping him with its history, traditions and values. Liverpool was a seaport town fading into oblivion. Located two hundred miles northwest of London, Liverpool was the launching point for the Cunard Steamship Line. It was a commercial port that brought in a wide variety of goods. Since 1840 the Cunard Yanks transported consumer goods from America to an eager British market. For a century a sophistication and prosperity reigned in Liverpool. A fine railroad line connected Liverpool to the United Kingdom and

Europe. The harbor not only brought prosperity but there was a sense of dignity among the locals.

The Mersey river is important to the Liverpudlian character. It is a wide and navigable river that made Liverpool the center of the world slave trade. Because of the slave trade there was a liberal political attitude and a strong commitment to egalitarianism. Local citizens commented frequently about the injustice of slavery. Because of this attitude Paul, like most locals, grew up with a pronounced sense of social justice. This was an important factor in shaping Paul's music.

Another key to the inherent strength and resolve in Paul's character is his dad. There are character traits which carried over to Paul and provided him with a solid foundation. The influences were musical and business ones, and they predict some of Paul's later attitudes.

Jim "Mac" McCartney was born on July 7, 1902, at 8 Fishguard Street, Everton, one of Liverpool's poorer sections. He was one of nine children and his parent's large family prompted Jim Mac to seek the bachelor life. He couldn't have selected a better time to enjoy himself. After growing up in a large and poor family, Jim Mac was ready to relax and enjoy himself.

During the 1920s and 1930s Liverpool developed into a jazz and big band mecca. The Cunard Yanks brought in records by American jazz, blues and dance band performers to feed local appetites. Jim McCartney frequently bought 78 records from the itinerant sailors in local pubs. His love for music led him to form the Masked Melody Makers. A name change to Jim Mac's Jazz Band allowed them to perform such well known songs as "The Birth of the Blues" and "Stairway to Paradise." To help his group achieve the American sound; Jim Mac collected records from the major U. S. labels. He loved to tell people that playing in a jazz band was a sign of making it in Liverpool.

The Liverpool Cotton Exchange employed Jim Mac and by 1930 he was a cotton salesman. After fourteen years of hard work, he thought he had a job for life. In the midst of World War II the cotton exchange closed. Eventually, Jim Mac went to work for the Liverpool Cleansing Department, as an inspector in the city sanitation department.

When he met Mary Patricia Mohin, he admired her fragile beauty. A quiet woman with a strong sense of family responsibility, Mary was an ideal prospective wife. He proposed and they married on April 15, 1941, at St. Swithens Roman Catholic church, Gill Moss, Liverpool. The traditional marriage in a full church ceremony was important to Mary who had dreamed about the perfect wedding.

The early years of the McCartney marriage were not easy ones financially. They established a household during one of the most troublesome periods in English history. Despite money pressures, the marriage was a solid one.

As World War II broke out, Liverpool was England's second largest port. The standard of living was excellent and employment high. In the center of town St. George's Hall with its stunning Greco-Roman architecture was a reminder of Liverpool's greatness. This magnificent structure, built in 1854, featured a law court, concert hall and mammoth public hall. It is the type of building that locals point to with pride. Yet, Liverpool was also a family town. The sprawling suburbs were full of children, and Liverpudlians prided themselves on their quality of life.

When Paul was nineteen months old, another brother, Mike, was born on January 7, 1944. Suddenly, the family home at 72 Western Avenue, Speke was too small, so the McCartney's moved. The new prefab family bungalow on Roach Avenue, Knowsley Estate, Liverpool now housed four people. It was a sparse but comfortable home that escaped the war's ravages.

After W.W.II, the McCartney homes were council houses. These small, poorly constructed homes were cold in the winter and hot in the summer. The council house built just after World War II to ease the population crunch was adequate but not necessarily comfortable. The first home that Paul remembered was a rent free house on Ardwick Road. He was proud of it.

These were happy years. The McCartney's had "Pound Nights." This was the practice of family and friends pooling food in festive celebration. After each person bought his or her pound of food, there was a sumptuous banquet. Paul loved these affairs. They provided a solid family base. Jim Mac often put the boys on his back for a ride as they cavorted around the living room.

Paul grew up in an average working class environment. It was a blue collar existence which promoted strong values. When Paul began his education at Stockton Wood Road Primary School, the family lived at 12 Ardwick Road. This home was on a street where the roads were unpaved and the ambiance was much like that of a frontier town. Located in the Speke area of Liverpool, the Stockton Wood Road School had over 1500 students making it the largest primary school in Britain. The new council homes and the large geographical area made it a perfect place for young families.

Before he attended school there was some discussion about Paul's education and the decision to send him to local schools was a financial and religious one. Although Paul was baptized Catholic, his dad preferred English schools. Jim Mac believed that there was too much religion and not enough education in the Catholic schools. He wanted Paul to reflect local traditions. English education had a profound impact upon young McCartney and his song writing.

When Paul left for school each day with his Stockton Wood badge displayed on his jacket, he showed his vanity by stopping to admire himself in the living room mirror. He smiled and stared at the badge. It was a black and yellow patch with a picture of a Spitfire flying over the Mersey River. There were also activities at school which were an important influence upon McCartney.

Each week a movie shown at school helped Paul develop a fondness for films featuring Crime Buster Dick Barton. This popular BBC radio figure was a hero to a generation of British youngsters trying to forget Hitler's menace. There was a romantic quality to these films that pitted good versus evil with good always triumphing. These images from Paul's school experience surfaced repeatedly during his Beatle days.

During these early years Paul dreamed about his future. He talked to his friends at length about the radio and the vivid images of a brighter world. Paul listened to his dad's music and admired the trad jazz and pop standards. It was the music which had a special place in Paul's life. As long as he could soak up the music he was content. Soon Paul felt confined at Stockton Wood school and grew restive.

As the 1950s dawned the population explosion created a demand for new English schools and a more sophisticated educational system. Consequently, the trend was to bus students into the countryside. Soon Paul and his younger brother Mike transferred to the Joseph Williams Primary School in Gateacre. This educational facility on Naylorsfield Road, Belle Vale, Liverpool 25 was a half-hour bus ride. The 9:30 to 4:30 school day proved to be a long one. Paul was a good student at Joseph Williams and had no trouble passing the 11 Plus examination for admission to the Liverpool Institute.

The Liverpool Institute was the most prestigious local high school with a long history of achievement. When the school was founded in 1825, as a mechanics institute, it shared a building with the Liverpool Art College. As the city's oldest grammar school, the Liverpool Institute had a reputation for turning out local leaders. Its graduates were teachers, businessmen and civic minded politicians.

As Paul entered the Liverpool Institute the McCartney's moved to 20 Forthlin Road in Liverpool's Allerton district. For the next nine years Paul grew into manhood in a home with a pleasant back yard that overlooked a police training field. Mike McCartney remembered: "Mum was mainly responsible for our move to better positions." The home was one that Paul remembered because of its indoor toilet.

Across a nearby golf course young John Lennon lived with his aunt, Mary Stanley (Mimi) Smith, but the two boys hadn't met. There was an irony to John growing up in an area that Paul frequented. When they met the common bond of their Liverpool childhood experiences forged a lifetime friendship. The boys also benefited from the lessons that they learned in school.

The sense of tradition at the Liverpool Institute remained intact. Gas lamps hung over the classroom doors. The foreboding iron gates placed in front of the school in the 1830s still loomed ominously. The boys continued to memorize the school motto: "Not for ourselves only but for the good of the whole world." A warm feeling filled the Liverpool Institute and Paul reveled in it. There was every indication that Paul would become an English or literature instructor. His English instructor, Alan "Dusty" Durband, remembers that Paul was an excellent student who loved classic English literature. His essays were among the most incisive in class. Paul had a critical facility that his peers lacked. He could evoke images of rust colored, fallen leaves or cut a literary figure to size with his wit. Yet, there were other diversions in young McCartney's life.

In 1956 Paul found a new interest-music. Elvis Presley's records invaded Liverpool and Paul eagerly listened to American rock and roll. Lonnie Donegan's hit record "Rock Island Line" popularized skiffle music and for the first time McCartney considered playing this new sound. He loved the makeshift instruments that were a part of the skiffle bands. The instruments prompted Paul to learn more about American rock and roll music. For the next few years he dedicated his energies to storing hundreds of rock songs in his memory. He became a human juke box, cataloging songs and singing to his friends.

The encyclopedic knowledge of rock music that Paul displayed made him a popular part of the Liverpool social scene. It was because of his interest in music in 1957 that Paul went to the Odeon Theater in Liverpool to see Bill Haley and the Comets movie **Don't Knock The Rock**. He watched Haley perform and came alive with his first rock and roll vision. Shortly afterwards, Paul saw Haley on television. In February 1957 a film clip featured Haley on BBC Television leaving an English train. "And then one night on television," Paul remarked, "the announcer was talking about Bill Haley and it was a scene of devastation... (as) Teddy Boys and Rockers...thrashed a few cinemas down in London...." During the next few years Paul went to see **Don't Knock The Rock, The Girl Can't Help It**, and **Twist Around the Clock**. Rock and roll movies provided Paul a sense of rock history. He began singing the songs from the movies as well as emulating the performers.

The birth of English rock and roll depended upon records by American rockers and Paul eagerly watched the drama unfold. Rock and roll emerged alongside a vibrant youth culture. One that depended upon the radio, records and the music newspapers. Like many teenagers, the radio was McCartney's constant companion.

Paul loved BBC radio. His family didn't own a record player until 1956, so they sat around the living room listening to BBC radio. "My dad bought a nice big family radio which us kids used to sit on the floor and listen to," Paul remarked. From 1955 until 1959 Paul spent an inordinate amount of time listening to the birth of rock and roll music on the radio. Such unlikely songs as Pat Boone's "I'll Be Home" blended with Fats Domino's "Ain't That A Shame," Little Richard's "Lucille," Wilbert Harrison's

"Kansas City," Lloyd Price's "Lawdy Miss Clawdy," and Elvis Presley's "That's All Right (Mama)" produced McCartney's earliest musical influences. As Paul remembered: "Bill Haley was the first stuff coming over...." But it wasn't Haley's sound that inspired McCartney. He was searching for a raw, tough sound. It didn't take long for Paul to find it.

"The first song I ever remember really coming through the airwaves that like shocked me was on the David Jacobs show," Paul remarked. "He played 'What'd I Say' and it was insane." After listening to Ray Charles, Paul rode his bike down to the local record shop and bought a number of American rock and roll records. However, life in Liverpool in the 1950s was not all rock and roll. There were other forces shaping Paul's character.

The McCartney's moved from Speke and its vapid factory smog to Allerton. The new house at 20 Forthlin Road pleased Paul's mother. It was the beginning of an idyllic period for the thirteen year old McCartney.

Then, without warning, tragedy struck. A few months after moving into the new home, Paul's mother developed breast cancer. She died quickly. Mary McCartney was buried in a Catholic cemetery. Paul and Michael went to live for a few days with their Aunt Jin at Huyton. After the funeral the boys returned to an empty house.

The legacy that Mary McCartney left was an enduring one. She cared for her children with skill and imbued them with a sense of honor and dignity. There was a no nonsense, hard working quality to her life. She was able to instill values in her sons and Paul's drive toward accomplishment was a part of her work ethic. It was Mary who emphasized the necessity of Paul striving for important goals. This lesson was one that served him well during his lifetime.

During his formative years Paul was close to his family. Consequently, his mother's death was a cruel blow, but one that he softened through rock music. The security that a young child shares with his mother was shattered, but Paul took this loss quietly and with dignity. There was a maturity to Paul that belied his years. Paul would make something of himself. His strong value system along with a positive self image allowed him to survive in the rock and roll jungle.

As Paul grew to manhood, he immersed himself in rock and roll music. He favored early American rock songs such as Little Richard's "Long Tall Sally," Eddie Cochran's "Twenty Flight Rock," Gene Vincent's "Be-Bop-A-Lula" and the Everly Brothers "Bye Bye Love." Like many young Liverpool kids he bought records from the Cunard Yanks. It was an American rock singer, Buddy Holly, who intrigued McCartney the most, and he asked the sailors not only for his records but magazine articles too. This began a life long obsession with Holly's music. Little did Paul realize that one day he would own Buddy Holly's music publishing rights.

During his years at the Liverpool Institute Paul practiced a number of rock and roll tunes. In Cliff Edge's History class, Paul played "Long Tall Sally" with members of the Remo Four. In 1960 Paul and John Lennon performed an Everly Brothers song as the Nurk Twins in Bending, Berkshire. These rare performances were ones in which Paul sang American rock and roll. He was also a keen student of British rock music. Paul was like any other British teenager hanging out in coffee bars with his friends.

From 1956 to 1960 the 2-Is coffee bar in London gave birth to a distinct form of English rock and roll. In Liverpool, as in most cities outside London, jazz dominated the music scene. Under the surface, however, there was a musical revolution brewing. It not only influenced McCartney but it set the stage for his emergence as a serious musician. Tony Sheridan who performed regularly at the 2-Is recalled the excited crowds in this small venue. "It was a magic time, we sang Elvis songs and covered tunes by black American artists," Sheridan remembered. When he first met Paul in Hamburg, they developed an instant friendship. "It was due to American roots rock and roll and the English coffee houses," Sheridan chuckled. The Beatles were one of many bands developing their own style. It was not only a musical evolution but one that emphasized a cool, clothing style.

The signs of change in fashion were revolutionary. The young Englishman who frequented the small music clubs wore a velvet jacket, a frilled shirt and narrow trousers. There were also a group who dressed like Americans from the 1950s. They were called Teddy Boys. It was a term which inspired people to love or hate this English youth. The Teddy Boy thumbed his nose at conventional British morality. He laughed at the admiration for the Queen and the good manners which typified the British. He was an incarnation of the American juvenile delinquent. When Gene Vincent came to England, he was the perfect embodiment of the Teddy Boy. He wore black leather pants, swaggered, and drank profusely.

In 1959, a day before Gene Vincent stepped off the plane at Heathrow Airport, the **New Musical Express** ran an article analyzing the American rock and roller's popularity in England for the past three years. The **NME** report attracted little attention, but it was a significant commentary on the British musical scene. Every fledgling rock and roller in England knew "Be-Bop-A-Lula" and when Vincent entered London Joe Brown played the tune. As Vincent toured England he inspired Britain's new rock bands. McCartney followed Vincent's tour with interest, and he listened regularly to Vincent's music on the Desert Island Discs program. This fantasy oriented radio broadcast asked listeners what record they would take with them if they were stranded on a desert island. Each castaway received eight choices and in the 1950s Vincent's tune was the most popular. Paul not only listened to the show, but "Be-Bop-A-Lula" was his first record purchase. Although John Lennon sang lead on the Beatles' version of "Be-Bop-A-Lula," Paul was the moving force in performing Vincent's tune. There was a realistic Teddy Boy approach to Vincent and the Beatles watched him with admiration. "I think Gene Vincent had a realism to his performance that inspired a generation," Bob Wooler remarked. Although the Beatles didn't appeal to the Teddy Boys, these musical fanatics were important in breaking the stringent conservatism of British society toward rock and roll music.

Once the Teddy Boys began listening to rock and roll music, they provided an audience for many newly created bands. They also built up a lucrative market for American records and concert acts. Elvis Presley's first two English albums were the staple of the Teddy Boy. Paul McCartney during his 1989-1990 world tour handed out a free concert book that recalled Elvis Presley's early influence. "Elvis was top of the list...we didn't know he was taking it off blues and Arthur Crudup," Paul explained. What Elvis did for McCartney was to inspire him to a musical career. Presley's sideburns, his cool clothes, his gyrating music all combined to form an indelible influence upon young McCartney.

It was a time when Gene Vincent, Eddie Cochran, Buddy Holly, Little Richard, Chuck Berry and Fats Domino not only sold their music to the record hungry British fans but created the initial rock and roll dream. The fledgling British rockers developed these early fantasies through American artists who offered a picture of a new musical world.

More Liverpool kids started buying records from local seamen who were making a lucrative living selling records bought in New York. Paul besieged the Yanks who came into Liverpool and the Cunard Line sailors who went to New York for records. Many of the records came from the five cent bargain bin and Paul discovered Arthur Alexander, the Cookies, the Toys, Chan Romero and others. Like Bob Wooler, the Cavern compere, McCartney bought whatever the Cunard Yanks had to sell. Paul had specialized musical tastes. He bought a different kind of rock and roll music. It was blues influenced, sometimes pop, but often straight ahead rock and roll. Paul's taste often ran to the obscure, but he was capable of purchasing mainstream American rock and roll. McCartney was an eclectic record collector.

A good example of Paul's esoteric taste occurred when McCartney purchased the Jodimars "Clarabella." The Jodimars were ex-members of Bill Haley's Comets who went solo, and, according to Marshall Lytle, they expected to become a popular rock act. After the Jodimars recorded Jimmy De Knight's "Rattle My Bones," they vanished into obscurity. In England, however, the Jodimars became a cult act with record collectors. McCartney was one of the Jodimars fans. The Beatles' performed "Clarabella" due to McCartney's insistence that the song fit their style.

Tony Sheridan laughs as he recalls the 1950s. "I found coffee bars all over England, they let me sing, so I quit art college." Like Sheridan, McCartney did likewise but continued his schooling. Sheridan's story was one repeated throughout England. The dank, sweaty coffee bars in Liverpool offered cool jazz, a hip owner, a group of hangers on and a sense of intimacy. The dull, dreary 1950s prompted Liverpool denizens to frequent a Chinese opium den, gay clubs and beer bars that let any band play.

Like most British teenagers, Paul went to see a film starring Glenn Ford and Sidney Poitier. Although this popular film was released in America in 1955, the movie didn't play Liverpool until early 1956. In this interim young McCartney read about the film. The movie, **The Blackboard Jungle**, was a case study in the futility of teaching juvenile delinquents. The musical score featured Bill Haley and the Comets' national anthem to rock music, "Rock Around the Clock." Since American music intrigued Paul, he hurried out to purchase Haley's record. He also made the decision to begin writing his own songs.

As a young man growing up in Liverpool, Paul took piano lessons with his brother Michael, but he had little interest in the piano teacher's pedantic style. Paul's friends remember a gregarious young man who loved music but hid his serious intentions. His dad helped to change his youthful doubts. There was a musical tradition in the McCartney house. Paul's dad, Jim, had led a ragtime group, Jim Mac's Band, which played at local dances and had a reputation for fine music. Paul not only learned from his dad, but he began searching for his own musical identity.

By 1956 fourteen year old Paul McCartney was seriously pursuing rock and roll music. From his record collection, Paul learned to play the roots rock of Bill Haley, Elvis Presley, Eddie Cochran and Little Richard. Quietly at home he practiced to the music of the pioneer American rock and rollers.

There were also concerts to attend. In 1956 McCartney lined up at the Empire Theater to see Lonnie Donegan and his skiffle sound. Like many aspiring rock and rollers, Paul left the Liverpool Institute during his lunch hour to catch a glimpse of Donegan. Showing up late for the mid-day rehearsal, Donegan stopped to talk to the fans milling outside the Empire Theater. Paul never forgot how accommodating Donegan was to his fans.

But Paul still viewed skiffle music as a curiosity. He wanted his own guitar, so he could play American rock and roll. He preferred Bill Haley's "Rock Around The Clock," and Elvis Presley's "Don't Be Cruel," "Hound Dog" and "Blue Suede Shoes" to the hit records of the British rockers. Paul's favorite American artist Little Richard was a continuing inspiration. In time Paul performed one of the best impressions of Little Richard in

Liverpool. The flamboyant American rocker had a strong impact upon McCartney's stage presence. Painfully shy, McCartney used Little Richard's image to overcome his own fears on stage.

There were other forays into music. Paul learned to play the trumpet. This was a temporary infatuation. Paul began searching for another instrument. While rummaging through a local junk shop, Paul picked up an inexpensive acoustic guitar. This primitive instrument allowed Paul to experiment with rock music.

There are other tales about musical influences. One is that Jim Mac bought his son an acoustic guitar to help him through the grief of his mother's early death.

The British music scene was a pop oriented one. The singular pop consciousness of rock moguls like Larry Parnes made it difficult for the raw rock acts who pioneered their sound on Little Richard or Gene Vincent to make it in the British rock world.

Larry Parnes was the most important British pop manager of the 1950s. He realized that the coffee bars in and around London were a bastion of musical talent. It didn't take Parnes long to milk this source. He found Terry Nelhams renamed him Adam Faith and from 1959 through 1966 he had twenty-five British chart records.

Another Parnes discovery, Billy Fury, was a local product. Fury was born Ronald Wycherley on April 17, 1940, in Liverpool. He grew up in the Dingle near Ringo Starr's home and in October 1958 he auditioned some of his songs for pop singer Marty Wilde. As Fury sang his tunes in the dressing room of the Essoldo Theater in Birkenhead, Larry Parnes listened intently in the corner of the room. He signed Fury immediately to a recording contract. Not only was Parnes impressed with Fury's song writing but he sensed a James Dean quality in his performance. In February 1959 Fury's self penned single "Maybe Tomorrow" began a lengthy pop career which was plagued by ill health and an early death in 1983. Fury was the model for many British pop singers.

There was a lesson in Fury's career which many British pop acts appreciated. From 1959 to 1966 Fury was a veritable hit machine as he charted twenty-seven British singles. In a moment of rock and roll incongruity, Fury's first hit "Maybe Tomorrow" was on the charts for three weeks and then dropped off for five weeks before reentering for another month and a half. The dreamy pop vocals that launched Fury's career had a strong impact upon British rock and roll. It created a sugary, watered down vocal sound. Although Fury was an original talent with a great deal to offer, the pop moguls, like Larry Parnes, never allowed him to venture from formula rock and roll. This constrained rock sound had a dramatic impact upon the Beatles and other British rock acts who desired artistic freedom.

As he grew to musical maturity, Paul watched the pop

icons, like Fury, that Parnes foisted upon the British public with a sense of commercial interest. Some Liverpool friends suggest that McCartney had a pop crooner's mentality and he went so far as to personally criticize Parnes' singers. He believed that there was a limp wristed Buddy Holly quality to Adam Faith whereas Billy Fury was an original artist with a special talent. Many kids in England emulated their rock and roll idols. Paul was no exception.

By early 1957 Paul and Ian James, a friend from the Dingle who also attended the Liverpool Institute, began hanging around Liverpool with guitars in tow. No one paid any attention to them as they played and sang Marty Robbins' "A White Sportcoat and a Pink Carnation." Paul's dad was afraid that his son would take up the Teddy Boy look. There was very little to worry about as Paul was not only a good student, but he was far from an unrequited rebel.

Ivan Vaughan, another of Paul's friends, also fancied rock and roll music. Vaughan wanted desperately to join one of the Liverpool rock groups. Ivan was a lonely boy who had lost his father, and he shared a common rock music interest with Paul. So together they searched out the fledgling bands emerging all around Liverpool. Eventually, Vaughan told McCartney that he was going to listen to a band that was playing at a local church celebration. Vaughan raved about one member of the band, John Lennon, and talked for hours about this free spirited individual. Not only did he believe that the band, the Quarry Men, were the best in Liverpool's suburbs, but they were looking for some new members. So Ivan Vaughan plotted to bring McCartney together with Lennon. An opportunity soon arose.

The annual celebration at St. Peter's was an important event for most of Liverpool. It allowed the locals to forget the dreary spring weather and depressing economic conditions. The July 6, 1957, carnival attracted a cross section of working class people and it reminded Liverpool that summer had arrived. The breeze blowing off the Mersey River dampened the day, but everyone was having a good time. The twang of Liverpool's scouse dialect was in the air and there was a good deal of alcohol for the fairgoers. Paul rode his bike to the affair. He parked his Raleigh three-speed bike behind the church and wandered through the fairgrounds. Ivan Vaughan rode on the fair rides with Paul and they talked about music.

There was a buzzing on the St. Peter's church grounds as English families talked of plans to go to Butlin's. The Butlin Holiday Camps were an inexpensive way to afford some recreation. They were also a nightmare. The food was terrible. The entertainment was amateurish. The accommodations were uncomfortable, and the English constantly made jokes about surviving Butlin's. Although there were other vacation alternatives, most Englishmen couldn't afford them. Those who could afford a vacation other than Butlin's traveled north to Blackpool to enjoy this working class resort city. During the St. Peter's celebration everyone stood around and talked vacation.

"I think that the English prided themselves on surviving Butlin's," Clive Epstein remarked. "It was the only vacation that the average worker could afford."

Paul was thinking about his vacation when he wandered into a summer garden next to St. Peter's Parish and saw John Lennon's skiffle group, the Quarry Men. They were a strange looking lot with DA haircuts, slightly dirty T-shirts, and engineer boots. The Quarry Men played skiffle music as well as American rock and roll cover tunes. Much of the interest in skiffle music was due to the use of make shift instruments. With these crude musical devices fledgling bands unsuccessfully tried to emulate Lonnie Donegan's hit song, "Rock Island Line." It was a crude, primitive brand of music that required neither musical ability nor professional instruments. So everyone who wasn't a soccer player in Liverpool fancied himself a musician.

As Paul observed the Quarry Men, he was struck by the ineptness of some members of the band. The banjo player, Rod Davis, and the drummer, Colin Hanton, were lost on stage. Not only were they woefully inadequate instrumentally, but they couldn't follow Lennon's lead. The other members of the band, Eric Griffiths, Pete Shotton and Len Garry were generally unfamiliar with American rock and roll music. They were John Lennon's friends, and this was the reason they were in the band.

The Quarry Men performed in an afternoon set and Paul watched with interest. After the set Paul was introduced to John by Ivan Vaughan who played a tea chest bass with the band. Pete Shotton's mother, Bessie, stood nearby beaming since she had booked the concert date.

It didn't take long for McCartney to become a member of the Quarry Men. The first day he met John, Paul showed off his extensive knowledge of American rock music. He told John that he could write out the lyrics to Eddie Cochran's "Twenty Flight Rock" or Gene Vincent's "Be-Bop-A-Lula." Then grabbing a guitar, Paul went into quick versions of Little Richard hits. After belting out a song, Paul stopped, smiled and handed John the guitar.

This display of musical virtuosity frightened Lennon. He had met his match. John needed time to think. Should he or shouldn't he ask Paul to join the band. It was Joe Flannery, whom Lennon talked to that afternoon, who persuaded the head Beatle to consider McCartney's talent. "Young John sat in my living room talking about this chap, I soon found out it was Paul McCartney," Flannery remarked. After listening to Lennon's description of McCartney, Joe urged John to bring him into the group.

The Quarry Men's performance at St. Peter's Church began at three in the afternoon and again at eight in the evening.

Neither performance was a memorable one. Colin Hanton failed to show up for the evening set and this may have prompted Lennon to consider bringing McCartney into the group.

What John Lennon remembered about meeting Paul is forever lost in history. It is unlikely that Paul joined the Quarry Men on the basis of meeting Lennon and watching this concert. A more plausible explanation is that John and Paul knew of each other without being close friends. A number of Paul's acquaintances remember Lennon catching the 86 bus into Liverpool, and McCartney remarked that he was fascinated with John's unique appearance. "Paul was an observer who astutely recognized Lennon's intellect and sense of style," Joe Flannery remarked. Liverpool was small enough for Paul and John to have spotted each other. Although they weren't yet friends, Lennon and McCartney knew each other in the provincial Liverpool social atmosphere.

Pete Shotton remembers riding his bike on Menlove Avenue and running into McCartney. They talked at length and Paul inquired about joining the band. Shotton went back to Lennon and told the Quarry Men's leader about McCartney's musical diversity. It was at this point that John invited Paul into the group.

It was not easy for the other band members to work with McCartney. He was precise and critical, whereas Lennon was calm and laid back. Colin Hanton's drumming skills were placed under Paul's microscope, and there were immediate hard feelings. When Paul sat down and showed Hanton how to play the drums, he considered leaving the group.

There were other changes that McCartney brought to the Quarry Men. He urged them to streamline their song selection, practice daily and search out new performing venues. There was a business like quality to young McCartney.

For the next eight months there was nothing to distinguish the Quarry Men from other local rock bands. "It was too early for the rock music scene," Bob Wooler remembered. "Everything was still jazz oriented but the Beatles, like other bands, gained a great deal from playing in the suburbs." Wooler's observation reveals how the Mersey sound began developing.

On February 6, 1958, the Quarry Men played Wilson Hall in Garston and Paul's fourteen year old friend George Harrison came along. They both loved American rock and roll and were mesmerized by John Lennon. Harrison was so taken with the Quarry Men's leader that he followed him around like a puppy dog. It was an ego inflating experience for John. Soon Harrison was invited to join the band. At this stage in the Quarry Men's career John, Paul and George were in a band that also included keyboardist John Lowe and drummer Colin Hanton. The group was eager to cut a record. The only problem was that they couldn't find a place to record.

This was remedied during the summer of 1958 when the Quarry Men cut their first record at the Liverpool studio of Percy Phillips. One side was a cover version of Buddy Holly's "That'll Be the Day" in which John sang lead. The flip side is a mystery. The song, "In Spite of All The Danger" is sometimes listed as a McCartney-Harrison song. This seems unlikely. When Mark Lewisohn interviewed Paul for his recording sessions book, Paul took full credit for the song. Harrison wasn't writing songs at the time, so it seems unlikely he was the co-author. To this day the mystery over authorship and availability remains a part of Beatle folklore. The Beatles had more serious problems than this obscure song.

In early 1959 Griffiths and Hanton left the Quarry Men, and the group no longer had a complete compliment of musicians. As a result the band had trouble securing bookings. Paul was frustrated by the Quarry Men's lack of progress. To change the look of the band, John brought his best friend, Stu Sutcliffe, in to play the bass. John and Stu lived together in a Gambier Terrace flat where they shared a common interest in art. This ground floor apartment was located just around the corner from the Liverpool Institute. Down a nearby alley, a local pub, Ye Crack, provided beer and good conversation. This began a period of ribald partying and intense music making. John told anyone who would listen that Stu was the reincarnation of James Dean. So maybe, Lennon reasoned, Stu could draw the poets, artists and writers around Liverpool to the Quarry Men's gigs. Paul was unhappy with Sutcliffe. He had neither musical talent nor physical presence. On stage Sutcliffe looked like a wounded puppy dog. At this stage in the Quarry Men's career most people believed that Paul would drop out of the group and pursue a teaching career.

The 1950s ended without fanfare for the Quarry Men. Paul McCartney was in his first band, but it was a second rate one. No one seemed to know or care about John Lennon's little group. Despite these problems the local music scene was booming. Clubs were opening up all over Liverpool, promoters like Sam Leach and Brian Kelly were making rock and roll concerts respectable, and Allan Williams' Jacaranda club was written about in the London newspapers. The Liverpool scene was about to burst open. It would give the Beatles a new drummer, a new venue and a new musical life. One that led directly to Hamburg, Germany and the first steps to musical super stardom.

II: THE BEATLES' MUSICAL EMERGENCE, 1960-1962

By 1960 the Beatles were making progress toward a new sound. John and Paul were writing songs, the band practiced regularly, and they had a positive attitude about the future. The only problem was that they couldn't find a drummer or places to play.

As the Quarry Men lingered in musical frustration, a new club opened in West Derby. On a quiet suburban road, Hayman's Green, the Casbah Club prepared to open for business. The West Derby district, located four miles from downtown Liverpool, was a quiet tree lined area with graceful Victorian houses and well-kept bungalows. It was home to Mona Best whose son was an aspiring musician. She opened a beat club in the basement of her home to provide her boy with a musical venue. Her eighteen year old son Pete was a drummer who loved rock and roll music. The large fifteen room Victorian house had plenty of room, so why not convert part of it into a London style Soho basement coffee house. Mrs. Best, a beautiful, stately woman, was an English and Indian mixture which gave her an exotic look and a great deal of sex appeal.

The driving force behind the Casbah was not Pete Best, it was his mother. She took the name from the 1938 movie **Algiers** starring Charles Boyer. After renovating the seven room basement the Casbah formally opened on August 29, 1959, with the Quarry Men as the house band. Generally, the Quarry Men played on Saturday nights at the Casbah. It was John Lennon's band, so few people remember McCartney's role.

The Casbah's opening night revealed fractious divisions within the band. They fought over song selection, the money split and where they would play in the future. After seven engagements at the Casbah Ken Brown, who played guitar, had an argument with Paul over fifteen shillings. When Brown left the group no one shed a tear. He had little talent and, according to John, looked like "a four-eyed school boy."

The Quarry Men weren't an outstanding band. "They were simply another suburban band that didn't stand out," Bob Wooler remarked. "I think that the Quarry Men were an amateur lot," Clive Epstein remarked, "but they had the desire to make music." Joe Flannery who managed his brother's group, Lee Curtis and the All Stars, remembers the Beatles as talented and unique. "I thought they had something very different from the beginning," Flannery remarked. "From the Quarry Men days John depended upon Paul to help craft his songs," Flannery continued. "They were both talented but there was something special in the collaboration."

By 1960 the Quarry Men had reached a turning point. They needed to develop a more professional sound and look, or simply wander off to other pursuits. John reasoned it was time to change their name. He felt a need to rid the group of the name taken from the school that they had attended. At one time or another in 1960 the Quarry Men were known variously as the Silver Beats, Silver Beetles, Silver Beatles, Beatals and,finally, simply in August, 1960-the Beatles. What contributed to this indecision? No one is sure. Lennon was caught up with the beatnik craze and he envisioned the band as an art form. Paul hoped to play with an American style rock and roll touch and he argued the "art band" idea was boring. Buddy Holly's band, the Crickets, were credited as the inspiration for the new name.

Sometime in 1960 a local Liverpool entrepreneur, Allan Williams, came into the Beatles' musical life. A Welsh-born Liverpudlian, Williams was a loud braggart with a penchant for drinking, story telling and rock and roll music. A swaggering self-promoter, he opened a series of coffee houses and beat clubs hoping to cash in on the popularity of the beatnik craze. In September 1958, Williams opened the Jacaranda amidst great fanfare. By 1960 it was the best known club in Liverpool and for two years the Quarry Men hung around the club. It had a beatnik atmosphere and a cup of coffee could be nursed for hours. Paul spent a great deal of time in the Jac and watched the Machiavellian behavior of the erratic Williams. It was hard to like Allan Williams. He was loud, brash, uncultured and prone to name calling. But he was the most significant promoter in Liverpool music circles. Other promoters, notably Brian Kelly and Sam Leach, were not as flamboyant as Williams, and while they were successful they lacked Williams' aura.

Of all the Liverpool promoters, Sam Leach was the one who had the Beatles' best interests uppermost in his mind. Because he promoted a number of Beatle concerts, Leach hoped to bring the boys along slowly. He realized that they were still developing their musical approach and Leach consciously attempted to feature the Beatles in the right local venues.

In 1960 Leach hoped to make his mark in the promotion business with groups like the Beatles. Among Leach's innovative promotions were plans for a series of dances at St. George's Hall. Leach hoped to give fledgling bands a chance to play their music in a small hall. However, a rival promoter hired a group of young girls to jump on stage and strip to their underwear. After this incident Leach was banned from renting the hall. So the Beatles were forced to play for the beer-breathed, wild man Allan Williams.

One night Williams walked into his club, abruptly threw up on the floor and asked the patrons for applause. It was in this atmosphere that the Beatles attempted to win musical converts.

The Jacaranda and other coffee houses featured American rock and roll music and benefited from the publicity surrounding Eddie Cochran and Gene Vincent's English visit. In January 1960, Paul watched Cochran on the British TV show, "Boy Meets Girl." The host, Marty Wilde, interviewed Cochran who also sang "Twenty Flight Rock." Paul was hooked. The Cochran sound was raw, his guitar hummed and his stage movements drove the crowd wild. The girls screaming in the background unwittingly provided the first signs of what would later become Beatlemania.

When Cochran and Vincent appeared at Liverpool's Empire Theater from March 14-20, 1960, Allan Williams and the Beatles were treated to a show that may have prompted Paul's decision to pursue a musical career. The top English promoter, Larry Parnes, dropped into the Jacaranda and Williams hobnobbed with the performers and Parnes.

When Parnes went to the Jacaranda after one of the Empire shows, he was impressed with the local musical talent. The lavish clothes, extravagant spending, gourmet food and the vast liquor supply stamped Parnes as an elegant gentleman. He managed pop singer Billy Fury and was considered the most significant English promoter. This was an opportunity that Williams wanted to turn to his advantage.

So he suggested that they co-produce a Liverpool rock show. Williams' announced that on May 3, 1960, at the Liverpool Stadium Eddie Cochran and Gene Vincent would be joined by a black American rock and roller residing in Liverpool, Davy Jones, as well as other local bands including Cass and the Cassanovas and Rory Storm and the Hurricanes in a live Boxing Day promotion. As ticket sales moved briskly, tragedy struck. Eddie Cochran was killed when he struck his head on the roof of a cab. Gene Vincent, who already had a badly infected leg from a motorcycle accident, suffered minor injuries. Vincent was devastated. His daughter, Melody Jean Vincent, recalls that the loss of Eddie Cochran was like losing a brother. "My dad was never the same after the accident," she concluded.

This incident increased Williams' erratic behavior, but he continued to promote the Boxing Day concert and added a number of new bands. The Quarry Men, now known as the Beatals, offered their services but were not signed for the show. Paul and John no longer had a drummer, and Williams refused to consider them. They sat ignominiously in the back of the auditorium as virtually every other Liverpool band cavorted on stage.

After the Boxing Day concert Parnes explained to Williams that he needed a group to back Billy Fury. The Beatals, as they were now known, picked up Tommy Moore, a truck driver in his mid-thirties, as the drummer for their Parnes audition.

Sam Leach was the Beatles only defender during the Boxing Day promotion and subsequent audition for the Fury tour. He urged Williams to reconsider his hasty actions. "I pointed out to Allan that he was punishing the boys for making fun of him," Leach remarked. It seems that John Lennon did an impression of Williams that broke up the Jacaranda regulars. The Beatles punishment for this indiscretion was to sit out the day that virtually every band performed before local fans. Allan Williams had his pound of salt. Only Sam Leach stood up to his bullying behavior.

As they prepared for the audition the paranoia over the group's name resurfaced. The name Long John and the Silver Beetles was suggested but John decided that Silver Beetles was appropriate. Paul liked it because the name was a take off on Buddy Holly and the Crickets.

When the May 10,1960, audition for Larry Parnes took place the Silver Beetles were nervous. It was early in the morning and they were only one of four bands selected by the mercurial Williams to audition for Parnes. Along with Billy Fury, Johnny Gentle and Duffy Power were going on tour. The band selected for this tour had to back up all the musicians and possess a wide musical knowledge. The prestige from this tour would help any fledgling band. So Williams was in a position of being a King maker.

The prospects of a professional audition frightened the Silver Beetles. Paul fidgeted. John walked around the room. George sat listlessly in the corner. The Wyvern Social Club at 108 Seel Street was the spot for the audition. Their drummer, Tommy Moore, hadn't arrived at the club so Johnny Hutchinson from Cass and the Cassanovas filled in. Moore appeared during the middle of the audition. Parnes and Fury were impressed with the Silver Beetles. But they didn't like Stu Sutcliffe's bass playing or his shy stage manner. When Parnes suggested that Sutcliffe not be included in the tour, Lennon withdrew the band.

During the audition John walked over and had Billy Fury sign an autograph. They chatted for a few minutes as Cheniston Roland took a picture. Fury wanted to use the Silver Beetles but since they were unwilling to replace Sutcliffe, another band was chosen.

To appease the group, Parnes offered the Silver Beetles a chance to back up Johnny Gentle on a nine day tour of Scotland. With only two days to prepare, the Silver Beetles were petrified. But this was a chance of a lifetime. So they swallowed their apprehension and began learning Gentle's pop tunes.

The van that took the Silver Beetles on this tour was cramped and tempers flared. Paul was quiet but unhappy. Although it was still John's band, Paul spent the nine days agitating Tommy Moore and poking fun at Johnny Gentle's pompadour. When the Silver Beetles returned to Liverpool on May 29, 1960, they were in a state of disarray. Allan Williams acted as their manager and he failed to negotiate an adequate fee.

Feeling guilty for selling out the Silver Beetles, Williams

booked them into the Jacaranda. The resident band, the Royal Trinidad Steel Band, was off on Monday nights and the Silver Beetles filled the spot. On May 30, 1960, a small and disinterested audience watched the Beatles perform.

In June1960, Tommy Moore played his last engagement with the Silver Beetles. They continued to play for Williams without a drummer and in July 1960, the bored and disinterested band played at Williams' New Cabaret Artists club located in a Victorian house at 174a Upper Parliament Street. It was a part of town where houses of prostitution, illegal liquor, gambling and casual dope smoking surfaced. A Manchester stripper, Janice, entertained as the Silver Beetles played standards like "Moonglow," "Summertime" and "Begin the Beguine." It was a new low for the boys.

Again they tried to find a drummer. Norman Chapman spent a few nights drumming with the band, but like Colin Hanton and Tommy Moore, he was an amateur. Things were not going well for the Silver Beetles. When they asked around Liverpool about new local drummers, they were surprised to learn that Pete Best had taken up the drums He had joined a band with bassist Ken Brown. For a brief time Brown played with the Quarry Men at the Casbah Club but he left the group over a money dispute.

In July 1960, Paul was sent to Best's West Derby home. Not only did Pete have an expensive drum kit, but he knew the American rock and roll songs. Paul didn't like Best's drumming and he was uncomfortable around him. So they delayed asking him to join the group.

It was the summer of 1960 and John, Paul and George had little to do. They played sporadic gigs and eagerly sought out places to play. They hung around Allan Williams' Jacaranda Club day and night hoping for a place to perform.

The regulars who frequented the Jac were a motley group of con artists. Willy sold rare carpets to unsuspecting tourists. An ad in the **Liverpool Echo** brought in customers who were easily bilked. An old man, Norman, sold watches. The Silver Beetles watched these characters in awe and learned a great deal about the public from them. But there were other concerns for the group.

They needed to find performing venues. There were some good moments during the summer. On July 2, 1960, as the Silver Beetles were performing at the Grosvenor Ball in Liscard, Johnny Gentle came in to see them. He jumped on stage and performed two of his hits. Gentle's dad had come along and he cheered as the excited crowd looked on. It was a magic moment. Gentle who was from Litherland north of Liverpool loved the Beatles' music, and showed his respect for their music by showing up to perform with them.

Like many local bands the Quarry Men played the Cavern Club. This basement jazz venue, located on Mathews Street, was adjacent to some of Liverpool's more popular pubs. The club at 10 Mathews Street had an entrance marked by a stark, low wattage light bulb. The Cavern was hot, cramped, uncomfortable and smelled of whatever was in the kitchen or behind the makeshift stage. The entry way was a maze as young rock and rollers walked down eighteen stairs and disappeared into one of the three tunnels that led to the main part of the club. The Quarry Men first performed at the Cavern on August 7, 1957, in a skiffle show with Ron McKay headlining. This engagement was not a triumphant one. The band's sound was primitive to an audience expecting traditional jazz.

Paul and John were frustrated by the Quarry Men's inability to develop their own sound. There were hundreds of bands in and around Liverpool, but very few developed a professional sound. Initially, the camaraderie, the girls, the good times and the dreams of stardom were enough to sustain the bands. Soon serious problems with the Quarry Men surfaced. For years John had brought his friends into the group. At first Paul didn't complain. Then in August 1960, Lennon began grousing that Paul wanted to shape the Quarry Men into his own band. McCartney didn't deny that he hoped to make the Quarry Men different from other bands. But Paul did acknowledge that it was John's band. This eased some hurt feelings, at least temporarily. It wasn't easy for McCartney to defer to Lennon. Finally, Stu Sutcliffe tested McCartney's patience beyond endurance. Personally, Stu agitated Paul. The reasons for the conflict are not clear but Stu often felt McCartney's wrath. It was an uneasy relationship from the day Paul joined the band.

During the summer of 1960, Hamburg, Germany night clubs began featuring English rock and roll. Tony Sheridan was booked from the London 2-Is Coffee shop and the Trinidad Steel Band left Williams' Jacaranda Club to play in Hamburg. The London clubs were visited regularly by German night club owners. In July 1960, Allan Williams traveled to London in an attempt to book his acts. Williams met Bruno Koschmider, the owner of several Hamburg clubs, and they talked at length about the Liverpool bands. Koschmider signed Derry and the Seniors who opened at the Kaiserkeller on July 31 to a raucous house. The Liverpool bands were an instant hit and Koschmider hoped to book other Mersey groups.

The Silver Beetles were not Williams' first choice for the Hamburg trip. He offered Rory Storm and the Hurricanes and Gerry and the Pacemakers a chance to play the Indra Club. They declined. Reluctantly, Williams approached the Silver Beetles, but they didn't have a drummer. So on August 12, 1960, Pete Best auditioned at the Wyvern social club and three days later became an official member of the band. The boys were ready for Hamburg.

In August 1960, during their first Hamburg trip Stu and Paul continued to have difficulties. Most biographers assume that

McCartney wanted Sutcliffe's job as bass guitarist. Nothing could be further from the truth. Paul simply objected to Sutcliffe's lack of musical talent. Because McCartney openly ridiculed Sutcliffe, there was trouble. "Paul wanted to agitate Stu," Tony Sheridan remembered, "and he did so constantly."

There was an egotistical side to Stu Sutcliffe that drove McCartney mad. One night, Tony Sheridan recalled, Stu announced that he could either fill in on the bass or drums. "Paul went bonkers when he heard that," Tony Sheridan laughed. "That silly little painter should stick to his craft," Paul remarked to Sheridan. A brilliant painter, Sutcliffe lacked the musical education to play either instrument and the Beatles were relieved when he brought a bass to practice. Paul also didn't care for Pete Best's drumming talent.

As the Beatles left for Hamburg, Pete Best's days were numbered. Even though he had just joined the group, Best did little to inspire confidence or loyalty. His days with the Beatles were ones of discord and disagreement and the decision to dump him was a smart one. As Tony Sheridan remarked: "Anyone who watched the early Beatles was amazed that Best was in the band. It was the young girls who loved Pete."

Because of the fan's adulation over Best, McCartney's role in dumping him is a pivotal one. As McCartney suggested to Bob Wooler, Best was a stone around the Beatles neck and they would sink with him. Best's lack of commercial success validated McCartney's thinking. "Paul didn't want Pete around," Tony Sheridan remarked, "he had no musical talent and took some of Paul's girls."

As the Beatles performed in Hamburg, this engagement had a dramatic impact upon McCartney's confidence. He realized that the Beatles were no longer a Liverpool band. They had made a connection with the outside world. McCartney was suddenly optimistic about the future.

The long bleak auto trip to Hamburg was unpleasant because of the loud mouthed, egotistical Williams. He provided the transportation and constantly badgered the boys about their music. The small van that he drove was a party caravan with the brash Jacaranda owner dominating the conversation. The lighter moments were due to the humor of Willie Woodbine. Commonly called Lord Woodbine for a cheap brand of cigarettes he smoked, the diminutive West Indian bongo drum player provided mirth and relaxation. It was a nice contrast to Williams drunken behavior and constant bragging. The Beatles were without a real manager and since Bruno Koschmider had called the Jacaranda, Williams weaseled his way on the trip to Hamburg. The Beatles knew that they could persuade Williams to grant a personal loan at any time.

In order to purchase some new clothes Paul asked Allan Williams for an advance of fifteen pounds. In an elaborate ritual

Williams made McCartney sign an I.O.U. and he lectured McCartney on his fiscal responsibilities. Paul simply swallowed his pride and ignored Williams. The reason that McCartney tolerated Williams was that he provided an entry into the German musical world. He viewed the Jac owner as a foolish man who lived for the moment.

The Hamburg club the Beatles opened in was little more than a converted basement with an electrical outlet. As the Beatles walked into the Indra Club on August 17, 1960, they were surprised at its primitive state. There was no stage and the small, damp room was ill equipped. The crowd was a motley crew of sailors, transvestites and curious tourists. There was a constant demand from the crowd to make music, so rest was impossible. After eight to ten hours on stage the Beatles fell into a cot behind a small movie theater, the Bambi Kino, and the boys went to sleep in a makeshift room smelling of cigarettes and urine.

In the morning the Beatles were awakened by the blaring of an American movie. The Beatles living arrangement at the Bambi Kino was less than inspirational. But they were playing rock music for a living and that was all that mattered.

Down the street from the Bambi Kino, Paul discovered the Blockhutte, a small tavern a block and a half from the Indra Club. He became friendly with Corey, the barmaid and owner's daughter, and enjoyed free food, beer and social pleasures. The Blockhutte, a country-western bar featuring local acts, drew an odd assortment of local characters. The German Hamburg cowboys who took the stage were unable to play or sing country tunes adequately. The pseudo-cowboy motif allowed Paul to unwind. There was a Kafkaesque sense to the Blockhutte that Paul loved to talk about.

In Hamburg, McCartney continued his fascination with Little Richard's music. Each night he belted out "Long Tally Sally" and other hits from the Georgia Peach. The reaction from the German audiences was always the same. They loved Little Richard's music and they didn't care who performed it. In 1960 Paul's lead vocals spanned a wide variety of songs. His cover versions of Elvis Presley's "All Shook Up," "That's All Right (Mama)" and "Blue Moon of Kentucky" were instant crowd pleasers. One of Paul's best live performances was a cover of the Jodimars "Clarabella." Thirty-five years after their flirtation with rock and roll fame, Marshall Lytle of the Jodimars remembered how eagerly the English kids warmed to their music. "I don't know if the Beatles ever saw us, but I was blown away when I heard a B.B.C. radio version of 'Clarabella' by the Beatles," Lytle exclaimed.

Ray Charles, Jerry Lee Lewis, Chuck Berry, Gene Vincent, the Coasters, Eddie Cochran and Carl Perkins were the artists that Paul covered during his first tour of Hamburg. By performing American rock and roll standards, McCartney displayed his encyclopedic knowledge of root's rock and roll.

From August 17 through October 3, 1960, as the Beatles performed in Hamburg's Indra Club, they received a valuable musical education. The more than 250 hours the Beatles played in these dreary venues perfected their musical sound. They became proficient as rock and rollers and moved to the Kaiserkeller Club. By late October the Beatles were the musical talk of this rough German city.

Since it was difficult to make friends in Hamburg, it was only natural for the Beatles to seek out fellow Englishman, Tony Sheridan. Not only was Sheridan Hamburg's most popular entertainer but he was a warm, gregarious person who welcomed their friendship. It was not long before Sheridan introduced each of the Beatles to the local intrigues. Sheridan was labeled "the Elvis Presley of Germany." He blanched at this title, but it was an indication of the esteem in which Sheridan was held. He was the perfect guide through the underbelly of Hamburg life. Soon Sheridan introduced the boys to the local girls, the best eating places and the out of the way spots to relax.

"Paul McCartney was the most energetic Beatles during the early Hamburg days," Sheridan recalled. "He loved to experiment with his music. It was Little Richard's 'Ooh! My Soul' that enabled Paul to develop his own cult following among the Germans." The exaggerated manner that Paul used to prance around the stage appealed to the Germans. Horst Fascher, the Beatles self-appointed bodyguard, remembers when he saw Paul perform for the first time. "He was the whole show." Fascher went on to suggest that McCartney's stage gyrations stopped the show.

For Paul the only negative part of the early Hamburg days was working for Bruno Koschmider. The short, dumpy German impresario treated the English rock bands poorly. He paid them a minimum wage, provided inadequate housing and ignored their requests for the simple necessities of life. The Reeperbahn was filled with impresarios like Bruno Koschmider. They were flashy dressers who lived in the suburbs and provided entertainment for foreign sailors, tourists and young Germans. There was a gangster touch to Koschmider's clubs, and Paul remarked that he dressed like a poor man's George Raft.

While performing in the Hamburg clubs, Paul and John faked fights or danced with one another. It was a way to relieve the long, tedious hours playing in the clubs. They loved to make the Germans holler. John would taunt the crowd by screaming "Nazis," whereas Paul was more subtle but equally provoking. Eventually, Bruno Koschmider wrote to Allan Williams, who had returned home, advising him that the Beatles had to behave in order to continue performing.

Williams immediately wrote to the Beatles about their obnoxious behavior. For years Williams belligerently attacked people and once opened a club in an abandoned house without paying rent or having any city permits. Williams was irate when Liverpool authorities evicted him. Paul laughed loudly when John read Williams' letter. Tony Sheridan remembers that Paul lit a paper doll effigy of Williams as the Beatles danced around it. Paul and John were never closer in their desire to rid themselves of "the little pissant" as they fondly referred to Williams.

Because of the Beatles' popularity, Koschmider moved them from the Indra into the Kaiserkeller at 36 Grosse Freiheit. As they performed from August 17 through October 3, 1960, in Hamburg the Beatles had forty-eight nights to perfect their musical sound. The change in the Beatles was enormous by the time they moved to the Kaiserkeller. "I had listened to the Beatles from their first few nights in Hamburg," Horst Fascher commented, "and they were a different band in the Kaiserkeller." Fascher suggested that they still looked like ruffians, but they played with a style and grace that belied their youthful appearance. The Beatles had perfected the key elements of American rock and roll while originating their own sound. During their first German visit, they performed one hundred and five different rock songs.

Hamburg's St. Pauli district was a fine place for a young Englishman. Unlike the stark, conservative Liverpool streets, the Reeperbahn was wide open and filled with excitement. Paul's angelic face attracted hundreds of young girls. The local prostitutes initiated Paul and the rest of the Beatles into pleasant sexual rites that they never forgot. The suburban girls showed up at the clubs and soon Paul was taken into the homes of some of Germany's finest families.

Like most tourists and Hamburg residents, the Beatles wandered into the Herbertstrasse. This was a square block that was walled off to isolate the prostitutes from the rest of the Reeperbahn. With the women standing in the doorways and in second story windows, Paul was offered a smorgasbord of female delights. One looked like a Nazi General, another smoked a pipe and looked like Daisy Mae from Little Abner's comic strip, another had on high heels and meshed stockings and Paul's favorites were the ones with the leather tops. Paul, like the other Beatles, extensively sampled the wares in the Herbertstrasse. Unlike Lennon, however, Paul was nervous at the crazy clothing and outlandish styles. The boots, whips and chains worn by some of the girls failed to excite Paul and the one he saw smoking a pipe wearing crotchless pants revolted him.

The Herbertstrasse was on the way to the Seamen's Mission where the Beatles walked in the morning for cornflakes and milk and some good conversation about England. Jim Hawkes, the Mission director, made them feel at home. They could talk with English visitors and eagerly catch up on the English news. The Seamen's Mission was a welcome relief from the German nights.

Paul often walked down to the docks and watched the ships come in. No one knew Paul and he reveled in the freedom. It was another world as German's bustled briskly to work oblivious of the young English visitor. A notebook was frequently in Paul's hand and his impressions of the locals created many song ideas. The creative impact of Hamburg was important, because it allowed Paul to craft his first songs independent of John's influence.

Tony Sheridan remembers the differences that erupted between Paul and John. They vied with each other for the best looking girls. John and Paul often had musical contests. They played a game to see who could play the most obscure American rock and roll. When Paul won it was due to his incessant search for records. When John won, he usually had just bought a record from some incoming sailor. It was all good fun, Sheridan remembers, but it sometimes had an ugly side. The two chief Beatles took their music seriously and they would argue over which record to cover in the clubs. "I think that John and Paul worked too closely together," Sheridan recalled. "Their song writing was like a marriage-happy at first but soon it fell on hard times." Sheridan was impressed by Paul's search for new songs. A day never went by in which Paul didn't search out a record store, thrift shop or sidewalk sale.

One of the earliest artists to occupy Paul and John's attention was the American soul singer, Arthur Alexander. During the summer of 1961, a Hamburg sailor brought in a copy of Alexander's Judd Record release "You Better Move On" backed with "A Shot of Rhythm and Blues." John and Paul loved this 45 but it didn't fit their style. Eventually, they discovered Alexander's "Anna," and it became a part of the Beatles' club repertoire. Alexander's music is an example of the diversity that Paul and John experienced in their search for an original sound.

While in Hamburg, Paul dated a bevy of local beauties. He was having a good time squiring the local girls around town. One was prettier than the next and they were all eager to please the English musicians. What Paul didn't realize was that these youthful romps would produce publicity that would haunt him for more than two decades. The tales of his sexual prowess continued for a long time. Long after the Beatles had left the small clubs in Hamburg, one of these buxom lasses, Erika Heubers, sued Paul alleging that her daughter, Bettina, was the result of an affair. In 1966 Heubers filed the suit just as the Beatles were preparing for an American tour. Fearing damaging publicity, Brian Epstein suggested a settlement with Heubers' German attorneys. McCartney paid 2,700 pounds but didn't admit paternity. The matter never surfaced publicly during the 1960s. Then in 1983, Heubers sued for admission of paternity, a spousal allowance and a share of McCartney's German royalties. The case was heard in a German Court. McCartney took a blood test. It proved that he was not the father. Once again Heubers had lost. There was not a shred of evidence to support her claim. The press was nasty and vindictive, infuriating Paul. He granted few interviews and was suspicious of the media. The London newspapers were the most abusive and irresponsible toward McCartney.

A good example of this tendency was demonstrated in a **London Sun** account of McCartney's life. The **Sun** charged that Philip Howarth, a young man who lived in Crosby near Liverpool, was McCartney's illegitimate son. The **Sun's** heavy handed reporting alleged that McCartney paid off the young man. There was no apparent purpose behind the **Sun's** reporting. There was also no proof for this sensational accusation.

After returning from his first visit to Hamburg, Paul went down to Allan Williams' new Liverpool spot, the Top Ten Club. Williams' was attempting to mimic the Hamburg Reeperbahn night club scene, but his club had little class. Williams was still the King of the Liverpool beat clubs, but there was competition from other promoters. There were also new bands. So Williams didn't feel that he needed the Beatles. A short sighted man, Williams believed that any band could fill his nondescript clubs.

The German music scene convinced Williams that he could duplicate Hamburg success with his Liverpool Top Ten Club. The bullying tactics of Bruno Koschmider appealed to Williams and he saw himself in the same mold as his Hamburg counterpart. Along the way, however, Williams offended some real local gangsters. Before he could open his new club it burnt to the ground. The Liverpool police announced it was arson but failed to investigate. There had been too many of Williams' schemes that had infuriated local politicians and businessmen. The local police were pleased that Williams' club burned so quickly.

From January through March 1961, the Beatles performed regularly in small Liverpool clubs where Brian Kelly did the booking. It was Kelly, a large, jolly man, who saw a future in the Beatles. "I knew the boys had something different," Kelly remarked. "When they played I loved the crowd's reaction." Kelly was not alone. Everyone was talking about the Beatles. Kelly promoted the "Beekey" dances in small halls in North Liverpool, they were considered the best dances in Northern England and helped to establish the Mersey music scene.

Kelly remains one of the most knowledgeable, if obscure, members of the Mersey sound. A gregarious personality with a penchant for a quick drink and a sly smile, Kelly booked the Beatles into many Liverpool venues. A larger than life figure, Kelly loved the music and the enthusiastic crowds. Kelly owned Alpha Sound and provided the Beatles with amplifiers. There was a party atmosphere at Kelly's dances and the Beatles loved playing for him. "I think the Beatles had a sound that was unto itself," Kelly remarked.

Bob Wooler recognized the Beatles new sound. "I couldn't believe how they had changed," Wooler remarked, "they weren't the band I had seen a year earlier." With his remarkable record collection and easy going personality, Wooler was the perfect candidate to manage the Beatles. In early 1961 he helped them book a number of dances and was instrumental in dealing with sympathetic local promoters like Brian Kelly and Sam Leach. Wooler had the Beatles' best interests at heart. He was friendly with John Lennon who envisioned him as a substitute father. There was talk of Wooler managing the Beatles. "I didn't want to manage the boys," Wooler remarked, "but I did everything I could to help them." The Beatles were drawing large audiences to their dances and the teen underground talked about their music.

The successes of the dances the Beatles played at Lathom Hall and the Aintree Institute were the result of Wooler's promotional genius. As a disc jockey, he was instrumental in developing the Mersey sound. He loved the bands and did everything he could to promote local groups. An accomplished artist, Wooler drew up stunning posters and provocative handbills. He wanted no more than to make the Beatles stars. There was a purity and kindness to Wooler that made many suspicious of him, but over the years he has remained true to the spirit of early Beatle music.

One of Wooler's earliest suggestions was that the Beatles tune their instruments, play some rough rock and roll backstage and prepare for their show. "I tried to tell the boys that they were like a soccer team," Wooler commented, "they had fans who expected a certain kind of performance."

At local clubs in 1961 the Beatles drew increasingly larger audiences. The Cavern featured them at lunch time and during nine noontime March appearances the first signs of Beatlemania surfaced. The Cavern owner, Ray McFall, recognized their drawing power. So he featured them at often as possible. This ended when the Beatles signed for ninety-eight nights at the Top Ten Club in Hamburg.

The return to Germany was like a coronation. On March 27, 1961, the Beatles opened at the Top Ten Club and were cheered by an adoring audience. The Hamburg crowd didn't recognize how musically tight the band had become. The Germans, never long on musical knowledge, loved the Beatles show. "I think the Germans simply liked any American music," Horst Fascher remarked, "they didn't care who did it or what it sounded like."

It was during this return trip to Hamburg that Paul and Stu fought over Sutcliffe's inadequate bass playing. Paul was still angry about Sutcliffe's inclusion in the band. He was John's friend but a lousy musician. When Stu quit the band to concentrate upon his art work, McCartney was free to be the sole bass guitarist. The myth has persisted that Paul wanted Sutcliffe out of the group so that he could become the bass player. There was no plot by Paul to become the Beatles' bassist, it was simply the logical position for McCartney to assume in the band.

When the Beatles concluded their Hamburg engagement, they were an accomplished rock band. Paul had learned to play the piano and drums and was working on his electric guitar technique, but they still needed to work on their song writing. "We thought John and Paul were strange because they wanted to write their own songs," Tony Sheridan remarked. "We didn't realize they were going to become millionaires writing rock and roll."

In July 1961, the Beatles returned to Liverpool. It was an idyllic summer full of girls, music and drink. The summer highlight was the August 25, Riverboat Shuffle. This was the first of four floating Beatles' performances aboard the Royal Iris. Acker Bilk, a traditional jazz clarinetist, performed on one of these cruises and praised the Beatles' music. As the Beatles played in and around Liverpool the question was raised about releasing a record. No one knew that the Beatles had already cut a record.

They recorded with Tony Sheridan for Germany's Polydor Record label. The session, supervised by German band leader Bert Kaempfert, led to the release of a single, "My Bonnie." Tony Sheridan sang lead on the song and the Beatles acting as Sheridan's backup group were renamed the Beat Brothers. The b side featured Tony Sheridan singing "When The Saints Go Marching In." The single was prepared for release in the German market. In June 1961, as John, Paul, George and Pete caught the train for Liverpool, the first Beatle single remained unreleased. "They didn't know what to do with the song or the Beatles," Tony Sheridan remarked. "I was a German star and made good money, the Beatles were unknown. So Polydor ignored their music."

The demand to release a Beatle record was helped by Bill Harry's **Mersey Beat** newspaper. This Merseyside music newspaper featured a column by Bob Wooler praising the Beatles. It also contained a short history of the band written by John Lennon, but **Mersey Beat's** most significant function was in promoting the Beatles.

A Beatle fan club was organized in September 1961, and a legion of young girls showed up whenever and wherever the Beatles played. There was a strong Beatle following and the record they cut in Germany was bought by mail order. The knowledgeable fans showed off the Polydor record, thereby creating a great deal of envy. It was only a matter of time before local stores were inundated with requests for the 45.

On a cold, wind blown October 28, 1961, Saturday, Brian Epstein came to work early to inventory the pop records. The perfectly manicured young men who worked at NEMS were not in the shop nor were the demure, polite girls that Brian hired to please the customers. Brian was thinking more about Anthony Newley's music rather than the Mersey sound. This changed when eighteen year old Raymond Jones walked into the Whitechapel branch of the NEMS wearing the uniform of the young rock and roller, a black leather jacket and dirty jeans. Jones said that he was looking for a record, "My Bonnie." It was a 45 by a group called the Beatles. Epstein listened to Jones request quizzically. Brian had not heard of the record. This bothered Epstein who fancied himself an expert. He knew the English record market inside out.

As was his habit, Brian wrote himself a note: "The Beatles, 'My Bonnie' Check on Monday." But before Brian could search for the record there were other requests for it. He was intrigued.

Like many local Liverpool music buffs, Brian had heard about the Beatles. Bob Wooler recalled that Brian had been on the music scene for some time. "I believe Brian had seen the Beatles when they weren't much of a group," Wooler stated. "It was after they came back from Hamburg that he took an interest." Wooler, like many people connected with the early Beatles, doubts that Raymond Jones was the sole reason for Epstein's interest in the Beatles. "It was glamorous to have a band of young boys working for you," Wooler maintained. "Brian saw it as a challenge."

As a result of the request for the Beatle record, Epstein showed up at the Cavern Club. Contrary to popular myth, Brian had been at the club a number of times. "Brian loved music," Clive Epstein remarked, "he watched jazz at the Cavern many times before he first saw the Beatles."

As Ray Coleman's biography suggests: "Brian Epstein in 1961 was the least likely person to enter the lives of four leather-clad, street sharp rock 'n' rollers." The twenty-seven year old Epstein managed the record section of his father's NEMS store which specialized in furniture and appliances. The record department was Brian's responsibility and he turned it into the most comprehensive record store in Northern England.

Since Brian had little knowledge of rock and roll music, it was up to one of Liverpool's rock and rollers to educate the young businessman. It was due to Bill Harry and the birth of his local music newspaper that Epstein learned of the Mersey beat. A Liverpool College of Art student, Harry was friendly with John Lennon and was a fledgling journalist. He had the dream of starting his own rock and roll newspaper. On July 6, 1961, the dream became reality with the publication of the first issue of **Mersey Beat.** This Liverpool based newspaper became the most influential rock music publication in the provinces. In its first issue Harry published a story by Lennon that traced the Beatles' early history. It was an interesting journalistic piece filled with puns, irony and allegory, the intellectual commodities that made Lennon a great songwriter.

It was difficult to make **Mersey Beat** pay. So Harry had to hustle for advertisements. This is how he met Brian Epstein. To promote his newspaper, Harry visited every record and music store in Liverpool. At NEMS, he talked to Brian and convinced him to take a dozen newspapers to sell in his store. Brian was skeptical. He didn't believe that there was a demand for a rock and roll newspaper. Brian was familiar with **Melody Maker** and the **New Musical Express** because they covered the music scene. Brain doubted that **Mersey Beat** would be of interest to most consumers but he took a dozen graciously. They sold out instantly.

When Brian called Harry at his 81a Renshaw Street office, he realized that the office was a mecca for local musicians. "What Brian learned," Bob Wooler remembered, "is that to make it in Liverpool if you were poor, you had to be a soccer player or a musician." It seemed everyone was in a band and Wooler maintained a list of more than 200 rock groups available for local clubs. "There was more music than we could present," Wooler concluded.

With keen interest Brian read the July 20, 1961, **Mersey Beat** with a headline which heralded the Beatles' recording contract with Polydor Records. While talking with Bill Harry, however, Brian decided that he would like to review records for **Mersey Beat.** After listening to the new music, reading the new rock newspapers and examining the pulsating club scene, Brian decided to spend some more time at the Cavern Club.

At noon the dank, sweaty, subterranean Cavern club was not a pleasant place to spend time. There was something about this dingy club that intrigued Epstein. He couldn't put his finger on it. Joe Flannery recalled: "Brian loved the ambiance of the Cavern, and even he couldn't explain why. I guess he just had show business in his blood." Brian also realized that it was the best place to watch the Beatles perform.

Brian's interest in the Beatles and trips to the Cavern Club helped establish Liverpool's rock and roll respectability. He was an influential record man who operated a thriving business. At Epstein's NEMS store a record could be made or broken, therefore rock musicians began frequenting the store in large numbers.

As Brian watched the Beatles perform at one of the Cavern's lunch time shows, he had an immediate impulse to manage them. He controlled that desire. Instead he took his assistant, Alistair Taylor, out to lunch and they discussed the Beatles at length. Brian's thoughts about the rock music business made Taylor uneasy. Epstein talked about the bright silver lining in the Beatles' future. Taylor countered that they were dirty, crude and musically unsophisticated. During the lunch Taylor was uneasy, because he disliked rock music. As Brian and Alistair sat in the Peacock Restaurant in nearby Hackins Hey talking about the Beatles, they were fascinated over the Liverpool rock music explosion.

After the lunch Taylor realized that Epstein was serious about managing the boys. Brian talked at length about setting up a separate company for the Beatles. But Brian was not a foolish businessman. He was uncertain about how to enter the management side of the music industry. So Brian spent a month quietly slipping into the Cavern. He took along members of his staff and solicited their opinions. "Brian came up to me one night," Joe Flannery remarked, "and began asking me all sorts of questions about rock music." They had been friends since childhood, so Flannery gave Brian free advice. Flannery suggested that Brian educate himself about the management side of the rock music business. Prior to becoming a successful hotel and wholesale grocery entrepreneur, Flannery was a comedian. So he had a sure knowledge of show business. For almost a month, Joe educated his old boyhood friend Brian in the fine art of music management. Since Flannery was guiding his brother's group, Lee Curtis and the All Stars, there was a wealth of knowledge for Epstein to pick up. "I didn't realize at the time how serious Brian was about the Beatles," Flannery concluded. Finally, in early December 1961, Brian invited the Beatles to his office. The purpose of the visit, Brian suggested, was to discuss a management contract.

On Tuesday night December 2, 1961, the Beatles performed at the Cavern. They told Bob Wooler that the following day they would discuss a contract with Mr. Epstein. The Beatles were concerned about acquiring a "proper manager." Under Allan Williams' management the Beatles had been taken advantage of in every sense. Williams' was more interested in bragging about himself than in helping the Beatles. The loud, brash, vulgar Williams was a sharp contrast to the gentle, effete Mr. Epstein. The meticulous, gracious Epstein used his charm to great advantage. The Beatles were swept away by his honesty, and a single-minded devotion to business detail.

When the Beatles met with Brian they were late. The boys spent a few hours in a local pub with Bob Wooler, and the beer they consumed heightened their nerve. Finally, Pete and George walked down to talk to Brian. Paul went home and a few hours later, as it neared 7:30 John and Bob Wooler walked into Brian's office.

This initial business meeting allowed Brian to size up the Beatles. He didn't like what he saw. They were crude, poorly dressed and lacked manners. Yet, Brian couldn't forget the reaction to their music. There was something unique to the boys and Brian was determined to find out what it was. "I think that Brian was overwhelmed with the scene and the Lennon-McCartney magic the first time he saw the boys," Alistair Taylor recalled. They also had a record that was selling well in Liverpool.

A part of the Beatles problem was their past association with Allan Williams. Like many Liverpudlians, Brian looked upon Williams with disgust. His clubs, the Blue Angel and the Jacaranda, were ones which Epstein described as amateurish. He found Williams personally repulsive as did almost everyone else in and around Liverpool. "Privately," Clive Epstein remembered, "my brother referred to Williams in most unflattering terms."

Despite his personal distaste for Williams, Brian sought him out for advice about the Beatles. Williams wasn't complimentary about the boys. He accused the Beatles of taking advantage of his management skills. Brian smiled. He sized up Williams' as a small minded man with a street smart sense of survival. Williams had been lucky, not skillful, in discovering new musical talent.

Brian made his decision, he would manage the Beatles. The next step was a proper contract. The Epstein family lawyer, Rex Makin, drew up the document, and the boys signed it. The agreement went into effect on February 1, 1962. The contract was for a five year period.

From the beginning, Paul was skeptical of Epstein. While Paul was gracious, his objections centered around Epstein's lack of experience in the management end of the music business. It was Paul's father, Jim Mac, who overcame these initial doubts. Because of his experience in the music business, Paul's dad saw another side to Epstein. He realized that the young Liverpool businessman had something to prove to his dad and family. Brian's younger brother, Clive, was the favored sibling and Brian would use the Beatles to establish his own independence. Jim McCartney's opinions were enough for Paul, and he dropped his opposition to the contract.

It was not until early 1964 that Paul expressed renewed doubts about Brian's management skills. From the day that he signed the contract with Epstein, Paul involved himself in business matters. He also gave Brian advice. Brian listened politely but failed to heed McCartney's advice. This bothered Paul, but these early differences faded in the glory of British and American Beatlemania in 1963-1964.

There was an electrifying presence to Brian that intrigued the Beatles and this explains why things went so smoothly on the surface during the early days. "I'll never forget when Brian walked into the Cavern during a lunch time concert," Bob Wooler commented. "It electrified the place." It was Thursday, November 9, 1961, and Bob Wooler remarked that Brian was hooked on the atmosphere. He had been in the club for jazz nights, but the rock and roll crowd made Brian shiver with excitement. He loved the young boys. The girls hooted and hollered and he drank in the excitement. "We had trouble with my brother for years," Clive Epstein remembered, "and when he went to the Cavern we thought it was another dalliance." But it was far from a hobby. Brian Epstein had a vision. He saw a commercial future in the Beatles and the Mersey sound. The time was right for a unique brand of British rock music.

Despite the well-publicized interest in the Mersey sound,

Brian's task was to secure a recording contract. This proved to be a difficult feat, because of the reluctance of the major English labels to recognize the commercial appeal of rock music. After making the rounds of London's major record companies, Epstein was turned down by every significant label. Eventually, Parlophone, a budget label, signed the Beatles. It was not important news in the entertainment industry.

George Martin, the producer at Parlophone assigned to the Beatles, knew very little about rock music. He had a reputation for honesty, integrity and hard work. He also worked for a large firm, EMI, a British corporation founded in 1931, that had little interest in rock and roll music. There were a number of labels that EMI supervised, with HMV being the most prestigious. The least significant was Parlophone. It was a budget operation which turned out novelty items. EMI executives hoped that the Beatles might find a market in the Woolworth record counters.

Alistair Taylor, Brian's assistant, remarked to me at a Beatlefest that after the Beatles couldn't convince the major English labels to sign the group, Brian blackmailed them into a contract. Since Brian owned the largest record shop in Northern England, NEMS, he could force EMI into a recording agreement. If they didn't sign the Beatles, Brian wouldn't sell their records. So, as Taylor recalls, Parlophone recorded the Beatles, and the corporate brain trust believed that they were doomed to fail with this budget label.

After months of negotiation Brian Epstein and Parlophone agreed on a contract. The June 4, 1962, agreement was a simple recording contract that did little more than give the Beatles a chance to record. Just two days after signing the contract, the Beatles drove to London's Abbey Road Studio to record their first songs. The tree lined streets leading to Abbey Road highlighted a suburban setting that surprised the Beatles. Although Abbey Road was a part of North London, it had a distinct rural ambiance.

In the studio, George Martin immediately saw something special in the boys' music. Once they went into the Abbey Road Studio the Beatles were put through individual musical tests. They passed with varying degrees of success. Martin liked Paul's pop voice and was struck by John's growling vocals. When a writer asked who the Beatles leader should be? Martin replied: "I should make Paul the leader." He quickly changed his mind when he realized it was John Lennon's band.

During this recording session, the Beatles were a pleasant surprise to George Martin and the people at Parlophone. They had an energy and enthusiasm that translated into excellent music. But Martin had no idea that he was producing what would become the most popular rock group of the 1960s.

Above: The Beatles conquering America.

Left: Paul chows down.

3: PAUL AND TWO PHASES OF BEATLEMANIA, 1963-1966

In January 1963, the cold London winter arrived early and the stoic English glumly trudged from home to factory. There was little to cheer in England as the economy staggered, the French bullied the British in Western Europe and London entertainment offered little that was new. At night the British dutifully turned on one of the two BBC television channels or the independent ATV network. Cliff Richard and the Shadows remained England's top rock music act. A pop version of Elvis Presley, Richard was the closest thing to a major rock and roll act in England. Other pioneer rock artists like Tommy Steele had escaped to legitimate theater. Generally, the English ignored rock music.

A genteel civilization long in decline, England was out of touch with most world trends. The economic, manufacturing, technological and banking skills that had once made Great Britain a formidable world power had vanished. What remained was a mediocre civilization. It was ironic that during this era of decline that the Beatles would become the nation's major industry. While the English loved the Beatles, they failed to recognize how important the Liverpool lads were to the economy. The English prided themselves on their civility, sense of world leadership and rational attitudes. As a result they found it difficult to recognize the impact of the Beatles' music financially.

As the Beatles' early records sold in large numbers, their concerts were a media event and the nation took notice. The post-war baby boom created a larger teen population who, despite the uncertain economic times, had money to spend. Teen consumers reached a stage of independence which allowed them to spend virtually their entire paychecks on records, concerts and clothes. The blue collar, working class kids eagerly looked for new music. The British music press helped with coverage of the rising English rock and roll sound.

The most significant force in publicizing the Beatles were the London based music newspapers **Melody Maker** and **New Musical Express.** While they blew alternately hot and cold about rock music during the Beatles' early days, they were still important news sources. Jazz, pop, show tunes, and English actors turned crooners dominated the English music charts. But it was the **Melody Maker** and the **New Musical Express** listings that made or broke an artist. The early English rock stars, Tommy Steele, Cliff Richard, Billy Fury, Terry Dene, Marty Wilde, Dickie Pride, Johnny Kidd and John Leyton among others had an American style. They appeared on stage with greased up hair dos, mohair suits and recorded silly pop ballads.

John Leyton was the perfect example of this phenomena. A successful television actor who dabbled in music, Leyton's 1961 single "Johnny Remember Me" was number 1 on the British charts. Eventually, after a number of hit records, Leyton left the music business and English television for a Hollywood career. He was typical of the British pop singer. An artist who couldn't decide between the stage, the movies or the musical theater. In the **New Musical Express** annual poll for 1961, Leyton was voted two top honors-"Most Promising Newcomer" and "Best Disc of the Year."

The state of British rock and roll was reflected in **Melody Maker.** This prestigious music magazine attacked many early British rock acts, and the jazz oriented writers made fun of the attempt to cover American rock music. When Van Morrison and Them came to London from Ireland to appear on the British TV show, Ready, Steady, Go, a reporter found it strange that they played American blues music. "I couldn't believe the British press," Morrison remembered, "they had a disdain for the blues and they didn't know their jazz." It was the constant criticism by pedestrian music critics and the provincial attitudes about the direction of rock and roll music which prompted Van Morrison to leave England for New York. "I needed to clear my head," Morrison remarked, "the English record producers wanted one type of song, it wasn't my scene." Van Morrison's remarks are echoed by many musicians who wanted more freedom in the studio. The thin skinned Morrison was upset by the non-scientific nature of the **New Musical Express** chart. **NME** reporters capriciously selected hit records and often ignored briskly selling records. **Melody Maker** rated records in a similar vein. The pompous, condescending jazz critics hated rock and roll. Because of the attitude of the music press it was necessary to treat them right. While not engaging in obvious bribery, no comfort was denied the rock critic.

Brian Epstein spent thousands of pounds entertaining **NME** and **MM** staffers. Since Top 40 radio didn't exist in England the music newspapers had an inordinate influence upon record sales. Ronan O'Rahily, the owner of London's Scene Club, was so outraged by the state of British rock criticism that he founded a pirate radio station. In May 1964, Radio Caroline began beaming signals to English rock and rollers. "I don't think the really popular music was being rated," O'Rahily commented. "I fixed that with the pirate stations." The Beatles loved Radio Caroline and her sister station Radio Atlanta. Their music was featured on these stations and Paul remarked that they were the "real record raters."

Because of their wit and sarcasm the Beatles' received **Melody Maker's** most vitriolic criticism. Since John Lennon didn't like photos with his glasses on, **Melody Maker** went out of its way to publish these types of pictures complete with insipid captions. **Melody Maker** loved to make fun of Brian Epstein and his sensible approach to rock and roll music. From October 4, 1962, until February 1963 **Melody Maker** virtually ignored the Beatles. Many of the significant rock music staff writers poked fun at Brian Epstein. "The underlings and small time writers loved to try to intimidate Brian," Bob Wooler remarked. When they did write about the Beatles it was often with disdain. **MM** didn't believe that the Beatles were an important act. This changed when the Beatles went on a well publicized and critically acclaimed tour of England in February and March 1963 with Helen Shapiro, Tommy Roe and Chris Montez. "I remember how the writers traveling with us marveled at the Beatles impact," Tommy Roe remarked. The reaction from the fans and the resulting newspaper publicity forced **Melody Maker** to take the Beatles seriously.

The **New Musical Express** was the key opinion maker in England, due to its polls and record ratings. When the Beatles' "Love Me Do" first appeared on the **NME** chart the newspaper's circulation increased by almost 300,000 copies. The early in-depth stories were bought up by eager fans. This changed **NME's** attitude toward British rock music. They not only supported the new wave of English rock bands but began to provide inside information on the groups.

The first sign of the Beatles' British success occurred on January 12, 1963, when they appeared on "Thank Your Lucky Stars." The Beatles were touring constantly, but they traveled to ATV's Birmingham Studio ready to put on a strong television performance. They had just returned from a brief tour of Scottish ballrooms and were musically tight. When they arrived at ATV's Birmingham studio the producer, Philip Jones, had no idea who the Beatles were or why they were booked on the show. This booking was due to music magnate Dick James. The Beatles song publisher realized that "Thank Your Lucky Stars" was popular with the kids who bought records. The show featured a teenage record critic, Janice, who urged the fans to buy some records over others. James hoped that Janice would like the Beatles, thereby spurring their record sales. The Top Twenty records were rated each week on the program. This appearance was their most important TV date and could make or break them.

In the midst of their early English commercial success the Beatles signed a song publishing deal with Dick James. Because their earnings grew so rapidly they were concerned about prohibitive British taxes. As Bob Wooler remembered, "James came to the boys with a solution to their financial problems, he was London's leading music publisher. I know John thought it was a marvelous opportunity." While James had reputation for honesty and integrity, he also was known for his shrewd business deals.

When James helped the Beatles form Northern Songs Ltd. in February 1963, he wittingly lined his own pockets. In its initial corporate structure Northern Songs Ltd. listed Brian Epstein and Dick James as directors. It was in the division of company shares that James caused the Beatles irrevocable financial harm. On the surface James owned no more stock than Lennon and McCartney. But in the contract's fine print the song writing duo was obliged to James until the mid-1970s.

The structure of the agreement also worked to James' advantage. The Northern Songs Ltd. stock was divided into A and B stock issues. The Articles of Association describe these stocks as a marriage between Lennon-McCartney and Dick James. The two interests would nominate a director and, in theory, all important decisions would be compromise ones. Since each side controlled a director, James told McCartney, they would work as a team. After the Beatles agreed to form Northern Songs Ltd., James restructured the contract and took control. The Beatles' earliest publishing copyrights were credited to Lenmac Enterprises Ltd. which was quickly sold to Northern Songs Ltd. for 284,00 pounds. What Lennon and McCartney didn't realize was that they sold the copyright of their tunes to James when he bought Lenmac Enterprises. This proved to be a disastrous business decision.

When Northern Songs Ltd. was reorganized in February 1965, James' influence and control increased. Because they grew suspicious of James' machinations, Lennon and McCartney formed Maclen (Music) Ltd. This was an agreement which granted Lennon and McCartney the first 50% of all song writing revenue. The remainder went to Northern Songs where Lennon-McCartney each had a 15% interest. What this contract did, however, was to bind Lennon and McCartney to Northern Songs Ltd. for another eight years. It was not until 1973 that the two chief Beatles would be free of Northern Songs. It was this agreement which began the Beatles' road to disintegration.

As the original deal was put together in the early months of 1963 no one realized the future value of rock and roll songs. In this business deal, Northern Songs and Dick James controlled copyright privileges. The irony of this provision is that when the Beatles organized the Apple Corporation and their own publishing companies, James quickly sold his share in Northern Songs Ltd. and ATV Music. In McCartney's view this was tantamount to treason. The Beatles, in the midst of these business negotiations, rehearsed diligently for the concert that would create English Beatlemania in its most rabid form.

On January 12, 1963, an unusually large English TV audience turned on the "Thank Your Lucky Stars" program and watched the Beatles perform. This show marked the beginning of England's preoccupation with the Beatles.

The Beatles performed inside a big metal heart. They

presented a unique entertainment picture. Their stylish suits were buttoned up to their necks, their hair was precise and cute, and the music was energetic American rock and roll. Yet, it wasn't an American song, it was a Beatle original-"Please Please Me."

As the new single "Please Please Me" was released the **New Musical Express** praised the Beatles' pop sound. The pompous, cutting intellectual edge that was typical of the British gave way to praise. "After all," a member of the House of Commons suggested, "they (the Beatles) are a comedy group." Maureen Cleve, a reporter for the **London Daily Standard**, was the journalistic exception as she wrote glowingly about the Beatles' music. Vincent Mulchrone of the **London Daily Mail** followed suit and suddenly they were a national item. The depressing conditions surrounding British life made the Beatles an innocent means of relieving national boredom.

The Radio Luxembourg disc jockey, Keith Fordyce, wrote glowingly about the Beatles in the **New Musical Express.** The positive reviews helped to attract a wide European audience for the Beatles. Brian Matthew, the MC for "Thank Your Lucky Stars," praised the Beatles, thereby assuring them of continued radio-television exposure. Brian Epstein was only too happy to oblige as he realized that this publicity was creating strong record sales.

As the Beatles popularity grew outside of Liverpool they were booked in every nook and cranny of Great Britain. Often the bookings provided abysmally low guarantees. But the experience that the Beatles gained playing nightly in small and large clubs, as well as the concert venues was invaluable.

While on tour, Paul loved to walk into record stores and purchase a Beatle 45. In February and March 1963, he delighted in finding his records in local stores. He also displayed a playful attitude toward other artists. Just before the Beatles appeared on a BBC radio show, Paul went to Oxford Street and bought John Leyton's hit "Cupboard Love." He began throwing it around back stage. One journalist asked:

"What is that, Paul?"

"The end of the old British rock," Paul smiled and held the end of the record up. The **Melody Maker** reporter walked away shaking his head. This was typical of McCartney's comical approach to the music business.

The Beatles national tour with Helen Shapiro, Tommy Roe and Chris Montez was the subject of countless newspaper and magazine articles. The tour created a screaming mob of girls who continually clamored for the Beatles. "I was closing the shows," Tommy Roe remembered, "but after three performances I went on before the Beatles. They were simply too tough an act to follow." They had to close each concert because of the screaming young girls. A few weeks later "Please Please Me" was number 1 on the **Melody Maker** chart.

While on tour with Helen Shapiro the Beatles were bored. It was night after night of endless concerts with the same musical set. There was too much free time. One night in Carlisle the Young Conservative Club invited the tour star, Helen Shapiro, to one of its dances. The Young Conservatives were a group of British public college students who were being trained for future leadership.This stuffy, pompous political club was similar to America's Young Republicans. They took themselves too seriously, thereby inviting the Beatles' blistering wit. They also had little understanding of or interest in rock and roll music. The Young Conservatives hoped to take advantage of the publicity of Helen Shapiro appearing at their dance to increase membership.

The thought of attending a Young Conservative Club dance was not a pleasant one for Helen Shapiro. So she asked the Beatles to escort her. They dressed up in leather outfits, combed their hair into greasy pompadours and took on a menacing air. It was all a good joke. When the Beatles arrived with Shapiro they were turned away and told not to come back. What started out as a joke turned into a well-publicized comment on the Beatles' popularity.

Every English newspaper featured the story. Helen Shapiro was asked to leave a dance due to her rough companions. Or better yet Helen Shapiro could stay, if her "thug friends" left. The version changed from paper to paper and the Beatles were featured as the newest danger to British teens. Record sales picked up after this incident, because the **London Daily Express** sensationalized the tale. The Beatles were touring, appearing on BBC-radio's "Saturday Club" and rising on the **Melody Maker** charts. So this incident only added to their popularity.

The Beatles were a national phenomenon. The NEMS office in Liverpool was inundated with fan mail and journalists descended upon the Beatles' former haunts. "I was surprised by the press reaction," Bob Wooler remarked, "there was no doubt in my mind that the Beatles were special...but I didn't realize how many people outside of Liverpool loved their music." Wooler recalled lending the Beatles many of his obscure American hits. "They loved to play my strange American records, as John called them. I didn't know any group that could cover the obscure hits from the states like the Beatles."

Their commercial success in Great Britain was unexpected. Many English rock critics wrote them off as a temporary change in the charts. The January 2, 1963, **Mersey Beat** article by Alan Smith was an indication that this opinion was an erroneous one. **Mersey Beat** announced that for the second year in a row the Beatles were the magazine's popularity poll winners.

Radio Luxembourg was the barometer that British teenagers used to select their music. On January 18, 1963, a live Beatle broadcast over the privately owned Radio Luxembourg featured John Lennon performing Chuck Berry's "Carol" and Paul and George singing "Lend Me Your Comb." In the 1950s Paul had listened nightly to Radio Luxembourg and now he was featured on it. The following day "Please Please Me" entered the **Melody Maker** chart at number 47.

During the next two months the Beatles' spectacular successes continued. Their concerts sold out and fans were turned away at every venue. In late January, Vee Jay Records, a Chicago based firm, signed the Beatles for the American market. Little Richard personally called Vee Jay to convince the label that the Beatles could be the first British act to succeed in the fickle American market. But it was the English market which concerned Brian Epstein. So he had the boys concentrate on taping songs for the BBC's "Talent Spot" and "Saturday Club" programs. "Please Please Me" went to number 1 on the **Mersey Beat** chart, Epstein informed the Beatles they were on their way to stardom. The London critics ignored this because **Mersey Beat** was considered their home magazine. The Liverpool based journal was staffed by close friends of Epstein and the Beatles, and they acted more like a public relations arm than rock critics.

Yet, there was no reason to ignore the Beatles' explosion. There were signs of popularity everywhere in England. They blended old and obscure American tunes with Lennon and McCartney originals which led to commercial success. The 45 record sales were strong, so it was time for the Beatles to record and release an album.

On March 22, 1963, the Beatles' first LP, **Please Please Me,** was rushed into record stores. This LP was a mix of Beatle originals and American cover records. They were gratuitous comments on the album jacket mentioning the Shirelles and the Goffin-King song writing team. It was still necessary for British groups to pay homage to American artists. Neither George Martin, the album producer, nor Brian Epstein, the Beatles manager, realized the LP's magnitude.

"When the Beatles' first album was released Brian was still tentative about the boys," Bob Wooler remarked. "He wasn't sure what he had." Echoing similar comments, Clive Epstein remembered that Brian had failed in previous endeavors.

It didn't take Martin and Epstein long to figure out the Beatles appeal. The girls loved their looks, the critics praised their "pop ditties" and the condescending British intellectuals heaped praise on Lennon and McCartney's song writing. As Brian and the Beatles trooped across the United Kingdom in 1963 they conquered a skeptical audience with the proper dress, the courtesy of the well bred and a slight touch of rascal behavior. This blend was one the English public loved.

Looking for heroes at a time of international decline, the British press played up the Beatles' working class background. The only problem was that the London tabloids failed to check their sources. As a result John was envisioned as a working class rebel while Paul's biographical sketch emphasized his education, cultural aspirations and middle class pretensions. The truth was that John had grown up in a permissive home with all the comforts, whereas Paul lived in a series of adequate, but drab, council houses.

Few people were concerned about the Beatles personal lives. Each week the British eagerly tuned in to BBC radio shows such as the Saturday Club and the Easy Beat to hear the latest Beatle record. The radio broadcasts built a large audience for tours and guaranteed abundant record sales. Beatlemania was building into a gigantic force. Each new Beatle record outsold the previous one.

When "From Me To You," the Beatles third Parlophone release, came out in mid-April, 1963, there was no question about their continued success. The story line in the song "From Me To You" was a fascinating tale. While on tour with the Helen Shapiro show, John and Paul spent an inordinate amount of time reading on the bus. They loved to peruse the music newspapers and laugh at the jazz oriented reporters. Brian scolded the boys for their attitudes and reminded them that the **New Musical Express** and **Melody Maker** could make or break them. In a moment of devious delight, John and Paul decided to write a song about the **NME.**

The result was "From Me To You" which was based on the **New Musical Express** column "From Us to You." In a party mood on the cold winter night of February 28, 1963, John and Paul were awake in the bus as it wound its way through the English countryside. To relieve the boredom they wrote "From Me To You." Fortunately for the Beatles, **NME** took the tune as a compliment." The Beatles made fun of the jazz oriented reporters," Tommy Roe remarked, "but Brian Epstein was always there to soothe things over."

Early 1963 was a blur for McCartney. He went from concert dates to radio and TV appearances to personal autograph sessions and into the recording studio. By June Paul was physically and emotionally exhausted. He was also preparing to turn twenty-one. To celebrate McCartney's symbolic journey to full manhood a party was set up. But it had to be planned in a remote spot. Even in the early days of Beatlemania it was hard to find privacy.

The perfect spot for a birthday celebration was Aunt Jin's home in Birkenhead. It was far removed from London's spotlight and the intrusive Liverpool fans could be kept away. John and Cynthia, Ringo and Maureen, George, Brian and Bob Wooler joined with some of Mike McCartney's friends to stage a crazy birthday. "Paul and the boys were happy with their success," Bob Wooler remarked, "but they partied like they were broke. It was a wonderful time."

It was at Paul's twenty first birthday party that Bob

Wooler noticed the first signs of tension. McCartney's role in Beatle affairs was a minor one. John received most of the publicity, Brian organized the tours and the subordinates handled the petty details. "Paul was thinking about the future, even at this early date," Wooler remembered. What Wooler suggests is that McCartney had a musical vision that went beyond traditional rock and roll.

"I think Paul's twenty-first birthday was a landmark," Clive Epstein remarked. "The Beatles were a unit, one for all and all for one, it was marvelous to watch." Clive claims that he didn't fully appreciate the Beatles success. "The boys were a much bigger entertainment act than most of us realized," Clive continued, "we thought that perhaps they were just another of Brian's flash in the pan schemes. We certainly were wrong." While Paul celebrated his birthday there were others who believed that the Beatles were the wave of the future. "I saw something in Paul's song writing that portended future greatness," Joe Flannery remarked. Others dismissed the Beatles. "There were a hundred groups as good as the Beatles," Allan Williams remarked. "The record companies came here and signed everybody." Williams' remark was an honest one. The English record charts were filled with hits by northern groups.

In July 1963, the Searchers' "Sweets For My Sweet" climbed the English charts to number 1 and opened the way for Merseyside acts. The Searchers charted eight British hits in 1963-1964 and this brought the A and R men to Liverpool in large numbers. Soon Rory Storm and the Hurricanes, Faron's Flamingos, Lee Curtis, Kingsize Taylor, Howie Casey and the Seniors and Gerry and the Pacemakers were signed to recording contracts.

The London A and R men didn't understand the Mersey sound, so they simply signed the groups to contracts based on their looks. Lee Curtis was the best looking singer in Liverpool. His brother Joe Flannery showcased Curtis' pop talent into a mainstream musical format. Not only was Curtis an exceptional singer, but he had the stage moves and personal charisma to melt the girls.

From 1961 to 1963 Lee Curtis played regularly around Liverpool and in Hamburg. In 1963 Decca Records released a single, "Little Girl" that seemed destined for pop success. At Hamburg's Star Club Curtis was not only a major attraction, but a rising German pop star. Such Curtis cover records as "Shot of Rhythm and Blues," "Nobody But You," "Mohair Sam" and "Come On Down To My Boat" were local Hamburg hits. But outside Liverpool and Hamburg the multi-talented Curtis failed to capture a rock and roll audience.

He never became a pop star, but his records offer a fascinating glimpse into popular English tastes. When Curtis' recorded "Baberock" which was based on "Finiculi Finiculi" from

"The Barber of Seville," it became a Liverpool hit. But this record doomed the handsome young singer's career. By identifying with show tunes, Curtis was unable to convince the rock and roll crowd that he was a serious contender.

Lee Curtis and the All Stars performed regularly at the Cavern where he was remembered as a magnetic performer. Curtis' cover versions of Bill Haley's "Skinny Minnie" and Frankie Laine's "Jezebel" excited local crowds. Curtis was comfortable with a rock song or a pop tune, but he failed to achieve mainstream commercial success. There were other Merseyside artists who had monster hits. Ironically, his new drummer for a time was Pete Best.

When Billy J. Kramer's "Bad To Me," a Lennon-McCartney song, reached the top of the English charts during the summer of 1963, the song vindicated Epstein's observation that the Liverpool area was a hotbed of new musical talent. A good looking kid who was active on the Merseyside music scene as the lead singer with Billy Forde and the Phantoms, Kramer changed his name and joined the Coasters. His cool good looks masked an uneasy stage manner but his talent caught Epstein's eye. When the Coasters refused to turn professional, Kramer persuaded a Manchester band, the Dakotas, to back him and he evolved into a major English pop star. From 1963 to 1965, Kramer had six British hits before fading into obscurity.

When Kramer recorded the Lennon-McCartney tune, "I'll Keep You Satisfied," he appeared destined for a lengthy career. But the Beatles' success shifted attention away from other Liverpool acts. In England the Beatles were major stars and dominated the charts. In America, however, the Beatles were having trouble finding an audience. The Beatles' first album was introduced in late July 1963, and it failed to cause a stir. Tower Records in Sacramento, California ran a $2.99 special for the **Introducing the Beatles** LP and found few takers. "Surf City," by Jan and Dean and "Easier Said Than Done," by the Essex dominated the **Billboard** Hot 100 and there was no interest in the Beatles.

In England, a small group of journalists trumpeted the Beatles' bright future. Among them Sean O'Mahoney, the publisher of **Beat Monthly**, was the most astute. He had a vision of the Beatles' future. Along with his friend Peter Jones, a **Record Mirror** reporter, O'Mahoney conceived a monthly magazine following the Beatles' activity. The result was the **Beatles Book**, a fan magazine which began in August 1963, with an 80,000 initial copy run. At its peak the **Beatles Book** printed 350,000 copies. When the magazine ceased publication in 1969 there were 80 issues that provide an excellent, in-depth historical record of the Beatles' career.

During the summer of 1963 the Beatles were a cause celebre in England. London newspapers vied with each other to uncover new tales of intrigue. The result was a publicity barrage that carried the Beatles to the forefront of the British entertainment world. But Brian Epstein was afraid that major London newspapers would turn on the Beatles. As a result he began a public relation campaign designed to reduce criticism of the band.

Taking a page from Barry Gordy's Motown book, Brian held a meeting with the Beatles to go over their press relations. Brain made it clear that proper attitudes, careful grooming and sparkling wit would win over the press. When Donal Zec, the show business columnist for the **London Daily Mirror**, began researching his full length feature on the Beatles: "Four Frenzied Little Lord Fauntleroys Who Are Earning 5,000 Pounds a Week," Brian was alarmed. He worried that Zec's feature might endanger the Beatles' popularity, so he arranged a cozy lunch between Zec and the boys. Not only were the Beatles on their best behavior, but they were charming, witty and complimentary to the columnist. Zec was won over and his article praised the Beatles' talent.

The **London Daily Mirror** also published **Melody Maker** and this once hostile music newspaper became a staunch Beatle supporter. By the fall of 1963, the incestuous London newspaper community stumbled over themselves to praise the Beatles. **The Beatles Book** appeared during a media blitz, and it quickly sold out. Why had the media changed its attitude toward the Beatles?

One reason for media interest was the personality of the new drummer Ringo Starr. After Starr joined the Beatles they became a tighter band. Not only did Starr's driving drums create a stronger sound, but he was a major personality transfusion in live performances. When Ringo became a Beatle he was the last link in their performing personality. On August 18, 1962, Ringo joined the band for a Horticulture Society Dance at the Hulme Hall in Bolton in Port Sunlight. For the next seven months, he became an integral part of the live performances. "I think the Beatles were on the verge of finding the right sound," Sam Leach remarked. "They worked harder than any Liverpool band and it showed. There were a special group at the small dances I promoted," Leach concluded.

It was not until August 1963, that Ringo girls began showing up in large numbers at Beatle shows. These young fans were instrumental in establishing his appeal. The wit, sarcasm and rings on his fingers made Starr an instant celebrity.

The British love affair with the Beatles was in full swing. In October 1963 the Beatles were scheduled for an appearance on the variety show "Sunday Night At the London Palladium." The British public eagerly anticipated this TV show as well as the Beatles' performance. It was not only the most popular show in England but was broadcast live on Sunday nights from a well-known London theater near Oxford Circus. The prestige of appearing on "Sunday Night At the London Palladium" was important to record sales. So Brian went all out to prepare the boys for this show.

During the rehearsals, which lasted all day, the Beatles were plagued by female fans. This bothered Epstein who believed that the stuffy British television moguls might react adversely to the young girls. These worries were premature, and the show was a successful one. Not only were the Beatles well received but the conservative London entertainment moguls praised the Beatles' music.

After the London Palladium show the press reported that the Beatles were the vanguard of a new entertainment phenomenon. The **London Daily Mirror** vividly recreated the euphoric teenage reaction and the **Daily Mail** and **Daily Express** printed front page pictures of the Beatles held captive by an adoring crowd. The Beatles were a welcome relief from government scandals, cultural indifference and the sagging morality of a nation in decline.

The revolution taking place in England resulted from a number of changes in the teenage population. The requirement that every young man join the army was eliminated. With the decline of national conscription, there was a new work force. Young people filled the expanding job market. Soon clothing boutiques, record stores and entertainment venues vied with each other for the youth dollar. It was in this milieu that the Beatles emerged.

In 1963 the Beatles became a symbol of swinging England. No one read or heard about the petty differences between Paul and John, the bizarre personal behavior of Brian Epstein or the carping of George and Ringo. The Beatles' story was a fairyland tale of success. The British press spent an inordinate amount of time covering Beatle activity and this translated into heavy record sales.

By December plans were underway to invade America. The **Beatles Monthly**, competed with small fan magazines to publish the latest Beatle secrets. When it was announced that Richard Lester would direct a Beatle film, **A Hard Day's Night**, the group was an entertainment blockbuster. America was another story, however, and Brian Epstein was cautious about the future.

When "I Want To Hold Your Hand" reached no 1 on the **Melody Maker** chart on December 7, 1963, it competed with four other Beatle tunes in the Top Twenty. By any standard the Beatles were racking up impressive sales.

To make sure that the Beatles didn't fade from public memory, Brian conceived the annual Christmas show. It was a variety affair replete with music, sketches and a chance to promote other NEMS acts. It was a way to thank the fans for their support while selling Beatle records and concert tickets. The concert was advertised as the NEMS Christmas show, thereby allowing Brian to introduce new acts.

The Beatles Christmas Show at the Astoria in Finsbury Park, England from December 24, 1963, through January 11, 1964, was a warm-up for their first American appearance. The Beatles were aware that the odds were not good for their success in the United States, and they were mindful of the failures of previous English acts. What the Beatles didn't realize was that Capitol Records was determined to break them in the American market. Quietly, without Brian's knowledge, Capitol executives flew to England to catch the Christmas shows. They liked the fan response and were surprised by the quality of the Beatles' music. Capitol executives realized that the Beatles had a unique commercial appeal. How to introduce them in the American market was another matter.

Capitol Records signed the Beatles and their first American single "I Saw Her Standing There" backed with "I Want To Hold Your Hand" was released with a great deal of promotional hype. Whether or not a program director or disc jockey liked the Beatles, they were an act that the media recognized.

On December 29, 1963, WMCA in New York played "I Want to Hold Your Hand". Although WMCA claimed it was the first station to play a Beatle record, there is good evidence that WWDC in Washington D.C. was the first to spin a Beatle record. In Chicago the Beatles were on the air in December 1963, as the Vee Jay label released a Beatle single.

In January 1964, the American press still paid no attention to the Beatles. When "I Want To Hold Your Hand" hit number 1 in Australia in early January, 1964, Jack Parr featured a Beatle clip on his NBC late night show. With a joking smile, Parr made fun of the Beatles clothes and music. A week later "I Want To Hold Your Hand" entered the **Billboard** Hot 100 at number 83 and eventually climbed to the number 1 spot.

At San Francisco's KYA Gene Nelson predicted the coming of Beatlemania. The young DJ talked about their music and played their records. "I saw the Beatles success coming," Nelson remembered, "and I urged my listeners to give their music a chance." Sal Valentino was one who listened and he formed a new group with a Beatle image. When the Beau Brummels approached Tom Donahue at Autumn Records, he was skeptical. Then Autumn Records production chief, Sylvester Stewart, soon to be known as Sly Stone, urged the groups signing. The Beau Brummels were one of many American bands to garner commercial success with a Beatle sound and look.

Tommy Roe, an American recording artist, whose hits "Sheila" and "Everybody," brought him to prominence in 1962-1963, was at a New York party in January, 1964. "The room was full of recording executives and everybody was talking about the Beatles." Roe was aware of the Beatles music but he was surprised by the intense interest in their records. "I saw the Beatles phenomena in its embryo stage before they appeared on the Ed

Sullivan show," Roe concluded. "They were responsible for a big musical change, and the music people didn't know what to make of it." As Roe suggested industry types couldn't wait to see the Beatles. It didn't take long. They were scheduled for Ed Sullivan's TV show and a mini-tour in February 1964.

In New York the rainy, chilly morning hours of February 7, 1964, were eerie ones. Local radio stations announced that the Beatles had boarded Pam Am Flight 101 for America. Curious listeners had no idea what or who the Beatles were and why there was such a fuss about a rock music group. Local talk shows conducted contests in which listeners voted on the Beatles' chances for American success. The promotion and hype was so great that it generated interest from even the casual listener.

Radio stations in New York vied for listeners in a tight market. Program managers at the major rock and roll stations envisioned the Beatles as the key to success in the ratings' wars. So WMCA tried to capitalize upon the interest in the Beatles by announcing: "It is now 6:30 A.M. Beatle time." Soon there was Beatle weather, Beatles news, Beatle fashions and naturally Beatle music. The music almost got lost in the promotional hype. It all appeared spontaneous, but few people realized that Capitol was spending more than $50,000 promoting this experiment in British music.

When the Beatles landed at New York's Kennedy Airport there was a screaming mob waiting to tear them apart. No one was more surprised than the Beatles. They stepped from the Pam Am airliner with a bewildered but happy look on their faces.

On February 9, 1964, the Beatles performed on the Ed Sullivan show before millions of curious American fans. As they waited for the Sullivan appearance, the Beatles were prisoners in the Plaza Hotel. Thousands of young girls stood outside the hotel screaming. Signs were everywhere. The charge was on to find a favorite Beatle. It seemed that every young girl in New York was involved.

The press conferences were successful and newspaper coverage praised the Beatles for their intelligence, spontaneity and fine music. While ensconced on the 12th floor of the Plaza Hotel the Beatles had their first chance to relax. They watched themselves on television and listened to their music on cheap transistor radios without earphones. It was a heady time for the Beatles. They had conquered America.

Even as their success was assured in America, there were business problems. A bootleg record of Beatle songs was selling in local record stores. Tollie, Vee Jay and Swan records flooded the New York market with Beatles records. MGM was preparing to release the Tony Sheridan sessions and Brian Epstein appeared to have lost control of the record market. Brian exploded in the Beatles' suite and was irritable at the reaction to his boys. He had hoped for success, but this was achievement beyond his wildest dream. Brian didn't know how to handle it. He stayed cool and appeared calm. This appearance was deceiving. Young Mr. Epstein was in over his head and the American promoters and record sharks were set to carve him up.

Paul reacted to Epstein negatively. He questioned many of the business transactions and wondered why the Beatles were on a mini-tour. Hadn't the reception been overwhelming? Brian told Paul to mind his own business. Yet, Paul complained long and hard about the mistakes in their itinerary.

After the Ed Sullivan appearance the Beatles caught a train for a Washington D.C. concert. Their first American concert at the Washington Coliseum was an unqualified success. All doubts were erased about the Beatles' commercial appeal. Unfortunately, much of the Beatles' early earnings went to businessmen outside of NEMS. Again Paul complained. Brian told him to leave the management end to the pros. Their differences foreshadowed future Beatle arguments over the disposition of the fiscal pie.

During his trip to New York, Washington and Miami, Paul experienced the fruits of stardom. A visit to New York's Playboy club resulted in a bunny, as the hostesses were known, taking McCartney home. In Washington the hotel was filled with admirers and the swimming pool in Miami saw Paul cavort in luxury amidst his new fame. The Beatles were hailed in America as the first rock and roll band with a penchant for intelligent music.

The Beatles cultural impact was debated extensively after the American successes. When the liberal English newsmagazine, the **New Statesman**, speculated on the dangers of Beatledom, this criticism improved Beatle record sales. There was a "rebel without a cause" syndrome to the Beatles among the staid, middle class English. The rock and roll fans knew that the Rolling Stones cut a much broader rebel path than the Beatles, but the general public approved of the Beatles' musical direction. Each Beatle assumed a distinct personality, and this led to commercial success.

Paul was the cute Beatle but he remained in the intellectual background. While John was considered a prose master, Paul was pictured as a hard working musician who shared top billing with his band mate. Over the years this distinction caused a great deal of tension between Paul and John. While on tour in 1965-1966, McCartney's life was a blur of one night stands. Only at home in London where he attended parties, frequented the West End theater, and made the rounds of the clubs which catered to the rock and roll aristocracy did Paul experience some piece of mind.

The white Aston Martin Paul drove in the mid-1960s was a familiar sight around London. As a famous Beatle, he had swinging London at his feet. There were many clubs that

McCartney enjoyed, but he loved the Speakeasy's ambiance. It was a prohibition era type club that catered to a trendy crowd and attracted the best in swinging London singles. The Ad-Lib was another night spot that provided the right setting for the rich and famous. Swinging London in the mid-1960s was akin to Paris in the 1920s. The pleasures, vices and ego manipulation available to McCartney created a pleasurable life. By early 1965 Paul had adjusted nicely to a baronial rock and roll life. But the changes in McCartney's life were reflected all over England.

England was transformed into a new civilization in 1965 as the Labor Party made a dramatic political comeback. In October 1964, Harold Wilson's Labor Party ended thirteen years in political exile with an electoral trouncing of the Conservative Party. "We have been in the wilderness too long," a Labor M.P. remarked. With the Labor Party came a new and exciting form of benevolent Socialism. After six months in power under Prime Minister Wilson the English economy underwent a dramatic change. Prices declined, welfare benefits increased and closer ties to the European Common Market brought in much needed consumer goods. Suddenly young Britons found themselves with more time and money. It was not surprising that this new prosperity found its way into the Beatles' coffers.

The era of Harold Wilson produced a hedonism unknown since the days of Henry VIII. Swinging London was a world wide euphemism for pleasure and young people from all over the world came to London to satisfy their appetite for music, clothes and freedom. "Cultural Magnets" is what Paul called the Beatle chasers who descended upon London.

To look and act like the London fashion plates was the credo of young American girls. The short haired, mini skirted London girls became a fashion statement that extended worldwide. Swinging London produced a look which popularized outlandish shirts, floppy hats, nehru jackets, Spanish boots and crazily cut suits. Fashion rules were abandoned and anything that the rock and roll royalty wore was instantly fashionable. Carnaby Street was a favorite of the modish dressers. This small, narrow street was filled with clothing stores, boutiques, second hand shops and zany import stores that rivaled each other for exotic merchandise. In 1965 Paul was seen rummaging through stores looking for pop art, clothes or exotic furniture.

Help, the second Beatle film, paid tribute to Swinging London. This movie combined music, art, aesthetic cinema and social criticism to produce a montage of London life in the mid-1960s. Director Richard Lester understood the national fascination with the Beatles and crafted a movie to unveil a mythical Beatle private life. The fans sat in movie theaters in rapt attention and watched the Beatles cavort in a setting reminiscent of the perfect London life. As the viewer watches the Beatles enter four separate but identical houses, but once they are inside there are no walls between the homes. So the four Beatles live in one big, grand playpen replete with toys, girls and camaraderie. The Beatle myth is well and alive in Lester's hands.

The British fascination with the Beatles extended to the royal family. Princess Margaret and Lord Snowden attended a number of social events with the Beatles. When the Beatles' **A Hard Day's Night** opened in London Princess Margaret had such a good time drinking and chatting at the party that everyone was afraid to begin eating the buffet. Paul looked longingly at the wide array of goodies on the table. Finally, George Harrison walked over and asked Princess Margaret if she was going to eat or leave the party. Laughingly, Princess Margaret exited the party and the buffet disappeared. The royal family loved the Beatles and this incident caused a great deal of humor in and around Buckingham Palace.

Press coverage had to be positive and controlled. Brian Epstein spent an inordinate amount of time influencing the media. It was necessary to perpetuate and maintain myths about the Beatles to continue their success. The Lennon and McCartney song writing myth was essential in the marketing of the Beatles records.

To promote this myth, Derek Taylor was hired by Brian Epstein in April 1964 to serve as NEMS public relations specialist. Taylor's first assignment was to ghost write Brian's memoirs, **A Cellarful of Noise**. Artful prose and an ability to diffuse sensitive issues were trademarks of Taylor's journalism and he had a charming manner with reporters. A plentiful supply of liquor, food and good conversation made Taylor indispensable to the Beatles. He had an organizational flair which made Beatle press conferences appear as off the cuff exercises in humor.

Ironically, it was the press conferences which first caused doubts to surface in Paul's mind about Beatle affairs. The swirl of early contract signings, the growth of record and memorabilia sales didn't swell the Beatles financial coffers. McCartney silently wondered whether Brian Epstein's management was as shrewd as the media suggested.

In August 1964, Paul voiced his first serious criticism of the Beatles' financial arrangement. The contract between NEMS and Seltaeb, the Beatles American merchandising company, expired and Brian renegotiated the Beatles cut of the profits from 10% to 46%. For some time McCartney had seethed about a royalty agreement that provided the Beatles such small profits on the multimillion dollar souvenir business. Brian's attitude was that it was none of Paul's business. Even though the Beatles didn't receive adequate compensation the sale of memorabilia helped record sales.

What prompted Paul's criticism of the Seltaeb deal was the failure of the Beatles to receive the past royalties due the group. In a move denoting monumental arrogance, Seltaeb refused to pay any past royalties. NEMS sued Seltaeb for not paying $55,000. Then Seltaeb countersued for five million dollars alleging breach of contract. Once the lawsuits became public, two American chain stores, Woolworth's and Penney's, withdrew one hundred million dollars of memorabilia orders. There were plans to install permanent Beatle counters in Woolworth and Penny stores, and these plans were abruptly scrapped.

As the Seltaeb drama unfolded, Paul tried to talk to Brian about altering the merchandising and business strategy. He urged Brian to establish a separate division in NEMS to handle the profitable trinkets associated with Beatlemania. "Brian was surprised that Paul had such a keen interest in business," Clive Epstein remarked. "He was unaware that Paul was watching the intake of pounds," Clive continued. "I think my brother misjudged Paul's business acumen." McCartney also had strong doubts about NEMS. Not only was Epstein's business arm archaic, but its employees were interested primarily in bodily pleasures.

By 1965 NEMS had moved it offices to a small, comfortable Argyll street location. The new offices were near Piccadilly Circus which afforded easy access to the West End Theater district, the alcoholic and sexual pleasures of Soho, and it was a short cab ride to the tranquil shopping area on Oxford street. It was an office adjacent to London's hedonistic pleasures. The media command center set up at the new offices was designed to bombard London newspapers, magazines, television and radio with Beatle news. It worked as 1965 became the year that serious Beatle press coverage inundated England. The boys, finally, were a part of the English cultural mainstream.

In the spring of 1965 the Beatles were awarded the Member of the British Empire (MBE). At first John Lennon wouldn't agree to accept this honor, but Brian convinced him it was necessary. Lennon also complained that he was losing control of the music and that the Beatles' second movie, **Help**, had little creativity. But John wasn't the only Beatle complaining about the whirlwind of recording, touring and promotional pressures that were tearing the group apart. Lennon had put on weight, Paul was not as jovial, Ringo sulked and George was silent. Yet, the publicity wheel continued to turn out the myth that the Beatles were inseparable.

Despite these press missives, there were open signs of conflict between Paul and John. George Martin was the first to comment publicly about these personality differences. As Martin suggested, these disagreements dated back to the Beatles first hit, "Love Me Do." From 1962 to 1965 there was less than a harmonious relationship between John and Paul on the song writing front. While they remained friends socially, there were ego conflicts regarding the music that were never made public. For three years, despite or because of these conflicts, the Lennon-McCartney song writing team continued to produce hit records.

The reason for the rift is a simple one. Paul didn't receive the credit he believed was his due. He was described as a "song writing lightweight." The press frustrated Paul, but Brian wouldn't allow him to shut out the media.

By 1965 Paul rebelled against the myth of the Lennon-McCartney song writing process. McCartney spent less time asking Lennon his opinion about new songs. A good example of Paul's new found independence occurred while he was writing "I'm Down." When he asked John for his opinion on the tune, Paul incorporated only a few of John's suggestions. This was an act of independence which indicated the erosion of Lennon and McCartney's relationship. When the song was released in the summer of 1965 "I'm Down" was a perfect reflection of McCartney's state of mind.   Had it not been for George Martin's sure hand the Beatles would have exploded into splinters. As egos got out of hand, the drugs became too plentiful or the mind games too excessive, Martin stepped in to guide the boys back into the creative process.

In recording sessions during 1965-1966, Martin increasingly depended upon McCartney's musical skill. Martin believed that Paul's professionalism and pop song writing guaranteed commercial success. But he was careful not to make this opinion public.

The level of creativity that the Beatles reached was demonstrated when Abbey Road's Studio No. 2 was turned into a Beatle rehearsal room. The Beatles no longer had to worry about studio time. But this freedom was far from a blessing. John and Paul monopolized the studio time, thereby creating new tensions with George and Ringo.

Ringo was the first Beatle to feel left out. He complained that he was a tag along Beatle. "I think Ringo felt abused, musically speaking," Clive Epstein remembered. The emphasis upon Lennon-McCartney songs, the prominence of John and Paul's lead vocals, and the media's interest in the two glamorous Beatles infuriated Ringo. He would sit in a stoic manner in the corner of Abbey Road Studio No. 2 patiently waiting to sing or drum. Because of his sense of humor and mild personality, Ringo's discontent passed unnoticed.

As 1965 passed into 1966 the Beatles were bored, dismayed and apprehensive. They were tired of the same questions during interviews. "We could send out waxwork dummies of ourselves and that would satisfy the crowds," John Lennon remarked. Beatle concerts, Lennon continued, were "just bloody tribal rites." Surprisingly, Paul didn't feel the same way. He loved the crowds, the concert ambiance and the media attention. John and Paul were estranged about the Beatles future and there was no way to mend their differences.

Beatle concerts were a happening but the music was no longer important. The end of the Beatles as a touring group began on December 3, 1965, when they opened a United Kingdom tour at the Odeon Cinema in Glasgow, Scotland. This ten day, nine city tour was a brief swing through some old concert sites. Paul was happy about going back on the road. The Beatles had finished recording the **Rubber Soul** LP and McCartney welcomed the chance to play live music. It was on this tour that Paul asserted himself in a number of ways.

Because he was concerned about live performances, Paul spent an inordinate amount of time working on the Beatles' concert sound quality. They played small theaters which allowed them to perform in an intimate atmosphere. The result was some of their strongest concerts.

This mini-United Kingdom tour provided some humorous incidents. On December 4, 1965, the Beatles performed at the City Hall in Newcastle-on-the-Tyne. Sitting in the basement munching his dinner, Paul looked around with dismay at the Beatles life. He couldn't believe the cloistered atmosphere they were forced to live in. The need for tight security robbed the Beatles of their freedom. The cold, sleet driven winter night was an unpleasant one. Paul was tired of the constant fan interruptions and the stupid questions. As he mused about the fans, a young man approached, smiled and spoke:

"Mate, eh, is Eric Burdon around?"

"Eric, who?" Paul mumbled with obvious irritation.

"You know, mate our Animal."

"Your what?" Paul continued.

"I thought you Beatles knew all the blokes."

"We Beatles are the blokes," Paul shouted.

He stood up and walked to the bathroom. He was in need of privacy. A stall in the toilet suddenly looked like a friend.

The following night the Beatles returned to Liverpool to play the Empire Theater. Their old friends eagerly anticipated the concert. Bob Wooler, Joe Flannery and Ray McFall organized a special party for the Beatles. Many of their original fan club members showed up at the show. The **Liverpool Echo** called the Beatles return a triumph for the local boys. The buildup and the hype failed to match the concert. Although the Beatles performed well, their old friends noticed that the fun had gone out of their performances.

On December 5, 1965, as the Beatles walked out on stage to play their last Liverpool concert, they were disheartened by the changes in their home town. It was an especially sad day for McCartney, because he had heard the news that the Cavern was in financial trouble. Quietly, Paul asked McFall if he could help. The answer was an unequivocal: "No." Paul wasn't told how difficult the financial crunch was for Ray McFall. The Cavern owner was virtually one step ahead of the tax man. Not even McCartney's money could have saved the Cavern. The fans no longer showed up and the string of excellent bands had vanished. A few days after the Beatles' concert the revenue authorities closed the

Cavern citing back taxes.

Paddy Delaney, the Cavern bouncer, came to see the Beatles at the Empire Theater. He lamented to Paul the passing of the old days. In a corner Bob Wooler, the Cavern compere, looked downcast as he recognized the tension and frustration in the Beatles' dressing room. "I couldn't believe how unhappy the boys were," Wooler remarked.

No one realized that the Beatles were embarking on their last tour. On June 24, 1966, they began the first leg of a world tour. Phase one involved dates in West Germany, Japan and the Philippines. On June 24, 1966, two shows were scheduled at the Circus-Krone-Bau in Munich, West Germany. These shows were a fitting, if ironic, place to inaugurate the Beatles' last tour.

Since 1960 when they opened at the Indra Club the Beatles had a special feeling for West Germany. The Beatles talked fondly about the old days at Hamburg venues- the Star Club, the Indra the Top Ten and the Kaiserkeller. Now they played large auditoriums, stadiums and venues that were more suited to a circus than a rock concert. On June 25, 1966, they performed at the Ernst Merck Halle sports arena in Hamburg. Tony Sheridan recalled that the Beatles played a lackluster thirty minute set. They were tired, bored and unable to perform professionally No one could hear the Beatles' music, they no longer were able to take pride in their concerts. Trouble was brewing.

As the Beatles flew the polar route to Japan, there was a great deal of complaining. Security was a problem. The stage sets and clothing that Brian selected were not right. "I think the boys had their own ideas, not only about the music, but their stage presence," Clive Epstein remarked. "I talked to John just before he left for Japan," Bob Wooler stated, "and he was ready to abandon the road."

The Beatles performed at the Nippon Budokan Hall in Tokyo to rapturous throngs of giggling young girls. There was polite applause and a Japanese compere that made the Beatles wonder if emotion had vanished in the Far East. The newspaper coverage and enthusiastic throngs prompted Paul to argue that the Beatles were more popular in Japan than anyplace else. There was also a light side to the time in Japan. Before and after their performances the Beatles enjoyed half a dozen geisha girls, brought Japanese goods and stayed in the sumptuous presidential suite of the Tokyo Hilton. They smuggled in a large quantity of marijuana and spent three days getting loaded with the delights of the Far East at their finger tips.

The usually reserved Japanese embraced Beatlemania. In Japan, Beatlemania translated into record, memorabilia and concert sales. The first concert at Budokan was filmed by NTV (Japanese television) for a July 1 broadcast. While the concert hall was relatively quiet, Tokyo buzzed with anticipation and excitement. The three days in Japan were pleasant ones, but then the Beatles last tour began falling apart.

The next stop was the Philippines. When the Beatles landed in Manila they found the most beautiful women in the world surrounding them during their stay. Drugs were plentiful but a group of Filipino gangsters hung around the hotel. Paul was the first to express fear. He noted these thugs and complained to Brian. When it was discovered that they were Filipino government officials the tensions eased. It shouldn't have, bribes and corruption prevailed. The Philippines were governed by a dictatorial President, Ferdinand Marcos, and his Machiavellian wife, Imelda. A social climbing, commoner with a penchant for power mongering, Imelda Marcos looked upon the Beatles as prized toys. Her spoiled young children wanted the Beatles to play for a private party. Her son, Bong Bong, was used to having his every whim satisfied. Consequently, the first lady of the Philippines, planned a Beatle lunch. In her younger days, Imelda was a singer and dancer, and she hoped to impress the Beatles with her talent. They viewed her as a mad woman. John laughed that Imelda sang as she talked. Paul thought that she looked like an aging cupie doll. The press was kept away and Brian told the boys that they would not have to meet her. This turned out to be a mistake.

When Mrs. Marcos announced that she would invite the Beatles to a lavish lunch, she failed to check with Epstein. The press reported that her children and their friends would listen to the Beatles at a private luncheon. When Brian discovered that the "private luncheon" was for more than 500 people, he was apprehensive. Mrs. Marcos was a ruthless and powerful woman. Gossip circulated in Manila that she had her eye on John Lennon. A special bedroom was made up in the Presidential Palace. It was replete with a British flag, tea and a sound system with Beatle records. Fortunately, the Beatles didn't attend the luncheon.

Because of their unintentional snub of Mrs. Marcos, the Beatles were almost lynched in Manila. When they refused to show up for the luncheon, fully armed Philippine troops invaded their hotel. It was a comic sight to everyone but the Beatles. They were scared to death. After their concert a $17,000 bribe was exacted by Philippine government tax collectors. The tax collectors were the same thugs who had hung out in their hotel. But it was worth this price to leave the Philippines.

The Beatles were upset by this incident. Paul was quiet but he wondered about the future. There was a serious security problem, the stadiums were growing larger and there were signs that some fans were growing disinterested. Could Beatle magic be wearing off?

As the Beatles began a tour of North America on August 12, 1966, a controversy erupted over John Lennon's remark that the Beatles were bigger than Jesus. This statement was an old one published in a London newspaper and Lennon had forgotten it.

Maureen Cleve, of the **London Evening Standard,** analyzed Lennon's religious ideas. Lennon's remarks were those of an innocent youth. He talked about the up and down nature of Christianity and organized religion. In a moment of mirth, he remarked that: "We're more popular than Jesus now." This innocent remark hit a nerve in the American South. In Dallas, Houston, Nashville, Memphis and Atlanta there were rallies against the Beatles' music. Few critics realized that the remark was five months old. Suddenly Beatle records were burnt in public. There were demonstrations planned in August 1966, outside of select concert sites.

The musical direction of rock and roll was changing. By the summer of 1966 Bob Dylan's electronic rock and roll vied with blues revival bans for the record and concert dollar. At the University of Chicago the Paul Butterfield Blues band played for fraternity-sorority gigs while two U. C. students Mark Naftalin and Elvin Bishop added punch to the band. It was another year before American blues bands became a top concert draw. The Fillmore East and West featured new blues bands who opened for acts like Howlin' Wolf and Muddy Waters. As popular musical tastes changed the Beatles were less and less of a novelty. This ultimately forced the Beatles to alter their musical direction.

Despite these problems, there was no reason to believe that the Beatles fourth American tour would be their last. To counter the controversy over Lennon's remarks about the Beatles being bigger than Jesus, Brian booked the Astor Towers in Chicago for a press conference. Epstein reasoned that a contrite Lennon could soothe American criticism. The Beatles and Brian had never experienced the mindless fanaticism of the American religious right. Disc jockeys, preachers, newspaper and magazine editors, and politicians indicted the Beatles' music. Most had never listened to it, but the chance to criticize "the infidels in the temple," as one Baptist minister remarked, was too good an opportunity for free publicity to pass up.

Capitol Records released a new album to commemorate the fourth American tour. The Beatles' **Yesterday and Today** LP was a compilation of songs from **Help** and **Revolver** as well as a few tunes from the forthcoming British LP. The cover overshadowed the music as it featured the Beatles wearing overalls favored by local butchers, carrying decapitated dolls placed strategically among pieces of meat. The butcher cover, as it became known, was an error in judgment. The outcry prompted the albums immediate recall and Capitol Records employed hundreds of people to past new covers over the LPs. Although the music was strong, the album art was beyond its time.

The controversy over Lennon's Jesus remark and the butcher cover obscured that Beatle concerts were no longer sure sell outs. By switching concert sites to large outdoor stadiums, the Beatles music was sacrificed. On August 29,1966, the Beatles ran out onto the second base area of Candlestick Park and performed for a screaming crowd that half filled the San Francisco baseball park. After more than 1400 concerts the Beatles finished their last show. The security was precarious, the music could barely be heard and the Beatles were tired. They evolved into a studio band.

As 1966 closed the Beatles had ambitious music and movie plans. There was no sign of the group breaking up, but they were dissatisfied with one another. The clashing egos, musical differences and business problems made the future a cloudy one.

The years from 1963 through 1966 were frenetic ones. The recording and constant touring had worn McCartney to the bone. He was ready to rest. Paul had plans for another Beatle album; it would turn out to be the revolutionary **Sgt. Pepper's Lonely Hearts Club** LP and it would change the Beatles' career dramatically.

4: PAUL AND SGT. PEPPER'S LONELY HEARTS CLUB BAND,1967

On November 24, 1966, the Beatles assembled at Abbey Road to begin recording tracks for the **Sgt. Pepper's Lonely Hearts Club Band** album. No one realized that this album would bring Paul McCartney to the forefront of Beatle musical production. For four years Lennon and McCartney had worked closely to produce a string of hit records. The **Sgt. Pepper** album, however, was a departure from past LPs. They would work independently of one another, thereby, beginning the first steps toward dissolving the Beatles.

There were pressures upon the Beatles that were tearing the group apart. The critical acclaim for their music led to increased demands for new and innovative songs. Intellectuals found the Beatles exciting. Marshall McLuhan dubbed Beatle music one electronic method of communication around the world. Aaron Copeland remarked that to understand the 1960s' one had to listen to the Beatles. Despite this praise the media sensed that Beatlemania was finished. The first sign of the Beatles' decline took place one day in 1966, when Ringo Starr was stopped at the gates to Abbey Road by an Independent Television News reporter. He asked Ringo about the end of the Beatles. "No comment at least until we break up next week," Ringo chuckled. Unwittingly, this reporter opened up wounds and tensions which were destroying the Beatles' cohesive fiber.

The Beatles were entering the age of psychedelic music. They would draw up a musical imagery in the **Sgt. Pepper** album which helped define one of the most creative periods in rock music history. Unfortunately, the **Sgt. Pepper** album would begin the long road to ending the Beatles.

Surprisingly, it was neither Lennon nor McCartney who expressed the first public doubts about the Beatles. George Harrison was the first Beatle to wonder publicly about their future. As the baby of the group, George took much criticism from Paul and John. He tired of this abuse quickly. "They misread me," George stated in a 1989 interview. What bothered George was the independent direction of John and Paul. "They no longer worked together," Harrison remembered, "so we didn't need the Beatles." Harrison's observations were sage ones. He talked at length in San Francisco in August, to Douglas Garbo, a Bill Graham employee, who was promoting his own rock band. "Harrison was disenchanted with the Beatles," Garbo maintained. This observation was one that many noticed in San Francisco. The Beatles were ready to get off the road.

After their last show at San Francisco's Candlestick Park,

Harrison remarked: "That's it, I'm not a Beatle anymore." Once the Beatles returned to England they stayed away from one other. There were individual music efforts; no one wanted to play together. Only Paul hoped to keep the Beatles intact. Soon he realized that this dream was impossible. As Paul brooded behind the walls of his expensive Georgian mansion at number 7 Cavendish Avenue in St. John's Wood, he thought a lot about the next step in his career.

Because he was unsure about the group's future, Paul agreed to score the music for a British film, **The Family Way.** This was McCartney's first movie credit as a solo composer and with George Martin's help he produced a solid twenty-six minute sound track. When a single from the album, "Love in the Open Air" and "Theme From the Family Way" failed to draw critical reviews or hit the British music charts, Paul ignored the failure. He was happy with the music and proud of the LP. He was increasingly at home in the Abbey Road studio and led a pleasant night life.

A satisfying social life made Paul not only happy but unusually creative. Paul hung out at the best clubs the Ad Lib, the Bag O'Nails, the Scotch of St. James, the Speakeasy, Sybilla's, and he frequently attended plays at the Savile Theater. Barry Miles, a journalist, was a constant companion as was John Dunbar, owner of the Indica Gallery. Through Miles, Paul met the American beat poet Allen Ginsberg and the writer William Burroughs. Burroughs, author of **Naked Lunch**, was a mentor to many rock musicians. In the early 1960s Burroughs participated in LSD experiments at Harvard University. His fame as a novelist intrigued McCartney. In 1964 when Burroughs' **Nova Express** was published to critical acclaim, the British embraced Burroughs' experimental attitudes. He appealed to a wide variety of intellectuals. McCartney loved Burroughs' skittish, stream of consciousness prose. He asked the questions that Paul found intriguing. After studying Burroughs work, McCartney met the experimental cinema giant, Michaelangelo Antonioni. This prompted Paul to produce two experimental movies, **The Defeat of the Dog** and **The Next Spring Then**. Film was only one of Paul's intellectual outlets. He expanded his musical interests to improve his song writing.

This early interest in film drew the attention of the British press. **Punch**, an entertainment magazine, reviewed the films. "They were like ordinary people's home movies," the critic wrote. The **Punch** reviewer also noted that the film was over exposed, poorly lighted and improperly cut. The music of the Modern Jazz Quartet and Bach blended professionally into the films. This was simply another way in which Paul stretched his creative genius.

One day Paul announced to John that he was considering producing an album entitled **Paul McCartney Goes Too Far**. It would consist of tape experiments completed at Paul's St. John's

Wood home. John simply raised his eyebrows.

Paul was infuriated. Not only did John not take his musical ideas seriously, but he ignored the intricate musical notions that McCartney suggested. On December 8, 1966, Paul showed up in the afternoon at Abbey Road to overdub his vocals on "When I'm 64." During the three hour afternoon session at Abbey Road, George Martin told Paul that John was unhappy about the first eight takes of "Strawberry Fields Forever." John complained to Martin that the acoustic version of "Strawberry Fields Forever" that he had played for Martin in November was now too heavy. John wanted to lighten the sound. To calm John, Martin told him that they would redo the song. Lennon mistook Martin's explanation and he informed the Beatles that they would return to the studio that night.

When the Beatles showed up at Abbey Road at seven, they learned that George Martin was at the premiere of Cliff Richard's movie **Finders Keepers**. At eleven o'clock, Martin arrived at the studio and found that Geoff Emerick and Dave Harries had produced new takes of "Strawberry Fields Forever." After completing fifteen takes of this tune, the exhausted group left the studio.

"I think that the Beatles were too heavily into psychedelic influences," Bob Wooler remarked. In December 1966, there was an incessant amount of mixing, overdubbing and musical experimentation in the studio. "Strawberry Fields Forever" redone in six separate studio sessions from December 9 through December 30, 1966 failed to satisfy the Beatles. When John asked George Martin to mix the beginning of one cut with the end of another, Martin shouted: "they are in different keys and different tempos." Lennon replied: "Well...fix it." The tinkering in the studio was only one aspect of the changes in the Beatles.

There were other influences upon McCartney. He admired Michael Hollingshead's World Psychedelic Center. Hollingshead's organization was a popular religion. It preached the intellectual benefits of LSD without adequate warning about the drug's side effects. The World Psychedelic Center attracted a strange collection of individuals, celebrity chasers and pseudo scientists. Paul found inspiration for many of his songs at this strange meeting place. American intellectuals flocked to London to learn of Hollingshead's drug experiments. This short lived experiment in mind altering drugs was a perfect reflection of London during the swinging 1960s. While living briefly in New York, Hollingshead acquired a full gram of LSD-25 which was enough for more than 10,000 doses, and when he flew back to London to open the World Psychedelic Center, he had found his God. Songs such as the Count Five's "Psychotic Reaction," the Electric Prunes "I Had Too Much to Dream Last Night," the Amboy Dukes "Journey To the Center of My Mind," and the Byrds "Eight Miles High" made LSD an in-joke with the rock music sub culture. In the

Beatles' **Revolver** LP, the first acid tinged song "She Said, She Said" appeared. It was written by John Lennon during a conversation with Peter Fonda while on acid in California.

Paul realized that the next Beatle album had to reflect the changes that LSD brought to their lives. When the **Revolver** album was released on August 5, 1966, it was an early indication that the "cute Beatles," as Bob Dylan referred to them, were a thing of the past. For the **Sgt. Pepper** LP, the Beatles selected a song that recalled their Liverpool roots. Consequently, "Strawberry Fields Forever" became the first song they recorded for the album. This Lennon composition caused many people to assume that he was directing the Beatles' recording activity.

Lennon was no longer nominally in charge of the Beatles' affairs, because he had little interest in maintaining his power. John was pursuing other interests. When Lennon wrote "Strawberry Fields Forever," he was in Almeria, Spain filming **How I Won The War.** He wrote the tune out of sheer boredom. While in Spain, John grew homesick. Longing for a familiar landmark, Lennon jotted down the words to "Strawberry Fields Forever." As a young child John played on the grounds of the Strawberry Fields Salvation Army home, so for Lennon the song recalled nostalgic images of a simpler time. That day in the Abbey Road Studio John laughed about the song and told Paul that it helped him get through the loneliness while on the movie set.

Charlie Lennon, John's Uncle, remembers how important "Strawberry Fields Forever" was to John. "He knew the Beatles were in trouble," Charlie recalled, "and John envisioned the song as keeping them together." John believed that Liverpool rooted music would heal the ego differences and petty grievances which were tearing the Beatles' apart.

While Charlie Lennon walked with me in Strawberry Fields he began to wipe his eyes. "I don't think the boys would have wanted it to turn out the way it did," Uncle Charlie remarked. I wasn't sure what he meant, but I didn't ask the obviously upset Lennon to elaborate.

As the Beatles prepared to record "Strawberry Fields Forever," Lennon's musical innovativeness was at its peak. He charged through the session with skill and was in command. The complex musical arrangement and instrumentation in "Strawberry Fields Forever" indicated that John was still a studio genius. The use of a mellotron to imitate other instruments was not only a startling breakthrough, but it portended a new era of musical experimentation. Long before the synthesizer was common in the recording studio, John programmed the mellotron to produce flute, bass and string sounds in the Beatles' music.

During the "Strawberry Fields Forever" sessions, Paul played the mellotron. This instrument not only intrigued McCartney, but he envisioned it as a means of expanding his music. For hours McCartney practiced with this instrument as he developed his ideas for a solo album. Suddenly Paul realized that he didn't need a band, technology made him superior to a studio band. It was a warm feeling; the Beatles were not necessary to his future.

At the conclusion of "Strawberry Fields Forever," Lennon appears to be saying "I buried Paul." What he actually said was: "Cranberry juice." Since this made no sense to the critics, it was reported that a rift between Lennon and McCartney had developed. There were mild differences between John and Paul and the media comments escalated these problems. The intense press interest in the Beatles' obscured the revolutionary impact of their music.

"Strawberry Fields Forever" was the result of four years of intense studio experimentation. The use of backward tapes, vari-speed sounds and the mellotron produced an eerie music with drug induced overtones. There was a dreamy, psychedelic nature to the music. On Thursday, November 24, 1966, during a seven and a half hour recording session, the Beatles produced one take of "Strawberry Fields Forever." This two minute and thirty-four second cut brought the Beatles' music into a new dimension.

Everyone noticed that there were increased pressures upon Lennon and McCartney. Sitting in the Holiday Inn in Liverpool in 1983, Clive Epstein recalled the Lennon-McCartney relationship. Clive remembered that Brian sent a note to EMI in October 1966, pointing out that there would be no new Beatle record during the upcoming Christmas season. "It was obvious there were problems," Clive remarked. "John and Paul had been sniping at each other for some time and John was losing interest in the Beatles' music." When he heard "Strawberry Fields Forever" Clive was horrified. Like many Beatle observers he didn't understand the music. Clive recalled that George Martin worried that the wit, sarcasm and ego battles were getting out of hand. Yet, Clive believed in the Lennon-McCartney collaboration. Clive suggested that Paul slowed John's excesses and contributed the commercial portions of the songs. Bob Wooler, the former compere at the Cavern, remarked that late in 1966 he saw the first signs of serious internal conflict. "The boys wanted me to move to London, but I refused. They needed someone to control the rumor mill." Looking back at that period, Wooler recalled that John was losing interest in writing. "He didn't want to cooperate with Paul, it was McCartney who wanted to continue writing hits songs," Wooler maintained. It was Paul who shaped the duo's music into complex rock operas. Few people close to the Beatles believed that the partnership could endure.

During production of the **Sgt. Pepper** LP, McCartney emerged as the chief Beatle. He didn't replace John and he wasn't heavy handed in rising to the top of Beatle affairs. There are many reasons for McCartney's ascension. Among these was

Lennon's move in new artistic directions. John no longer was interested in Beatle music. He looked to the literary life. Lennon's ideas for solo songs, and his writing was moving beyond the Beatles. Paul took over the Beatle mantle by default.

For years McCartney operated in a creative role equal to Lennon's, but his efforts weren't recognized by the press. Paul vowed to end this inequity. He did so by organizing the concept behind the **Sgt. Pepper** album. Since the Beatles no longer toured, there was little of the boy's night out atmosphere that had created so many of the Lennon-McCartney hits. Once Paul quit hanging out with John, he had an intense desire to write his own songs. He tired of Lennon receiving half the credit for songs that were essentially his compositions.

In the past, writing half the songs with Lennon had been enough for Paul, but during the **Sgt. Pepper** album, he took over production duties. For years Paul experimented in the studio, but it was not until **Sgt. Pepper** that his production talent was recognized.

Contrary to many biographies, Paul was not brooding behind the walls of his St. John's Wood mansion. During the **Sgt. Pepper** sessions, Paul was busy writing new songs and planning solo recordings. While Paul, George and John were embarking quietly upon solo careers, the public relations machine continued to perpetuate the myth of unity behind Lennon-McCartney songs.

As McCartney's individual talent surfaced commercially, rock critics assumed Lennon's creative powers were diminishing. What all but the most astute observers failed to realize was that Paul had a unique commercial musical talent, whereas John was more political and esoteric.

When the **Sgt. Pepper** album went into production, Paul used some of his dad's musical ideas. Jazz, show tunes, experimental rock and classical music fused, thereby allowing Paul to develop a new sound. There were also intellectual influences which were changing McCartney's mind set.

By 1967 Paul religiously read the **LA Free Press,** the **Berkeley Barb**, the San Francisco based **Oracle** and the **East Village Other**. These American counterculture newspapers provided the key ideas for many of Paul's new songs. There was a historical quality to McCartney's observations as he recognized the changes in youth culture. He hoped to use these themes in rock and roll songs. In October 1966, the California legislature passed a bill outlawing LSD. Paul was horrified by the public hysteria over the drug. But Paul didn't share his ideas with the press. Brian Epstein was relieved that there would be no new controversies. He was concerned that the growing reaction against the counterculture revolution would hurt the Beatles' record sales.

Epstein also fretted about the ego tensions between Lennon and McCartney. Brian's worries proved unfounded. Lennon didn't resent McCartney assuming control of the **Sgt.**

Pepper album. The Chief Beatle looked for new creative outlets. Bob Wooler remembered: "John had kept the Beatles afloat with his songs. John was tired, it was time for Paul to write a batch of tunes." Paul was eager to do so and Lennon was happy to have his collaborator grind out the hits. Bob Wooler and Clive Epstein, remarked that during the production of the **Sgt. Pepper** album there was little serious discord over the music. "The press made up a series of spats and problems," Clive Epstein remarked, "and for the life of me I couldn't remember any of it." As Bob Wooler remarked: "It's not that the Beatles didn't fight, the point is these spats didn't hamper their creativity."

As the Beatles recorded the **Sgt. Pepper's Lonely Hearts Club Band** LP from November 1966 until March 1967 there were the usual rumors of excessive drug use, incessant partying and loud shouting matches. These rumors resulted in an inordinate amount of negative publicity. McCartney was the Beatle stung hardest by this criticism. Not only were the media tales unfair, but they were seldom close to the truth. The **London Evening Standard** called Paul McCartney a "culture chaser." Other London newspapers followed suit. The press featured Paul's girlfriend, Jane Asher, his show dog, Martha and his St. John's Wood home regularly. The fans couldn't seem to get enough of McCartney. So one enterprising journalist founded a fanzine devoted entirely to Jane Asher. This fanatical little tabloid detailed the intricate details of McCartney's chief lady. Not only was Paul's private life subject to odious scrutiny but his music was analyzed, criticized and dissected by everyone from college professors to amateur magazine editors.

Despite the rumors surrounding McCartney and the Beatles, they continued to record quietly in Abbey Road Studio Number 2. This marvelous recording facility was constructed in 1931 to produce the best in classical music, and it was the perfect setting for the Beatles' classical form of rock music.

It was a comfortable private hideaway insulating the Beatles from the outside world. The neat white house that Abbey Road occupied was well kept, and the short driveway led to a series of high front steps that kept the fans away. The quiet neighborhood seemed unaware of the Beatles as business executives, nannies and curious tourists wandered by the Abbey Road recording facility.

Rock writers have criticized the Abbey Road Studio for its primitive instrumentation and crude recording facilities. Abbey Road is, in fact, a unique recording facility that was far enough from the musical mainstream to foster experimentation. It was one of the first English recording studios to allow for advanced musical technology. In 1966 a special phaser was developed for the Beatles. The phaser became an integral part of the Beatles music, and allowed the band to expand beyond the traditional rock and roll boundaries.

George Martin had a great deal to do with the musical progress. He continually encouraged the Beatles' avant-garde experimentation, and he was a constant source of ideas. Martin's integrity and vision was significant to their success. He didn't praise the Beatles when they deserved criticism. Martin's loyalty, careful working habits and attention to detail was important to their success.

While recording the **Sgt. Pepper's Lonely Hearts Club Band** album, Martin was not happy about many of the songs. During the planning stages of the **Sgt. Pepper** album the Beatles were enthralled with electronic gadgetry. For years Magic Alex Mardas urged the boys to "use electronics to their fullest...." They heeded Magic Alex's advice. John included a pair of electric organs in "Being For the Benefit of Mrs. Kite." Because Lennon believed that the organ sound would create the proper ambiance for this tune, no time or expense was spared. But the organ effect didn't work, so Lennon used recordings of Victorian steam organs playing traditional tunes. These sounds were pieced together from more than a hundred concerts, thereby creating a series of carousel noises and a unique circus background.

The inner circle surrounding the Beatles had a chance to witness a musical revolution. Clive Epstein dropped into Abbey Road from time to time to watch the Beatles work on the **Sgt. Pepper** album. He was amazed at how Paul joked with George about forming a new band; one that would end the bickering, egoism and perpetual musical differences which limited the Beatles.

"I was still in Liverpool," Bob Wooler commented, "but I knew that things were changing." As Wooler recalled the Beatles used pleasant parts of their past to forget their problems.

While the Beatles spent long hours in the studio recording the **Sgt. Pepper** album, they recalled the Liverpool-Hamburg years. Images of eating fish and chips or German sausage came to Paul's mind. These were thoughts that Paul entertained to get through the long evenings at Abbey Road. For the last few years his dad, Jim, had retired in Rembrandt just outside Liverpool. The 8,750 pounds that Paul paid for the house gave him a sense of satisfaction. Paul also purchased a 183 acre farm in Scotland near Campbeltown. This isolated, yet beautiful, retreat was characterized by a rock terrain with a jagged look. The furnishings were primitive, the terrain was stark and the house was isolated. Local villagers smiled at McCartney, but they left him alone. It was the perfect place to get lost amidst the pressures of fame and fortune. The stark contrast between the Scotland home and the St. John's Wood mansion was one that Paul appreciated. He never forgot his working class roots. The Scottish retreat reinforced these origins.

As McCartney produced the **Sgt. Pepper's Lonely Heart's Club Band** album, there was a dadaist sense to the music. Paul delighted in this form of highly personalized anarchy. By employing dadaist images, the Beatles could deny history and wander off into a personal world; one without responsibility, one without a future.

Another example of dadaist forces was John's collaboration with Yoko Ono. They created an art form that hastened Lennon's transition into an avant garde intellectual world. When Paul urged John to reexamine his childhood roots, this suggestion was the catalyst to Lennon's new song writing direction. "Strawberry Fields Forever" resulted from this conversation.

This poignant reminder of Lennon's Liverpool youth has been badly misinterpreted by rock and roll historians. In Albert Goldman's book **The Lives of John Lennon**, "Strawberry Fields Forever" is dismissed as "a product of LSD...." This conclusion is the result of Goldman's reliance upon interviews by a **Liverpool Daily Echo** journalist. As Lennon's friends were interviewed they provided sensational answers that had little to do with John's career. The subtle nuances of Lennon-McCartney songs, and the sense of their Liverpool past is ignored. The reason is a simple one. Goldman judges the Beatles by the standards of another generation.

Goldman matured intellectually during the 1950s and had an inordinate interest in the beatniks, jazz and J.D. Salinger's fiction. As one critic observed: "Goldman is the finest mind never to leave prep school." He viewed Lennon through this narrow perspective. When Goldman writes that Lennon mimicked the language of the beatniks, he misses the key elements in John's personality. Goldman failed to recognize the sense of anarchy, the elements of dadaism and the birth of a new cultural form in the Beatles' music.

A good example of Goldman misinterpreting Lennon's music is his analysis of "Strawberry Fields Forever." Goldman alleges that it was the first time that Lennon "gave full voice to his puns in song." Had Goldman taken the time to read James Sauceda's book **The Literary Lennon**, he would have realized that puns were an integral part of Lennon's early intellectual development. Since the 1950s Lennon had employed simple anecdotes and puns in his songs.

Goldman misrepresents Lennon's working relationship with McCartney by calling "Strawberry Fields Forever" an example of a tune that "was not simply John Lennon's playground," but "his spiritual home." This observation ignores the creative impact that McCartney had upon this seminal tune. Often Lennon and McCartney argued over their music, but the results were invariably impressive ones. During the recording of "Strawberry Fields Forever," Lennon and McCartney's differences created a strong song. Since Lennon thought "Strawberry Fields Forever" was too pop, he persuaded McCartney to produce it with a touch of Phil Spector's Wall of Sound. With a spiraling cathedral as an inspiration Lennon's "Strawberry Fields Forever" became a much different song. There were some problems that were difficult to overcome.

Again internal difficulties surfaced during the "Penny Lane" sessions. On January 4, 1967, the Beatles resumed recording "Penny Lane" in a tension-filled atmosphere. The next night after Paul overdubbed yet another vocal onto "Penny Lane," he began creating a sound effects tape for the "Carnival of Light." This was a highly experimental show to be held in London featuring a tape combining various electronic sounds. George Martin shook his head in disgust, he couldn't believe the waste of tape and studio time. Patrons who saw the show at London's Roundhouse Theater disagreed; they believed that it was an excellent example of 60's avant garde music.

Paul spoke fondly of this experiment which had produced a tape of electronic noises which was much like "Revolution 9." This strange musical melange of sounds included distorted sounds, a hypnotic drum, various organ bursts and a misplaced lead guitar. A church organ and gargling water were added to the track. For no particular reason John and Paul screamed "Barcelona" and "Are you allright?" It took Paul fourteen minutes to create this strange piece of tape. This electronic game eventually bore important commercial results during the **White Album**.

When the January 5, 1967, session was completed, George Martin remarked: "This is ridiculous." Few disagreed with Martin. What were the Beatles doing? The answer was simple. They were experimenting with musical change, thereby creating a new form of Beatles music.

The crazy loop of electronic music diverted the Beatles' attention from the "Penny Lane" cuts. On Friday, January 6, 1968, the Beatles arrived at Abbey Road at seven in the evening and worked for six hours overdubbing "Penny Lane." Paul's bass guitar, John's rhythm guitar and Ringo's drums were not working to full efficiency. From January 9 to 17 "Penny Lane" was completed. On Tuesday night, January 17, 1967, Paul McCartney sat down and listened to "Penny Lane." It still needed work.

To relax from the strain of the "Penny Lane" sessions, Paul turned his television set on to watch the BBC 2 series Masterworks. One of the musicians on the program, David Mason, played a trumpet that intrigued McCartney. As Mason performed Bach's "Brandenburg Concerto, Number 2 in F Minor," Paul had a vision. Suddenly, he knew how to complete "Penny Lane."

Getting in touch with David Mason was easy, the musician's union stumbled over themselves giving McCartney his home phone. Mason was surprised when Paul called, but he agreed to work on a Beatle session. To complete "Penny Lane,"

Paul employed Mason's New Philharmonia Orchestra sound. The added trumpet, Paul reasoned, would give "Penny Lane" a unique commercial flavor. Mason took nine trumpets to the session and the intricate "Penny Lane" sound was completed. It was Mason's trumpet overdubs and his instrumental solos in the middle and toward the end of the song that gave "Penny Lane" its distinctive flavor. Mason remembers that McCartney was completely in charge of the Beatle session. He was the one who produced the final cuts of "Penny Lane," Mason concluded.

For the remainder of January 1967, the Beatles worked on "A Day In The Life" and completed a mono remixing of "Penny Lane." As the Beatles recorded "A Day in The Life" they had no idea that it would make such a magnificent climax to the **Sgt. Pepper** album. As the Beatles worked on "A Day In The Life," the old Lennon and McCartney magic clicked again. Geoff Emerick remembered: "McCartney had a middle but no ending for the song and Lennon had a beginning and end but no middle. It didn't take long for Lennon and McCartney to meld their ideas into a coherent song."

The February 1, 1967, Beatles recording session created the song that gave the new album its name. The tune "Sgt. Pepper's Lonely Hearts Club Band" was completed during a marathon seven and a half hour recording session. The following day Paul's lead vocal was added to "Sgt. Pepper's Lonely Hearts Club Band" and a demo remix was completed.

Overdubbing on "A Day In The Life" and eight takes of Lennon's "Good Morning, Good Morning" occupied the Beatles' for the next week. The album was progressing nicely, and the constant experimentation created a promising musical direction.

During the **Sgt. Pepper's Lonely Hearts Club Band** album sessions, Paul had the opportunity to record in a new studio. On February 9, 1967, Paul drove to the Regent Sound Studio at 164-166 Tottenham Court Road to cut "Fixing A Hole." This was the first Beatle session for EMI. The Regent Studio had a fine reputation for producing hit records, and Paul was excited about entering the studio that produced the Rolling Stones' early hits.

In the small, cramped Regent Studio McCartney used a harpsichord and bass simultaneously on "Fixing A Hole" to create a new sound. The evening of recording brought a new enthusiasm to Paul. He wanted to go back into the studio the next night. Paul had a plan for yet another musical experiment.

On February 10, 1967, McCartney hired ninety musicians to complete "A Day In The Life." Although Lennon wrote the first and last parts of this song, it was largely a McCartney composition. The concept and execution indicated Paul's musical creativity. In "A Day In The Life" the orchestra was recorded four times before the sound was mixed down to one final take. It was much like using one hundred and sixty musicians, and the completed sound was a stunning musical gem.

As McCartney conducted the orchestra, he seethed with an inner joy and yearned to make his own solo music. The musicians from the Royal Philharmonic and the London Symphony orchestras were more than happy to play with the Beatles. Many of them wore red noses, funny hats and balloons. This festive atmosphere contributed to a harmonious atmosphere which in turn produced a quality record.

Since this session was filmed, everyone assumed that it would be included in a television special about the **Sgt. Pepper's Lonely Hearts Club Band** album. The presence of many old friends including Mick Jagger, Keith Richards, Donovan, Mike Nesmith and Marianne Faithful added to the party like ambiance.

The first cut of "A Day in the Life" was not a strong one, so on February 22, 1967 McCartney returned to Abbey Road to finish the tune. The problem was how to end "A Day In The Life." It was up to McCartney to finish the song. To complete it John, Ringo and Mal Evans joined in on three pianos and they all hit an E major note simultaneously. "A Day In The Life" was completed. David Crosby of the Byrds sat in a corner watching this frenetic studio activity. Paul had been a friend of Crosby's for some time. When the Byrds played their first British tour, Paul saw the group and took Crosby and Roger McGuinn home in his Aston Martin. "Scared us to pieces because he was driving drunk," Crosby recalled, "but he was very kind to us." It was typical of McCartney to hang around other musicians. Crosby and McCartney talked late into the night about music. "Paul was excited," Crosby remembered. "He talked at length about finishing the new album."

When the **Sgt. Pepper's Lonely Hearts Club Band** LP was nearing its final stages in March 1967, McCartney jetted off to America to meet his girl friend, Jane Asher, who was touring with the Old Vic Theater Company. After spending months recording the **Sgt. Pepper's Lonely Hearts Club Band** LP, McCartney was eager for a vacation. He looked forward to spending some time in California. Los Angeles was McCartney's favorite city for business but San Francisco was his cultural mecca. The balance between these two towns, McCartney informed a close friend, drew him to California.

In April 1967 McCartney accompanied by Mal Evans flew to San Francisco and met with the Jefferson Airplane. After landing in San Francisco, McCartney dined with members of the Airplane and toured the local clubs. He spent some time with Ken Kesey and the Merry Pranksters. They talked at length about the psychedelic revolution. Not only did Kesey preach that LSD liberated the mind, but he continually pointed to his own literary creativity. Paul was impressed. This bearded, balding guru with rippling muscles attracted a strange crowd but they were hip and in touch with the Beatles' music.

As McCartney wandered through the San Francisco he recognized that the **Sgt. Pepper** album was part of the emerging psychedelic sound. On a stopover in Los Angeles, John Phillips and Cass Elliot of the Mamas and Papas accompanied Paul to a Beach Boy recording session where Brian Wilson was working his masterpiece, a rock opera known as The Four Elements Suite. Paul was impressed. He knew that the **Sgt. Pepper** album was in a similar vein. Upon his return to England, McCartney inspired by Kesey and the Merry Pranksters and the Beach Boys' **Pet Sounds** concept, scribbled his impressions of the trip on a piece of Apple stationary. This short sketch developed into an idea for a movie. Eventually, it became the **Magical Mystery Tour** film. Paul informed close friends that the blend of San Francisco and Liverpool created a new twist in his thinking. One that blended film with music thereby creating a new avenue for his creativity.

Barry Miles was an astute observer of McCartney's life. This avant garde thinker was a student of American radicalism. He supplied McCartney with copies of the **Berkeley Barb**, the **LA Free Press** and the **East Village Other**. Miles also lent albums like Frank Zappa's **Freak Out** to McCartney and provided a different intellectual vision for his Beatle friend. A student of beatnik poetry and a close friend of Allen Ginsberg, Miles cut a wide path in English pop history. In October 1966, Miles founded London's premier underground newspaper, the **International Times**. Because of his fondness for Miles, Paul provided much of the financing for **IT**. In turn, Miles shared his varied intellectual interests and sense of style. In fact, Miles later wrote the famous **In His Own Words** books on the Beatles.

Since 1965 when Allen Ginsberg visited London, Barry Miles was a teacher, provocateur and guru to McCartney. When Bob Dylan visited London in 1965 and again in 1966, Miles was instrumental in bringing Dylan and the Beatles together. McCartney had heard Dylan's music in New York and turned the others on to the laconic folksinger. In 1966, during their second meeting, Miles brought Ginsberg in to break the tension between the superstars.

"I remember going to see Dylan when he was at the Mayfair Hotel and we went to pay homage," Paul remarked. It was not a pleasant meeting as Paul was forced to wait his turn with the Rolling Stones' Brian Jones and Keith Richards to meet Dylan. There was a sense of adventure to Dylan and Paul loved his disjoined comments. Paul confessed to Miles that he found Dylan "too loose."

As Miles and McCartney sat in the small waiting room adjacent to Dylan's suite they laughed about the "God like aura" surrounding the American singer. The change in the musical climate due to Dylan was important, and McCartney felt a sense of musical and personal freedom. Miles did most of the talking as they laughed about the regal air surrounding the "Dylan coronation." After a few drinks they were heard loudly in the small room.

"You'd think the bloke was us," Paul laughingly remarked.

"Thank god he's not you," Miles retorted. "You'd be stuck with all these boring people."

"I think I've been already," Paul continued.

"Remember, he made fun of you," Miles lectured.

"I forgot," Paul remarked. McCartney looked in a nearby mirror and suddenly was in deep thought. "I don't think we should get into a newspaper thing with Dylan," McCartney concluded.

This exchange offers some insight into the Beatles long standing anger over Dylan's comments. He had not only made fun of their dress, music and life style, but he implied they lacked a visionary talent. Paul had a long memory, but he was smart enough to stay away from a press confrontation. There were more pressing matters for McCartney. He needed to develop a life outside the Beatles. His friend Miles helped in this transformation.

By early 1967 it was Miles who inspired McCartney to wear long, flowing robes. Miles also turned Paul on to the music of Pink Floyd. In December 1966, Miles helped launch the UFO Club which became a vehicle for underground music.

The UFO Club in London featured Pink Floyd on a dozen different occasions. Not only was Pink Floyd the house band of the underground, but they performed alongside some of the best experimental films of the day. Kenneth Anger's film **Fireworks** was one of McCartney's favorites. He frequently snuck into the UFO in disguise and the crowd was too hip to recognize the famous Beatle. As one survivor of the UFO Club remarked: "The trendy London intellectual believed Pink Floyd's 'Arnold Layne' was too pop and that the guy who looked like Paul McCartney should get another disguise." It was all good fun for Paul.

Miles often accompanied McCartney to Abbey Road to hang out during the recording sessions. When the Beatles were in the final stages of the **Sgt. Pepper** sessions, Miles mentioned that Pink Floyd was in the next studio. Immediately, Paul walked over with George and Ringo to say hello.

When McCartney began talking to Pink Floyd he made it clear that he was not only a fan but appreciated the art of their music. To close friends Paul confided that Pink Floyd was the only British band "to bring together electronic music and studio recording techniques in an art form."

On October 15, 1966, Miles launched the **International Times** during a Roundhouse celebration featuring Pink Floyd, the Soft Machine and a psychedelic light show. The San Francisco influence was unmistakable during this strange evening. Kenneth Rexroth, a San Francisco poet, covered the concert for the **San Francisco Examiner** and the beat poet demonstrated little understanding of rock music. When Rexroth complained about the music, Miles realized that the grouchy poet had stepped out of his generation. Rexroth didn't realize that he was witnessing a moment in rock history.

This was Pink Floyd's first big concert and it had an enormous influence upon Paul. Whenever he had some free time in London, Paul went to the UFO club to watch Pink Floyd. Because the UFO reminded him of Liverpool's Cavern Club, Paul referred to it as Pink Floyd's "trippy adventure playground." Syd Barrett's pop song writing intrigued McCartney. Not only was the chief architect of Pink Floyd's sound a promising art student but he seemed to have a vision beyond rock music. Film was a medium that Barrett enjoyed. This intrigued McCartney who hoped to branch out as a filmmaker.

Throughout 1967 Paul and Miles had long talks about music and film. McCartney believed that film was the next medium for the serious rock musician. A sensitive, art form brand of rock music, McCartney continually lectured Miles, was in the future.

Paul remembered: "The funny thing is John's ending up as the one that's the avant garde guy because he did all that with Yoko." While John was living in the suburbs, Paul complained, he and Miles were experimenting with new literary, poetic and musical forms. "I helped start **International Times** with Miles, helped start Indica Bookshop and Gallery where John met Yoko," Paul complained. Obviously, McCartney felt a sense of not being fully appreciated for his intellectual contributions.

"I had a very rich avant-garde period which was such a buzz, making movies and stuff," Paul continued. Living on his own in London, Paul was away from his three married Beatle partners. It wasn't that his life was intellectually richer, Paul simply had the time and freedom to follow his interests.

Paul was bursting with new ideas and he assumed naively that others would open up to his vistas. "I think Paul experienced a personal crisis during the **Sgt. Pepper** album," Clive Epstein remarked, "and I believe it was due to psychedelic drugs. I always thought that he had a psychedelic hangover," Epstein concluded.

Once Paul experimented with LSD, he changed the rules for his song writing. On "Penny Lane," for example, McCartney wrote about a single street in Liverpool and wove lyrics around its meaning. He concentrated so heavily upon this one dimensional street that it evoked broader memories than the street possessed. Some critics complained that drugs were the reason for the strange references and narrow symbols in McCartney's music.

The **London Daily Mirror** criticized Paul for taking LSD. The **Daily Mirror** stated: "Paul McCartney is one of the oldest teenagers on record..." and is "behaving like an irresponsible idiot." After the **Daily Mirror's** critical article, Barry Miles and Derek Taylor went to see McCartney. They urged Paul to insulate and isolate himself from the press. Consequently, McCartney was careful in subsequent dealings with the press. Paul believed that he had to look deeper within himself for musical creativity.

Many changes surfaced in McCartney's personality. When he returned from his visit to America, Paul looked forward to a period of new creativity. The **Sgt. Pepper's Lonely Hearts Club Band** album was in its final production stages. Brian Epstein was in a hospital with drug problems and the Beatles finances were in shambles. Robert Stigwood was attempting to take over NEMS and Brian was numb from business pressure.

Because he had been so ill, Epstein didn't hear the **Sgt. Pepper** album until its final mix. Brian realized instantly that the 12 songs set a new standard for rock music. The album had taken four months to record and cost $100,000. It so stunned other musicians that after the Beach Boys' Brian Wilson listened to it, he gave up work on his forthcoming concept album.

As Paul guided the **Sgt. Pepper** album through its final production stages, Brian was trying to keep the Beatles' empire intact. On May 16, 1967, Brian left his New York hotel to meet with long time friend and Beatle attorney, Nat Weiss. After elaborate discussions, Brian granted Nemperor Artists in New York the exclusive right to book NEMS artists in the U. S. and Canada. Not only was Weiss a good friend but he was a shrewd businessman and adept at promotion. This deal indicated that Brian had a number of new Beatle tours planned for the next three years. He also had old and new acts he hoped to present. Epstein's untimely death, the Beatles' financial problems and the emergence of the Apple Corporation altered these plans.

After returning to London, Brian hosted a party for the Beatles forthcoming **Sgt. Pepper's Lonely Hearts Club Band** LP. In deference to Epstein, all the Beatles appeared at the party and Brian rigidly supervised the press questions. Reporters had trouble talking to the Beatles without Epstein's smiling countenance.

At this May party Paul's influence over Beatle affairs was demonstrated in a number of ways. Sir Joseph Lockwood, the President of EMI, had objected to allowing the excesses of the **Sgt. Pepper** cover. The fear of law suits was ever present in Lockwood's mind. Paul single handily convinced him to use it and guaranteed the money needed to defend against potential legal action. The use of famous personalities on the Beatle LP cover worried many in the record industry. As McCartney suggested, this was nonsense. Everyone wanted their face on a Beatle album. When a **New Musical Express** reporter questioned Paul about Lockwood's objections, McCartney made it clear that the Beatles had great power with EMI due to exorbitant record sales. Paul informed the reporter that a 50 million pound bond was guaranteed against possible law suits, and the Beatles would stand by the album. "The music, the album cover and even the design of the water closet is our choice," Paul remarked jokingly.

Once the **Sgt. Pepper** LP was released on June 1, 1967, it was praised as the perfect rock and roll album. The cover, designed by pop artist Peter Blake, was a collage of 62 personalities which included Marilyn Monroe, Marlon Brando, Carl Jung, Edgar Allen Poe, Bob Dylan and Stu Sutcliffe among others. But it was a concert in America which was responsible for highlighting the musical genius of the **Sgt. Pepper** album.

The Monterey Pop Festival held from Friday, June 16 through Sunday, June 18, 1967, was a catalyst to the brisk sales of the **Sgt. Pepper** album. This three day rock and roll extravaganza featuring the best of Los Angeles and San Francisco rock music was responsible for the emergence of a number of acts notably Janis Joplin and Big Brother and the Holding Company, the Steve Miller Band, Jimi Hendrix, the Quicksilver Messenger Service and the Electric Flag among others. During intermission the strains of "Sgt. Pepper's Lonely Hearts Club Band" wafted over the sound system out into the marijuana laden air. Rumors of the Beatles appearing surfaced hourly.

Jann Wenner, a fledgling journalist, loved the **Sgt. Pepper** music and he tried to interest **Look, Life** and **Hi-Fi** magazines in a feature article. When Wenner failed to sell a story on the Beatles, he teamed up with a San Francisco journalist, Ralph Gleason, to found **Rolling Stone** magazine. The Beatles' influence went far beyond rock music. Wenner's concern for intelligent rock journalism prompted him to found the magazine that was the first mainstream publication to take rock and roll seriously. Not coincidentally, **Rolling Stone** featured the Beatles in most early issues.

From his Monterey motel, Derek Taylor, the former Beatle press officer, phoned **Disc** to report the extraordinary Monterey Pop Festival. The **Disc** story stressed the Beatles impact upon Monterey. They were the most talked about rock group even thought they didn't attend the festival. The music from the **Sgt. Pepper** album was everywhere and it dominated a festival which included some of the best rock bands. Paul was pleased that his **Sgt. Pepper** concept went beyond the English market. As a token member of the Monterey Board of Governors, Paul had lent his name to the festival. The rumor of McCartney and the other Beatles surfacing in Monterey disguised as hippies was a marvelous one. The Beatles were safe in London watching **Sgt. Pepper** climb to the top of the charts.

In England the **Sgt. Pepper** album sold more than a quarter of a million copies during the first week. **Sgt. Pepper's Lonely Hearts Club Band** remained at the number 1 spot on the British album charts for twenty-two weeks. On the American **Billboard** album chart **Sgt. Pepper** was no. 1 for fifteen weeks. By January 1971, the **Sgt. Pepper** album sold more than seven and a half million copies. Six years later the album exceeded ten million copies in the world market. By 1991 almost twenty million copies had sold in the world market. In 1978, **Sgt. Pepper** again appeared on the **Billboard** Top Twenty. The lengthy commercial success of this album was in part due to its controversial nature.

There was immediate controversy over **Sgt. Pepper's** music when BBC banned, "A Day In The Life." It was because of Paul's lyric "found my way upstairs, had a smoke/somebody spoke and I went into a dream." This was a song about pot, BBC alleged, and a BBC editorial denounced the tune. What BBC failed to realize is that "A Day In The Life" employed a 40 piece symphony orchestra assembled at the Abbey road studio number 1 with the musicians wearing tuxedos and black ties. There was no indication of drug use in the song's lyrics nor in the context in which it was written. But the red flag of British conservatism made it impossible to stifle BBC's criticism.

The controversy continued over Lennon's "Lucy In The Sky With Diamonds." The lyrics celebrated "tangerine trees and marmalade skies." Again the critics cried out. It was a song obviously inspired by LSD. In reality, Lucy was a friend of John's son, Julian, and the phrase "Lucy In The Sky With Diamonds" was a description of a drawing John made of the little girl. It was Lennon's fascination with Lewis Carroll's writing which helped him to write "Lucy In the Sky With Diamonds."

Yet, the controversy continued, John was subjected to intense scrutiny by the media and the general public. It was easy to understand Lennon's songs. "Getting Better" was John's confession about the women in his life. "Being For the Benefit of Mr. Kite" was taken from a 19th century circus poster. Because of the phrase, "Henry the Horse," some critics assumed that the song was about heroin. This was a ridiculous conclusion, because Lennon bought a poster in a London antique shop. The famous nineteenth century circus poster featured a picture of a woman next to an acrobat balancing on a pole. The posters were sold all over England and had nothing to do with drugs. It was the poster that inspired John to write the tune.

The rock critics whose reviews were published in **Rolling Stone**, **Melody Maker**, the **New Musical Express** and **Disc** concluded that the Beatles finest song on the **Sgt. Pepper** album was "A Day in the Life." Because of this song, the major newspaper and magazine critics congratulated the Beatles for their innovative approach to rock music. They were enthralled by the use of a 40 piece orchestra on "A Day In The Life."

"Strawberry Fields Forever" and "Penny Lane" were originally scheduled for release on the **Sgt. Pepper** album. But in January 1967, they were packaged as a single, thereby escaping the LP. When **Sgt. Pepper** was finally released on June 1, 1967, Chris Welch in **Melody Maker** wrote: "it is a worthwhile contribution to music." The **New Musical Express** reviewed **Sgt. Pepper** track by track and unequivocally praised Harrison's "Within You Without You" as the best song on the LP. Ray Coleman, the editor of **Disc** and **Music Echo**, considered the **Sgt.**

Pepper album the "very zenith of rock and roll music." Not only were Coleman's reviews incisive commentaries on the Beatles' music, but he was one of the few critics who recognized their natural evolution into a band with a new sound that would rock the world.

Although he had opposed the Beatles' new direction, George Martin changed his mind. In Martin's autobiography, **All You Need Is Ears**, he recalled: "The time had come for experiment. The Beatles knew it and I knew it...we had had an enormous string of hits...we could try anything we wanted." This observation was one from the vantage point of hindsight. At the time **Sgt. Pepper** was conceived and recorded, George Martin worried that the Beatles were destroying themselves. Martin failed to see the changes coming to rock music. Perhaps the most innovative one was the merging of the rock and art world. The **Sgt. Pepper** album cover was the catalyst to this marriage of rock music and pop art.

On March 30, 1967, when the album cover for the **Sgt. Pepper** LP was shot at Michael Cooper's studio at 1 Flood Street in Chelsea, no one realized its revolutionary impact. This picture session took three hours and there was an enticing aroma of Moroccan hashish in the studio. Large jugs of wine were everywhere and bottles of gin, vodka, scotch and coke filled in the refreshment budget. It was time for adult beverages and the Beatles and their cohorts imbibed in excess. When it was finished **Sgt. Pepper** changed the direction of rock and roll album history as the cover became a selling point. The differences over the album's direction ignited a quarrel between Paul and John that escalated into the battle that helped to break up the Beatles.

The **Sgt. Pepper** LP is an important turning point in the Beatles' musical, artistic and business direction. In 1968 Paul continued to come to the fore and take over the musical and business forces necessary to continued success.

The historical dimensions of the **Sgt. Pepper** album are important ones. In 1987 **Rolling Stone's** critics poll proclaimed it as the best LP of the past twenty years. As Bill King and Al Sussman remarked in **Beatlefan**: "**Sgt. Pepper's Lonely Hearts Club Band** may not be...the greatest pop music album ever made....But there's no denying it ranks as their most important and influential work...."

5: A NEW ERA: JANUARY-FEBRUARY, 1968

In January and February of 1968, Paul McCartney began placing his business and personal life in order. The period of mourning the death of long-time manager Brian Epstein had passed, and McCartney planned to straighten out the Beatles' affairs.

The unexpected death of Brian Epstein changed the direction of Beatle affairs. In late August 1967 Brian planned a weekend in the country. The circumstances surrounding Epstein's death were strange ones. Brian was happy and upbeat, according to close friends, and his personal and business life was running smoothly. He had invited a number of guests for a weekend at his Kingsley Hill country home, but Epstein abruptly returned to his London home at 24 Chapel Street, Belgravia, not far from Buckingham Palace.

Brian locked himself in his bedroom for two nights. Eventually, Maria, Epstein's Spanish housekeeper, called close friends, and they arrived to find Brian dead in his bed. It was an apparent suicide. Yet, rumors persisted that Epstein was murdered. No evidence of a homicide surfaced.

Paul McCartney, like the other Beatles, was shaken by Brian's death. The Beatles were in India when Epstein died. So Paul had a great deal of time to think about the circumstances surrounding Epstein's death. Eventually, McCartney was critical of Dr. John Flood's inquest. Paul believed that the coroner had not completed an in-depth report on Brian's death. The official report was that a buildup of Carbitrol, a sleeping pill, was the cause of death. McCartney disagreed with this conclusion.

London newspapers had a field day with the story. Soon the question of Epstein's death was mixed with rumors of gangland retaliation, drug abuse and a mysterious and jealous homosexual lover. The strange business deals and the lack of liquid assets added to the mystery.

To forget Brian's death, McCartney plunged himself into Beatle business affairs. The rumors of fiscal problems, the slow decline of royalty payments and the pressure to make commercial music intensified McCartney's work habits. There was also time to play, and there were also new cultural elements in McCartney's life. Robert Fraser, the Indica Gallery owner, helped Paul purchase some inexpensive Magritte paintings. They adorned the wall in his 7 Cavendish Avenue home, giving it an air of good taste.

Bashful and sensitive, Paul seldom displayed his intellectual side publicly. Finally, in early 1968, he rebelled against the press picturing John as the "intellectual Beatle" and

Paul as the "culture chaser." In his St. John's Wood home, Paul held court with a celebrated cast of rock stars, writers, artists, sculptors and intellectuals of varied disciplines. Paul showed his movies to Italian film maker Antonioni, expressing a desire to move into a new medium. Andy Warhol sat for hours in Paul's back yard freely stating his opinions on the Beatles' music and pop culture in general. "It was like a salon," Paul explained. "Brian Jones, John, Mick and Marianne were always around there."

The assorted group of musicians, writers and artists discussed the film **Magical Mystery Tour.** Paul remembered: "The movie was just a mad idea...why don't we do a film, really offbeat." But McCartney wasn't prepared for the negative reaction to his home movie.

The artistic failure of **Magical Mystery Tour,** and the problems with British tax authorities created new tensions with the other Beatles. They viewed the film as a waste of resources. Paul disagreed. If the Beatles' were to reach their full artistic potential, they must grow artistically as well as financially. John thought this was a contradiction, considering how tight McCartney was with money. Privately, Paul expressed reservations about the money he spent on the **Magical Mystery Tour** film. This was not surprising, considering his background.

He had never forgotten the cold Liverpool nights, and the depressed northern England economy. He still nurtured fears of bankruptcy. The Beatles' inability to collect full royalties intensified Paul's economic concerns. He realized fame was fleeting, and the prospect of a decline in the Beatles' music sales was foremost in his thinking. There were images of poverty, failure and an overwhelming sense of isolation which created McCartney's omnipresent fears. Consequently, Paul was determined to develop a detailed business plan to ensure Apple's future.

The first signs of the new McCartney occurred during a visit to his father's house on New Years day, 1968. This home had a special and symbolic meaning. For Paul McCartney it was the culmination of his dreams. Three years earlier, Paul encouraged his father to retire after almost half a century in the Liverpool labor market. Then Paul bought his father a 8,750 pound home on Baskervyle Road, in Hewswell, Cheshire. When Jim retired, he met and married Angela. With a five year old stepdaughter, Ruth, and a young wife, Jim began a new life. Not only was Paul happy for his dad, but he encouraged the relationship. In this relaxed atmosphere, Paul talked incessantly about the future. The question of a master plan for the Beatles was foremost in McCartney's thoughts. It was time to change the time tested musical formula for the Beatles. But there were also other concerns.

Paul informed his dad that he intended to assert himself

in the Beatles' affairs. He wrote out an elaborate list of things to accomplish and at the top of Paul's notes a huge pound sign was visible. In a nostalgic mood, Paul talked fondly with his dad about his youth. Yet, deep down, some of the distasteful experiences of the early Liverpool years remained. As a young man Paul was unable to bring people home because there wasn't enough food in the refrigerator. Although he was a multi-millionaire, McCartney worried about money. The specter of poverty haunted him.

When Paul informed the other Beatles that they needed to reorganize their finances, they laughed at him. The reason for the Beatles' lack of concern about their finances was a simple one. They were wealthy. The were also well thought of in the music business. Increasingly, the Beatles were praised as a major influence upon the radical American left. The mainstream media, as well as the counterculture press, proclaimed the intellectual significance of the Beatles.

Student rallies on college campuses invariably featured Beatle songs. Black radicals and anti-war advocates praised the subtle nuances of Beatle lyrics. They were part of the revolution. So John suggested they spurn corporate organization. Ringo and George taunted Paul about his nine to five business mentality, his three piece suits and his bowler hats. It was easy for Paul to ignore George and Ringo, but he was tempted to answer Lennon. In the end, Paul took the high road and refused to become involved in a debate with John. Because of these differences there was an unhealthy air of tension and animosity both in the recording studio and in the Apple offices. Paul offered the only solution he knew to solve the differences between the Beatles-hard work.

In retrospect, it is surprising that John looked upon Paul as a member of the establishment. McCartney was viewed as someone who would do anything to make a dollar. The other Beatles were just as eager to cash in on their fame. As McCartney attempted to salvage his personal fortune, the remaining Beatles'were working in the movie industry. Ringo had finished a small part in the art movie, **Candy**. George was recording tracks for the film **Wonderwall** at EMI Studios in London. John was actively pursuing movie and literary interests.

The creation of the Apple Corporation was the first step toward restructuring the Beatles' empire. The Apple concept was a simple one. Paul would write, produce and record his songs. The other Beatles would have the same freedom and the creative atmosphere was to be an open one. By controlling their own music, the Beatles would promote promising new artists. Clive Epstein urged the boys to branch out. "You need a tax deduction," Epstein retorted shortly after his brother died. "Any business you go into will make money, you're the Beatles." It wasn't nearly that simple. The Beatles had neither training in business nor management skills. It would not be easy to organize and run an entertainment empire. Paul realized the enormity of the task the Beatles faced, and he urged John, George and Ringo to involve themselves actively in the venture. Most Apple staffers remember McCartney as the only Beatle to show up at the Apple office daily to direct business affairs.

The Apple Corporation made some premature decisions which delayed the initial business direction. McCartney signed a psychedelic band, Grapefruit, to a contract with the Apple Music Publishing Company. This proved to be a hasty move as Grapefruit, for unknown reasons, didn't release its first single on Apple Records. Grapefruit's music intrigued McCartney. Their song, "Elevator," was a psychedelic tune that Paul loved. Because of his interest in the group, McCartney produced a three-minute film clip of the group at the Albert Memorial Statue in Hyde Park. "Paul loved Grapefruit," Clive Epstein said. "He had a penchant for bringing in these bands with the psychedelic sound. I couldn't understand it."

Only Paul dreamed of a business empire. In explaining Apple's mission, Paul remarked: "If you have paperwork and bills and royalties and accounts...they all have to be handled...." McCartney continued by suggesting that without management controls the tax man would end the Beatle dream. "The main downfall is that we were less businessmen and more heads," Paul later confessed in an interview. It was clear in 1968 that McCartney was no longer interested in "sex, drugs and rock and roll." He wanted to be a full-fledged corporate executive. His mission was to save the Beatles.

In January 1968, the other Beatles considered whether they would join McCartney and sort out their affairs or continue to be avant garde pop intellectuals. The hedonism surrounding the pop music world and the luxurious life that came with the financial rewards made corporate organization difficult.

John, George and Ringo wanted to make music. The thought of the corporate world was distasteful to them. They would leave the business decisions to accountants, lawyers and managers. This was the main reason that the Beatles' affairs were clouded. There were too many fingers in the fiscal pie. The Apple experiment was diluted by hangers on, poor management and sycophants who clung to the psychedelic vision. It was a pleasant atmosphere but not a healthy business environment.

A major part of the Beatles' problems stemmed from their revolutionary attitude toward the entertainment industry. Rather than going through agents, auditioning new talent or scouting the clubs, the Beatles depended upon audition tapes and direct letters to sign new acts. This was a naive approach. It led to inane proposals from fans. The result was a circus atmosphere of letters and a barrage of personal visits from the untalented legion who followed the Beatles.

There was so little original talent that Paul came to

believe it was a mistake to have placed these ads. The other Beatles took great delight in reading the mail. Ringo, George and John loved to read aloud the applications from the acid drenched artists who were unable generally to produce music, poetry or prose. Many hours were spent in the Apple offices drinking and reading the addled-brained suggestions of would be artists. A California girl wrote to propose that the Beatles sell plaster of paris penises. From Chicago a fan asked to buy poems and Christmas cards from each Beatle. In San Francisco a Beatle incense was suggested by a Haight-Ashbury renegade. Clive Epstein grabbed these letters and read them aloud. As John Lennon walked by one day, Clive grabbed him in the Apple foyer:

"John, look, look, what wonderful ideas." Clive's belly jiggled, he smiled. John thought he looked like a stuffed toad.

"What?" A startled Lennon remarked.

"There's more to the market than music, John," Epstein continued.

"Bye, mate," Lennon said as he walked rapidly to the front door.

"John, John, listen," Epstein hollered hurrying after the Beatle.

This was one of many instances where letters to the Beatles created tension at Apple.

As letters flooded into the Apple Corporation the Beatles were praised effusively. Not only were the Beatles looked upon as saviors by newcomers to the record industry, but they were thought to be the conduit for new talent into the **Billboard** Hot 100. Hadn't they promised to end the unfair world of big business record production? Wasn't every deserving artist going to get his or her own record contract? Didn't the Beatles have a responsibility to their fans? These questions weighed heavily upon one Beatle mind who believed that they were becoming too entrepreneurial.

John Lennon reasoned that if the Beatles became businessmen, fans would turn away. Paul quickly dismissed this argument. For years Paul had complained about the 94% British income tax. Many rock groups were changing their approach to royalties, expenses and record contracts. The Rolling Stones were living abroad to avoid taxes. A number of British musicians had relocated to Los Angeles to take advantage of American tax laws. When Donovan moved to a California desert town east of Los Angeles, he let Paul know the living was good and the tax advantages were even better. The Beatles could not bear to leave England, so they had to consider a new business arrangement.

As a result, John and Paul disagreed about the direction of their business affairs. These tiffs were complicated by Lennon's intense involvement in American politics. Not only was Lennon involved in the American New Left, but he was an ideological oracle for this tempestuous movement. The gurus of radical

American politics were as fond of quoting Lennon's lyrics as they were of ignoring McCartney's contributions to the music.

The consensus was that Lennon was the brains behind most Beatle songs. The truth is somewhat more complicated. In the early years of their song writing career, Lennon dominated the process. It was after all, John's band. By 1965 McCartney equaled Lennon's song writing productivity, and during the following three years Beatle tunes were generally McCartney songs. By early 1968 the two songwriters were going their separate commercial ways. The songs were increasingly evolving into either Lennon or McCartney tunes, and the Beatles were fighting constantly with one another. As a result of this squabbling, the first two months of 1968 brought signs of change in the Beatle empire. McCartney was writing more of his own tunes and spending less time with Lennon on Beatle songs. The press paid very little attention to this change. The publicity wheels continued to turn out the myth that Lennon and McCartney were happily at work on new tunes. Many of the changes taking place in Paul's life were the result of his changing relationship with his long time girlfriend Jane Asher.

It was not just his partnership with Lennon that bothered McCartney. His relationship with Jane Asher had grown stale. He was still friendly with the Asher family but Paul felt strained around them. They were suddenly not as friendly. Jane's dad was prone to erratic mood swings. Her brother Peter Asher was involved in Apple Records production but the working relationship between Paul and Peter was uneasy. For years Paul had depended upon Jane's parents for a normal family atmosphere. Lately, however, he had uneasy feelings about the Asher's.

It is understandable that Paul had second thoughts about ending his relationship with one of England's most eligible women. When McCartney met Jane Asher in May 1963, she was seventeen. An aspiring actress, Asher rated records for the TV program Juke Box World. Her picture was in every British magazine and she was the symbol of the perfect English bird. Slight, stylish and well dressed. Asher's middle-class roots and sense of style appealed to McCartney.

An independent person with a fine dramatic flair, Jane Asher was pursuing a successful acting career. Only three years after her birth on April 5, 1946, Jane was taking singing and dancing lessons. In her early teens, Jane developed an interest in pop music. The 17 year old Asher still lived with her parents. Paul was impressed with her class, sense of style and physical beauty. They became a London celebrity couple seen at the best spots.

For the next three years, Paul was close to the Asher family. They insulated him from the critics and the pressures of musical super stardom. Jane's father, Dr. Richard Asher, was a comforting figure to Paul. Dr. Asher was considered one of the best physicians to consult for blood disorders and mental diseases. Her father constantly reinforced McCartney's ego while providing intellectual sustenance. But Dr. Asher was only one member of the family who was an accomplished professional.

Margaret Asher, Jane's mother, was another member of the Asher family who enjoyed Paul's fame. A professor of classical music at Guildhall School of Music and Drama, she was renowned for her wide musical knowledge. Mrs. Asher had once taught George Martin to play the oboe, and she was proud of her long list of famous students. Margaret Asher, the music scholar, was the cement that held the family together.

To Jane the Beatles were much more than a musical group. They were national celebrities who validated her importance. She loved the limelight and basked in their glow. Jane's brother Peter, a musical prodigy, was a composer and musician of extraordinary talent.

The Asher family home was a showcase five-story terrace mansion on Wimpole Street near the West End. Each night around the dinner table they offered a fascinating selection of conversational topics that delighted Paul. Beneath this happy family surface, however, a monster lurked. There are a number of London locals who remember Dr. Asher cursing the Beatles' success. His relationship with Paul was a love-hate one. In his lucid moments, Asher was a model of decorum, but during violent, drunken outbursts he was uncontrolled and threatening.

From 1963 to 1966 when McCartney lived with the Asher's, he learned a great deal from them. To this day Paul has only delightful things to say about Jane and she refuses to talk openly about him. As one person very close to the couple remarked: "they simply weren't meant for each other."

After Paul bought his St. John's Wood home, he reflected on his life with the family. "I found the family warm, charming and living in luxury. It was a heady experience," Paul concluded. It was certainly different from his own upbringing. The McCartneys' working class background and strong sense of their place in English society, made them strong and resilient.

One of Dr. Asher's pet dinner table talks was the relationship between tension and lack of productivity. As Paul listened to these dissertations, he was increasingly concerned about his place in the Beatles' musical hierarchy. Unwittingly, Asher pushed Paul into a position of greater leadership in the Beatles business career.

The constant tension among the Beatles also prompted McCartney to reflect on his life. He felt he wasn't in charge. Not only did John get too much credit for the Beatles music, but Lennon was referred to in the press as the "serious, intellectual Beatle." Not only were the Beatles at a crossroads, but the group had developed different musical interests. Yet, Paul smiled about some of the positive changes in his life. He had established some degree of independence. It was this coming of age, at least in his mind, that made Paul look at Jane with misgivings.

Paul was overjoyed with visions of his St. John's Wood home. The large, detached three-story house adjacent to the House of Lord's cricket ground and around the corner from the Abbey Road recording studio was a comfortable hideaway. The purchase price of 40,000 pounds was considered a bargain. Always frugal, Paul decorated the home with an eye to a strict budget. It was not long before the weeds grew to such length that there was a shabby nature to McCartney's place. He didn't mind the stare of the neighbors.

Each night as Paul walked up the paved courtyard that led to his front door he basked in his success. To the left of the main house a detached double garage housed two fashionable automobiles-a Mini Cooper and an Aston Martin. The high brick wall that surrounded the home and the large iron gates provided needed security. A sophisticated electronic answering service connected the front gate to the house allowing Paul to peruse the front gate. The **London Daily News** reported that his home had the largest number of female fans milling outside the front gate than in front of any other Beatle home.

When he was lonely, Paul could call up Mal Evans, Alistair Taylor or Neil Aspinall and they would bring their Liverpool accents to St. John's Wood. When he needed to rest, Paul vanished into his bedroom. The large L-shaped room had a decorative bed highlighted by an enlarged headboard. There was a sense of style and class to this room. To Paul, the St. John's Wood residence was a grand home. It was a modest sort of luxury that befitted McCartney's standing in the rock music world.

One of the more interesting conversation pieces in McCartney's house was the Paolozzi sculpture in his study. Paolozzi was Stu Sutcliffe's former teacher and the statue remained an ominous sign of his former band mate.

Paul had taken control of his life, and he was ready to make business and recording decisions. A few days after returning from Liverpool, McCartney learned that the album to the Beatle movie, **Magical Mystery Tour**, was number 1 on the **Billboard** album chart. Not only did this boost McCartney's ego, but it was a source of comfort during this critical period. Paul was uneasy about taking over Beatle affairs, he was sensitive to the entertainment and movie writers who unmercifully ridiculed the Beatles' movie.

But not all critics panned the movie **Magical Mystery Tour** and **Time** magazine reported that it earned a two million dollar profit. The critics were ignoring the Beatles' art, but they grudgingly pointed out the economic success of this venture. Richard Goldstein, a **New York Times** critic, remarked that: "when the Beatles' work as a whole is viewed in retrospect, it will be **Rubber Soul** and **Revolver** which stand as their major contributions." It was obvious to Paul that many of the critics were unaware of the changes taking place in rock and roll music. So how could they legitimately recognize a revolutionary movie like **Magical Mystery Tour**? It was not just movie success that inspired McCartney. The Beatles had contributed to the rise of the concept album, the extended length single, new freedom in the studio, and recognition of literary images in rock and roll music. They had made rock and roll a respected part of the arts.

The changes in the direction and context of rock music encouraged McCartney to develop his art. He didn't need Lennon to write songs, perform or publicize the music. Hadn't numerous artists recorded McCartney's compositions? Many of these songs had little input from Lennon. Paul believed he could write his own hit tunes. Clive Epstein remembered in January 1968 how excited McCartney was about his music. He spent more time than ever inside his St. John's Wood home working on tunes. It was not the Beatles that McCartney considered leaving in early 1968, it was his dependence upon Lennon's co-song writing skills.

The cold London winter prompted McCartney to stay indoors. He drank, smoked marijuana and was optimistic about his musical future. Paul was thinking along movie lines. He also spent an inordinate amount of time reading. Critical studies of the French and Italian film makers, the literature of Herman Hesse and the politics of the emerging New Left occupied McCartney's literary pursuits.

In quiet moments, Paul reflected on the film, **Magical Mystery Tour**. He had created the movie. It was designed for a mass market audience but ended up on British television. This didn't depress McCartney. He likened it to the Beatles' Hamburg recordings. It was a learning process. Paul was proud of **Magical Mystery Tour**. He had hired the actors, written the script, composed the songs, directed the shooting and edited the film. Although it was coolly received by the critics, **Magical Mystery Tour** found a ready-made audience among college students.

The Christmas 1967 showing in black and white of **Magical Mystery Tour** on British television prompted London critics to use terms like "blatant rubbish" and "contemptuous nonsense" to describe the film. McCartney pointed out that critics didn't understand the message. So Paul was determined to produce music that would earn him the recognition he deserved, but he viewed the film as a useful experiment.

Chris O'Dell, an employee at Apple in 1968, recalled how important McCartney was to Apple's early business activity. A twenty-two year old blonde from Tucson, Arizona, O'Dell was Peter Asher's secretary. She kept a log of everything that went on at Apple. Foremost in her scribbled notes were references to Paul's work habits. Not only did McCartney spend hundreds of hours on business affairs, he planned for new musical directions.

This trait eventually made Apple an artistic, if not

financial, success. O'Dell remembers how organized Paul was during the Abbey Road recording sessions. He had a clear vision of what the Beatles needed to accomplish in recording sessions.

Each morning O'Dell watched McCartney enter his Apple office just after nine and settle down to work. In fact, Paul worked so hard that he didn't realize Peter Brown and Derek Taylor, who had been brought back into the Beatles' fold, had hired two cordon bleu chefs to make them lunch. After Paul discovered the chefs and the expensive wine cellar that was part of the Saville Row offices, he closed down this extravagance. A take charge individual, Paul looked into all parts of the Apple empire. In fact, as O'Dell recalls, many insignificant areas occupied McCartney's attention. She smirked as Paul checked the toilet paper each night before going home. The little details were the ones that McCartney loved.

There was a broader side to Paul McCartney. He was determined to make the Apple experiment work financially. When the formal incorporation papers were filed in February 1968, Apple was broken into a number of divisions: Apple Music Publishing, Apple Electronics Ltd., Apple Films, Ltd., Apple Retail, Apple Wholesale, Apple Television and Apple Records. An agreement with Capitol Records allowed Apple to be distributed in America, Canada and Mexico. EMI was licensed to distribute Apple to the rest of the world. When the press heard of the new name Apple, they were curious.

"It's a pun," Paul McCartney remarked. "Apple Corps.," Paul shouted like the Core of an Apple but instead Apple Corps." Clive Epstein stepped in to soothe Paul's feelings. "I won't explain Corps. as Core one more time," Paul shouted to a **Melody Maker** reporter.

On paper, the Beatles looked and acted as if they understood the business world. There were continual references made to Henry Pinsker, the head of Bryce-Hammer, Brian Epstein's accounting firm. Since Pinsker was part of the Apple Corporation, it must be a responsible and precise business entity. Nothing was further from the truth.

The office atmosphere at Apple was total mayhem. Alistair Taylor remembers that Derek Taylor's monthly liquor bill was generally for three cases of scotch, three cases of whiskey, three cases of gin, three cases of vodka, twelve cases of cola and fifteen cases of beer. One day Alistair remarked to Derek Taylor in jest: "Isn't the liquor bill a bit low, mate?"

Alistair smiled knowingly and walked away. The next month the bill was double. Alistair Taylor never complained again about the liquor bill. The typical Apple employee had a field day with open bars, a choice of exotic drugs and numerous groupies.

Apple employees were hip, counterculture types connected to the official circle or brought in by those close to power. Neil

Aspinall, Managing Director, Alistair Taylor, General Manager, and Mal Evans, Director, were responsible for hiring most Apple employees. There was no simple reason for selecting employees, but nepotism ruled. Alistair Taylor had a business sense and a concern for money. In contrast, Aspinall and Evans placed neither controls nor restrictions upon Apple employees. They were amateurs playing the role of entertainment moguls.

Neil and Mal hired Gene Mahon, a designer who had worked on the **Sgt. Pepper** album sleeve, to photograph an Apple and create the new record label. It took six months for Mahon to finish the Apple logo. There was a considerable amount of debate over the color of Apple's label. George Harrison commented that Paul wanted the Apple green. To show his independence Harrison argued that the Apple should be orange. John coyly suggested a white Apple and Ringo preferred a blue one.

The genius of Gene Mahon made the concept work. In the acid drenched atmosphere of the late 1960s Mahon shot the whole apple for side one and a sliced apple for side two. On some releases "This Side" was used to indicate the hit song and the "Other Side" was designated for the b tune. The label was an immediate hit with record buyers and it caused a curious reaction from the critics. The strange label also helped to establish Apple as a unique company. One that offered something different. The employees were concerned more about the music than the monetary return.

Peter Asher was Apple's most knowledgeable staffer. The twenty-three year old Apple artist and repertoire man was part of the pop singing duo Peter and Gordon and a shrewd judge of pop talent. Asher recognized mainstream, pop hits, and he produced one hit record after another but not for Apple.

Peter and Gordon had recorded a Paul McCartney composition, "A World Without Love" which was a hit in the spring of 1964 in both England and America. Asher was also an investor in the Indica Gallery and was well thought of in the pop music world. A studious looking, quiet, bespeckeled young man, Asher had strong musical opinions and a talent equal to McCartney's. As a result, Paul's relationship with the young producer-recording artist was strained.

As Paul fought with Jane, Peter found it difficult to work at Apple. Eventually, Asher left for America where he continued to produce hit records. Had McCartney not broken up with Jane, Peter might not have gone beyond producing James Taylor.

The scientific brain behind the Beatles' sound system was twenty-seven year old Alex Mardas. This self proclaimed electronic genius was a Greek technician who fed the Beatles ego and talked incessantly about sophisticated sound systems. Much of what Magic Alex prophesied never came to fruition, because he wasn't able to invent a sound system. Yet, many people in the Beatles empire had special talents. Among these people, Ron Kass was the most important to Apple's long term success. A thirty-three year old American, Kass headed Apple Records. He had worked extensively in the recording industry with Liberty Records. Kass, a dashing figure in his specially tailored suits, was the perfect embodiment of the record company executive. Hip. Hyper. Hustling. Every important business decision within the Apple empire required in-depth knowledge of the music industry. Kass not only provided this information, but he was an honest, hard working executive. Unlike many of the Beatles old Liverpool friends, Kass took the Apple experiment seriously.

Peter Brown, thirty-two, the former assistant to Brian Epstein, scurried around the edges of the Apple empire looking for a way to increase his authority. Richard DiLello, twenty-three, was the house hippie who served everyone tea and kept copious notes on Apple projects. DiLello, a gifted writer, provided the best historical record of the Apple experiment in his book **The Longest Cocktail Party**. Most Apple employees occupied their days with excessive liquor consumption, smoking copious amounts of marijuana and sex. This preoccupation with getting loaded and feeling important meant there was seldom a sense of business.

As Paul arrived at Apple to spend each working day, he was upset by the attitudes and work habits. Most of the people appointed to positions of power were old Liverpool friends. They failed to produce and created the general party atmosphere. The other Beatles were disinterested in the Apple business experiment. It was the key people in charge of Apple projects who bothered McCartney.

In deference to his friends not only did Lennon not work in his private office, but he was critical of Paul's input. When Paul criticized any of John's friends, he went to the press to praise their work. As a result an unhealthy atmosphere developed. This gave the press a chance to reveal small tidbits of gossip. Often deeper problems were exposed. The press realized that during the first few months at Apple there were no controls over spending, and financial matters at Apple were reported eagerly by the press. No matter how intensely the Beatles fought amongst themselves, there had been an unwritten rule not to go public. The Apple experiment ended this truce.

The hard work Paul put in to expedite Apple's success created an open rift with John. When the **London Daily Mirror** reported that John and his father Alfred had reunited, attention was diverted from McCartney's frantic business reorganization. No one knows if Paul resented Lennon's apparent lack of interest in Apple.

There were other forces splitting the Beatles. When John Lennon appeared on the cover of **Look** magazine in mid-January, 1968, a number of Lennon's close friends needled McCartney. The American media didn't recognize Paul's talent. This was a bone of contention with McCartney. To take his mind off the media's love affair with John, Paul praised the other Beatles. He hoped to bring a cooperative working atmosphere to the fore at Apple. A few days later, McCartney confided to a friend that he was not only happy that George was composing the music for the film **Wonderwall**, but that Apple would "publicize the hell out of George's efforts."

While Harrison was recording in Bombay, India, Paul pondered Apple's future. There was a great deal of criticism directed toward Apple. These comments divided the Beatles. McCartney wanted to keep the group together, but the other Beatles were disinterested. The press continually referred to McCartney as "snobbish," "hostile" and "prone to tirades." This hurt Paul. He hoped to continue the Beatles' musical success and straighten out their business affairs.

When McCartney suggested that the Beatles' British fan club move its headquarters from Liverpool to London, he did so to consolidate their business interests. Paul was also concerned about the Beatles' publicity efforts. The move to London would allow Paul to monitor fanzine publicity as well as guide fan club press releases. The news items were important to the Beatles' continued success.

The need to promote Beatle records was the result of a cash flow problem. Not only were the Beatles broke but they had a difficult time putting their hands on liquid assets. Collecting song writing, publishing and mechanical royalties was not an easy task. There were other financial problems. Expenditures for alcohol, food, entertainment and furnishings had gotten out of hand. With two Cordon Bleu chefs, finely furnished rooms, a well-stocked wine cellar and a petty cash fund that was exorbitant, it was time for change. Paul tried to restructure Apple so that both employees and artists were financially accountable.

The behavior of a collective group of fashion designers and artists who worked under the name The Fool brought the issue of monetary responsibility to the surface. The action of this group of fashion designers and artists was a hot topic of conversation. They turned out a product with little thought to profit or marketability. While under contract to Apple to provide clothing for the boutique, The Fool was accused of systematically stripping Apple of clothing. In a rage, Paul instructed John Lyndon, the head of Apple retail, to warn The Fool of their malfeasance. In a strangely worded February 1, 1968, memo from Lyndon to McCartney the head of Apple retail stated that The Fool needed controls.

The business practices which made The Fool's product too costly were reviewed. Paul sent a memo to Lyndon alleging that The Fool was duping Apple. Not only did The Fool order the most expensive raw materials for their clothing designs, Paul pointed out, but they often gave away or carried out the finished product. There was no accounting to anyone, and Lyndon recommended tight restrictions on The Fool. Paul immediately set up an internal auditing system.

Once McCartney restricted The Fool, they spread scurrilous rumors about his "nasty behavior." The British press was only too happy to repeat these tales with little or no backup research. The stories were too good to be verified. Again McCartney was pinching shillings.

The counterculture search for truth, the mystical influences of the Summer of Love and the desire for spiritual regeneration led the Beatles to the Maharishi Mahesh Yogi. A short, silly Indian guru with no understanding of rock and roll music, the Maharishi was knowledgeable about making a buck. Tony Barrow, the Beatles public relations person, was the first to dub the Maharishi the "giggling Guru." The name stuck in an affectionate way. The squeaky voiced little Guru envisioned the Beatles as a quick source of wealth. The Maharishi was struck with how naive and trusting John and George were during their initial contacts with him.

In London, the Maharishi's following of approximately 15,000 eagerly embraced his doctrine of Spiritual Regeneration. Patti Harrison was the first Beatle insider to follow the Maharishi. She thought that he was cute. An elf with a pixie smile, the Maharishi's teachings attracted Patti and others like her who desired simple answers to complex questions. As her own life fell apart she increasingly turned to spiritual avenues. She joined the Spiritual Regeneration Movement in February 1967, to calm her jangled nerves. It was not long before George embraced the Maharishi.

On Thursday, August 24, 1967, the Beatles, out of deference to Harrison, attended the Maharishi's lecture at the Park Lane Hilton Hotel. The Maharishi offered a soothing message. A half hour of meditation each day would cleanse the soul. This appealed to John because he had dabbled with meditation for some time. Ringo was willing to be a part of it. Paul was not so sure. The diminutive guru talked about "inner peace" and chided those whose fortunes were too large. This message appealed to the Beatles. They also were struck by the small seven shilling admission fee. Perhaps the Maharishi was not in it for the money.

Since the Maharishi didn't know that the Beatles were in the audience, they received no recognition and no preferential treatment. This simple mistake worked to the Maharishi's advantage. The Beatles believed they had met a man with integrity, one whom was not intent on taking advantage of their celebrity status.

The Beatles agreed to attend a ten day seminar at University College, Bangor, North Wales. It was the first trip that the Beatles had taken without Brian. The Beatles were joined by Mick Jagger and journalist Hunter Davies. There were no substantive talks at this meeting but the Beatles did hold a press conference to announce that they had given up drugs. This early flirtation with the Maharishi was not serious. It would take a more significant crisis in the Beatles' life for the guru to influence them.

The first important conversations with the Maharishi Mahesh Yogi occurred shortly after Brian's death. To escape his untimely demise, the Beatles embraced the Maharishi's teachings. Among trendy London intellectuals, the Maharishi's book, **The Science of Being and the Art of Living**, was a popular piece of propaganda. There was a plastic spiritualism to the Maharishi that made this dull little book required reading for members of London's hip underground. The emphasis upon peace, love and understanding was inspirational to a generation lost in the fog of Vietnam, the racism of world politics and the greed of corporate takeovers. The Maharishi seemed to offer a better world. At first the other Beatles were skeptical about the lithe Indian guru. Tony Barrow credits George Harrison with influencing the other Beatles to listen to the Maharishi.

The Beatles searched for a new spiritual direction at a time when they were all becoming increasingly political. The first sign of a public political commitment occurred when the Beatles became involved in a movement to legalize marijuana. After signing a petition to support this legislation, three of the Beatles left for a Greek vacation. George Harrison flew to California and visited the hippie Haight-Ashbury district of San Francisco. As Douglas Garbo remembered: "Harrison was struck by our unique culture. He had never seen anything like it." Garbo, a rock band manager, worked for promoter Bill Graham and his job was to make sure that Harrison was comfortable during his visit. It was Garbo who explained the Hippie ethic to Harrison. After Harrison's problems with the rock music business, he listened intently as Garbo extolled counterculture virtues. When he returned to London, Harrison was the catalyst in bringing the rest of the Beatles to the Maharishi.

The small guru, with a constant smile and incessant giggle, intrigued the pop stars. They had the time and money to indulge their fantasies. The Maharishi was no fool. He realized that the Beatles, the Beach Boys and Donovan among others would be useful in spreading his teachings beyond England, India and Sweden. For some time the Maharishi had appealed to a group of wealthy, elderly Swedish dowagers, but the Beatles' support promised to carry his teachings into a broader market.

Since this was a transitional point in the Beatles' lives, they were easily influenced. Paul was the exception. He saw through the Maharishi's addle brained ideas and intellectually inconsistent teachings. From the first day John talked to Paul about the Maharishi, McCartney looked upon the giggling, confused charlatan as another groupie.

Paul remembered the posters in the London subway advertising the Maharishi's books. They were highly commercial ads designed to make the Maharishi a cult figure. In the 1960s people were increasingly attracted to eastern mysticism. The summer of 1967 created significant changes in London as beads, bells and flowers proliferated along with LSD, hashish, peyote and other popular mind expanding drugs. The opening of two new rock emporiums, the Roundhouse and the Middle Earth, created the venues for elaborate rock shows. At these gatherings Indian music was an integral part of the London cultural milieu. The music persuaded Lennon to argue that the Maharishi's message was divine. Paul reluctantly agreed to consider the Maharishi's limited intellectual offerings and erratic lifestyle.

While Paul was poking gentle fun at John's fascination with the Maharishi, George engaged McCartney in serious conversation about meditation. Like many 1960s rock stars McCartney believed that Spiritual Regeneration had some positive points. So he flew to India to listen to the Maharishi's teachings.

On February 19, 1968, Paul McCartney, Jane Asher, Ringo and Maureen Starr flew from London to New Delhi. A squealing crowd of mini-skirted young girls stood at Heathrow Airport to cheer the Beatles. As the newspapers headlined the gory details of the Tet offensive in Vietnam, the world press left for India to camp outside the Maharishi's Himalayan foothill retreat. After landing in India the Beatles began the rigorous 140 mile jeep ride to Rishikesh. The countryside intrigued Paul as he rode to the holy city located near the majestic Himalayan Mountains. The sight of disheveled people riding donkeys, the primitive houses and the abject poverty was unpleasant.

When Paul arrived in Rishikesh, he was surprised that the Maharishi's compound was a European style luxury hotel. The bedrooms were elaborately furnished. A swimming pool, gourmet food and other amenities prompted Ringo Starr to suggest that the Maharishi's layout "was a bit like a Butlins Holiday camp." With a sly smile Ringo remarked, "Even the foods the same, fine, but not really good." Butlins was noted for its poor food, inadequate service and boring atmosphere. While the other guests were awakened at three in the morning, the Beatles slept comfortably until seven or eight o'clock. This special treatment did not escape McCartney. From the beginning Paul was the only Beatle skeptical of the giggling holy man. Paul's criticism began with breakfast.

The vegetarian breakfast the Beatles consumed was a disaster. They ached for sausage and eggs. After breakfast, the Beatles retreated to small caves under the temple to meditate. There were gains from the ashram life. The bland diet, combined with yoga, released personal tension. In time, however, they became bored with this regime. Initially, however, it was a welcome diversion.

After ten days Ringo fled back to London. He informed **Melody Maker** that he not only disliked the food but the living conditions were primitive. It was the London night life that Ringo missed but he also complained about the other guests at the ashram. There was a group of celebrity prima donas who were difficult to be around. The worst of these celebrities was Beach Boy lead vocalist Mike Love. Because he was determined to avoid controversy, McCartney generally ignored Love's malevolent actions.

On March 15, 1968, shortly before he left India, McCartney sang "Indian Ropetrick" and "Happy Birthday Mike Love" to celebrate Love's birthday. These songs were released on the bootleg album **Indian Rope Trick**. Paul later commented that the songs helped liberate the Beatles. They convinced the group to leave the Maharishi's retreat.

Yet, Paul appreciated the changes the diminutive guru brought to his life. There were positive results from the Rishikesh experience. The Maharishi's Meditation Academy offered privacy, intimate contact with creative people and a chance to stretch the mind. Paul took advantage of his time. He thought about new songs and scratched furtively on note pads. Soon the words and music evolved into brilliant new tunes.

Paul meditated daily and experimented with mind control. He believed that his song writing needed more discipline and the Rishikesh experiment convinced McCartney to work harder. He began to spend more time alone. A new maturity was obvious to Paul's friends.

There was also time for fun and games. One of Paul's favorite activities was to walk in the gardens and hide from curious fellow campers. While the Maharishi regulated activities, the Beatles were allowed free run of the compound. Paul loved to appear and then vanish. It was a pleasant way to alleviate the boredom.

The London press followed the Beatles' activity in India with great interest. Although the Beatles initially praised the Maharishi, they soon changed their minds. When it was learned that the Maharishi was negotiating for an ABC-TV Special in America, the Beatles turned on the Holy Man with a vengeance. Peter Brown was instructed to warn the Maharishi about using them for commercial gain. But Brown was neither forceful nor convincing, and the diminutive little guru continued to abuse his relationship with the Fabulous Four.

Magic Alex Mardas was instrumental in destroying the Maharishi's credibility. When Ringo Starr left the ashram after ten days it was Magic Alex who convinced Ringo that the Maharishi had serious character flaws. John and George ignored Magic Alex and continued to follow the daily ritual prescribed by the Maharishi.

In conversations with McCartney, Magic Alex was equally influential. He reinforced Paul's belief that the Maharishi was using the Beatles for his own personal gain. The Maharishi's ritualistic and tedious environment reminded McCartney of school.

After the Maharishi invited a pretty blonde nurse from California to a private chicken dinner and made sexual advances toward her, the Beatles became wary. This may have been the reason that Paul left the gurus' paradise. McCartney had been used too many times in his career to allow a second rate holy man to intimidate him.

On March 26, 1968, Paul and Jane returned to London. The trip to India brought changes in McCartney's life. He realized that the Maharishi was no different from hundreds of others who hoped to exploit the Beatles. This made Paul more determined than ever to redo the Beatles financial affairs. The Apple Corporation was on his mind and it was time to make it work. But Paul was also depressed over the prospect that the Beatles might not return to live performances.

He recalled the times in the late summer of 1967 when Brian Epstein discussed the Beatles touring again. McCartney loved the road, but Brian's untimely death ended this dream. The Beatles' had planned a mini-English tour during the Christmas holidays, followed by a short European jaunt in the spring and a full fledged American tour in the summer of 1968. None of these plans materialized, because Brian Epstein was no longer around. So business became the order of the day. Apple Records and the various corporate outlets occupied Paul McCartney's attention.

During the next few months there were organizational meetings and plans to make the Apple Corporation a business empire. This proved successful, but it was another step in dissolving the Beatles.

6: A PERIOD OF REORGANIZATION, MARCH-APRIL-MAY, 1968

On the plane returning home from India, Paul abstained from alcohol and considered his future. It was late March 1968 as he flew to London a week ahead of John and George. McCartney thought a great deal about the cache of songs that he had written in India. Not only were they commercial ones, but the themes broke out of previous song writing patterns. Paul had grown immensely as an artist. The visit to the Maharishi provided an inspiration for McCartney.

After enduring the Maharishi's retreat, Paul looked forward to the release of a new Beatle album. McCartney planned a new direction in Beatle music. The next batch of songs, Paul exclaimed, would reveal an even stronger commercial side. Paul loved to tell people that the old days of one dimensional hits were gone. No song was more suited to this philosophy than "Lady Madonna."

On March 15, 1968, as the Beatles' seventeenth single "Lady Madonna" was mixed at Abbey Road, there was heady optimism. After listening to the song, George Martin saw no need to spend much time remixing it. So the mono mix was completed during an hour and a half, and, initially, the record was released without a stereo mix.

To promote "Lady Madonna," Paul spent an inordinate amount of time designing an attractive advertisement. Because of his new business intensity, Paul hoped to make the single a hit as it would be Capitol's last American Beatle record. In the publicity surrounding "Lady Madonna," McCartney mentioned that he had used an old song, "Bad Penny Blues," as the model for the tune. In 1956 the Humphrey Lyttleton Band issued the song, and, ironically, it was produced by George Martin. It had been almost six weeks since the Beatles recorded "Lady Madonna" and Paul felt strongly about its commercial potential.

One of "Lady Madonna's" ironies was its profound influence upon fledgling rocker Elvis Costello. It was the type of song that New Wave musicians like Costello preferred. In 1978 Costello told **Crawdaddy** magazine that "It's a bit sad when you have to wait for a ten-year-old record to come on the radio to turn it up." A decade later Costello wrote music with McCartney and helped to produce the **Flowers In The Dirt** album.

As soon as "Lady Madonna" began wafting out over the airwaves it became an instant American number one hit. It was not only a hit song but one backed with an exciting George Harrison tune, "The Inner Light." In the American market there was a great deal of critical acclaim for Harrison's song, but commercial airplay concentrated upon "Lady Madonna." In the studio Paul aided Harrison's emergence as a composer. "The Inner Light" generated favorable reviews; yet, there was no mention of McCartney's contribution. Paul used his considerable studio experience to help George while remaining quietly in the background.

"The Inner Light" was a song based on the cult book **Lamps of Fire**. This was an English translation of the **Tao Te Ching** and it was an indication of Harrison's spiritual nature. The book was sent to George by Juan Muscard, a Sanskrit Professor at Cambridge University. When George began writing "The Inner Light," he used the first verse from the book verbatim and then added his own interpretive lyrics. The result was a strong tune which was eclipsed by the commercial success of "Lady Madonna."

By March 20, 1968, "Lady Madonna" entered the English charts at number 6 and went to number 1 within two weeks. In England "Lady Madonna" sold more than a quarter of a million copies. The song remained in the Top Ten for five weeks and the Top 30 for seven weeks. Soon world sales soared over two million and "Lady Madonna" was number one in America, Germany, Poland, Denmark, Sweden, France and Australia. Suddenly everyone felt secure about the impending Apple Record experiment. It couldn't miss if the Beatles continued to produce hit songs.

After Paul wrote "Lady Madonna" in February, 1968, it was produced in a recording session in which George and John played their guitars through the same amplifier while Ringo stroked the drums. Later Paul added bass guitar and his voice. This session also included key jazz musicians Ronnie Scott, Harry Klein, Bill Povey and Bill Jackman all of whom played saxophone. This was Paul's last minute idea as he reasoned that these well-known jazz musicians would add credence to the record. Paul also played piano on "Lady Madonna" and all four Beatles sang with their hands cupped around their mouths.

McCartney's songs were being released by other artists. For more than a year Paul was busy writing new songs. On March 8, 1968, McCartney's "Step Inside Love," was released by Cilla Black in the United Kingdom. The demand for Lennon-McCartney songs was continual, but Paul was more interested in releasing his own tunes. He had broken his co-song writing bond with John, however, the general public wasn't aware of their differences. This was an ominous sign. Lennon and McCartney songs were now less of a collaborative effort.

While McCartney was in India there were new honors for the Beatles. On March 9, 1968, the **Sgt. Pepper's Lonely Hearts Club Band** album won four Grammys. The National Academy of Recording Arts and Science annual award was the most important event in the recording industry. Not only did the

Beatles receive the best album award, but they also won for best contemporary album, best album cover and best engineered recording. As was common after the American Grammy awards, Capitol Records reported that in-store record sales had exhausted the supply. Paul McCartney was gleeful. This was a sign of continued success for Apple. It also made Capitol Records very cooperative with Apple. Capitol had worked out a lucrative distribution deal, and they would profit immensely over the next few years.

While he was at the Maharishi's retreat in India, Paul McCartney received word that the March 14, 1969, film clip of "Lady Madonna" which appeared on British TV's "Top of the Pops" was praised in **Melody Maker**, the **New Musical Express** and **Disc**. This made it easier for McCartney to adjust to the food and meditate. Ironically, the video showed the group singing "Hey Bulldog" with the words to "Lady Madonna" dubbed in.

After leaving India, Paul wrote triumphantly to his brother, Mike, pointing out that "Lady Madonna" was the last record that the Beatles owed Parlophone. This pleased Paul, it was time for the Beatles to provide not only the music, but the promotion for their music. When the Hollywood Palace, a popular American television show, featured a clip of "Lady Madonna," the song moved from 23 to number 4 on the **Billboard** Hot 100. American television, Paul thought, was the key to increased record sales. But how much difference did American promotion mean? McCartney began examining the foreign record sales and realized that the Beatles were missing out on foreign markets.

A few days after Paul returned from India, he scrutinized accounting reports on the Beatles' partnership. Business records indicated that the Beatles' financial worth combined with those of the Apple Corps Ltd. had escalated to one and a half million pounds during the past sixteen months. This was the last statement of earnings that Paul would receive during his years with the Beatles. As late as December 1970 there was no further accounting of the Beatles' business partnership.

A week after arriving home from India, Paul and Jane Asher celebrated her birthday. It was not a pleasant party. The trip to India had strained their relationship. Since their return, the problems with the Beatles' finances consumed McCartney. Despite the tension between Paul and Jane, there were ego strokes that kept McCartney going.

The London pub and party scene was still a lively one. Yet, McCartney was growing weary of fame and fortune. He had been in the media spotlight for half a decade. The absence of a private life bothered Paul. He needed to find a comfortable middle ground between fame and a normal life. Cilla Black, an old Liverpool friend, shared Paul's feelings. As he crafted a hit record for Cilla, Paul discussed his relationship with Brian Epstein. Not only was McCartney upset by Epstein's management direction, he also considered him a fiscal amateur.

For years Paul had complained to the other Beatles about Brian's lack of precise financial planning. "Brian and Paul were never compatible," Clive Epstein remembered, "they developed a mutual distrust that never ended." Many Liverpudlians recall Paul's complaints about Brian's management. "Paul told me that he had a dream about Brian," Bob Wooler, the Cavern disc jockey recalled, "he dreamt Brian sold the Beatles to the devil." Wooler laughed and continued to recall how seriously McCartney took the Beatles' music. "Without Paul's concern for the future, they might have remained just another bar band." In a more serious vein Wooler reflected on McCartney's fears. "He feared poverty, bankruptcy, legal problems," Wooler maintained. "Funny, some of those fears came true." As Wooler reminisced about McCartney, his affection for the "handsome Beatle" was obvious.

He also had some insights into Paul and Brian's relationship. For a time, Bob Wooler told me, Paul called Brian's office daily with business suggestions, but these were ignored. This lack of communication made the working relationship a difficult one. Ironically, Brian and Paul were alike in some respects. They both hoped to save the Beatles' fortune. For years Paul confronted Brian with his cavalier management style and predicted that he would lose clients.

When Cilla Black left Epstein's management stable, Paul's prediction was realized. Clive Epstein was given the impossible task of attempting to bring Cilla and Brian back together. When Cilla Black broke her contract with Brian in 1967, it was because of his amateurish decisions. During this time of turmoil, Cilla Black leaned upon McCartney. He not only provided her advice but urged her to stand up for her musical convictions. Out of this mutual distaste for Epstein's professional guidance, a musical partnership was born between Paul and Cilla.

On April 6, 1968, **Melody Maker** had Paul's song, "Step Inside Love," recorded by Cilla Black, as the number 7 tune on **MM's** Top 30. Paul was now virtually living in his office while attempting to sell Apple's music. He tried to promote every type of Beatle product as well as concentrating upon developing new acts.

There was a sense of satisfaction for McCartney when the press reported that **Magical Mystery Tour** had been sold for television broadcast in Japan and that "Lady Madonna" was certified as a Gold record. To commemorate these sales, John jokingly made a sign for the men's washroom that read: "PAUL SELLS MORE THAN TOILET WATER."

As Paul sorted out the Beatles affairs there was constant publicity surrounding John's activity. Not only did Lennon's return from India dominate the press, but his impending divorce took attention away from more substantive Beatle matters. The press ignored the success of the Beatles' new music publishing company, Phyton Music Ltd. The role of this new publishing venture was to generate revenue as well as protect the Beatles' new songs.

The Beatles were preparing to go back into the studio. They met with George Martin at Abbey Road Studio to sort out the songs they had written in India. When John appeared for these meetings, Yoko, his recent girlfriend, was at his side. The Beatles had an unwritten rule that no one was allowed in their meetings or in the studio. While this rule had never been enforced, it did cause John and Paul to bicker over Yoko's presence.

Paul was flustered by Yoko's appearance, but he was determined to maintain John's friendship. Rather than challenge Lennon, Paul tried to maintain the precarious Beatles' unity. The new Beatle album was foremost in McCartney's mind.

As Paul planned the **White Album,** he continued to publicize Apple's products in the United States. From the Beatles' publicity office, Derek Taylor directed a campaign to bring the Apple Corporation into the mainstream of the American record buying market. Paul realized as soon as he placed Taylor in charge of American publicity that he was virtually useless. One day in April 1968, Paul stormed into Derek Taylor's office distraught.

"What the hell are we paying you for?" McCartney screamed. Paul huffed and puffed. He lit a cigarette. Taylor sat in a stupor and said nothing. There was a scurrying of feet outside Taylor's office. A belch in the hall punctuated the silence.

"Huh," a surprised Taylor responded.

"The kitchen or the bar is your home," Paul screamed.

"You bugger, you bugger, you bugger," Taylor whispered. He picked up a cold leg of lamb and munched on it.

"Where are the bacon butties and caviar?" Paul shouted. "You should do some god damned thing for your money."

"I'm working for John, fuck off mate," Taylor finally screamed hysterically. Getting up from his chair, Derek put on his overcoat and stormed out of the building. Welcome to Apple Records. The musical experiment was successful, but the business arrangement was falling apart.

Chris O'Dell remembered how little Taylor did to help the fledgling Apple Corporation. He spent most of his time drinking or directing the house hippie, Richard DiLello, in carrying out meaningless tasks. Only Peter Asher, the head of A and R, and Alistair Taylor, the General Manager, had specific ideas about Apple's future. As Asher sorted through tapes looking for new talent, he recognized the enormity of Apple's task. They had to find new talent and develop it. That meant traveling to America and evaluating musicians, singers and songwriters. So America became the vocal point in the search for legitimate new talent.

On May 11, 1968, Paul flew to New York with John Lennon, Neil Aspinall, Derek Taylor, Mal Evans and Ron Kass to promote Apple. As Paul and John journeyed to America, a San

Francisco benefit at the Straight Theater featuring the Beatles' **Magical Mystery Tour** was screened to a large, appreciative audience. The event, sponsored by radio station KMPX-FM, was a celebration of the Beatles' artistic accomplishments. San Francisco was the logical ally for applauding the Beatles' new artistic direction.

While the Beatles concentrated upon the American market, their records slipped off the British charts. There were no Beatle songs on the **Melody Maker** charts for three and a half months as they turned their attention to America.

Shortly after they arrived in New York, Paul and John appeared on the Tonight Show. Johnny Carson was on vacation and the show was hosted by the former baseball player and TV sports commentator Joe Garagiola. He had no knowledge of rock and roll music and had trouble understanding Paul's explanation of the Apple corporation. Garagiola appeared dim witted as McCartney commented that Apple was "a controlled weirdness, a kind of Western Communism." Garagiola smiled.

Paul continued: "We want to help people, but without doing it like a charity." Garagiola went to a commercial. In the midst of the Tonight Show Joe asked Paul to write a song for him. McCartney refused. It was all in good fun and this American television appearance was one that Beatle fans savored.

The Tonight Show appearance was intended to promote Apple's broad cultural vision. Paul finished his explanation of Apple by announcing that a foundation had been set up to discover new talent.

Once McCartney announced the Apple Foundation For the Arts, American intellectuals, would-be artists and the general hanger on descended upon London. They couldn't believe McCartney's comment: "We're in the happy position of not needing any more money, so for the first time the bosses aren't in it for profit. If you come to me and say, 'I've had such and such a dream.' I'll say to you 'Go away and do it." As Paul extolled Apple's virtues, he unwittingly began a revolution. McCartney's spiel was cut short by the drunken behavior of actress Tullulah Bankhead. She leered at the two Beatles and at the same time told them that they were beautiful. Bankhead then ran her hand up Lennon's leg and grabbed his privates during a commercial break. Paul laughed. John winced.

The Tonight Show began a new era in McCartney's life. He was definitely through with Jane Asher. For some time McCartney had maintained a bachelor apartment close to the Claridge Hotel in Mayfair. There he entertained many young women. He also increasingly confided to friends his negative thoughts about Jane. Since Christmas, 1967, Paul and Jane had fought like two school kids. Paul was miserable. Jane acted like a princess who had been jilted by a pretender to the throne. It was not a healthy relationship. Finally, in New York, Paul was free, and he vowed to make the most of it.

After finishing the taping of the Tonight Show, Paul prepared for a press conference announcing Apple Records' entry into the American market. At this press conference, McCartney shook hands with a young American girl, Linda Eastman. Paul didn't remember that he had previously met her in London. She had been a regular in the chic London clubs. McCartney again struck up a brief conversation with her. After they talked awhile, Linda slipped her phone number into Paul's pocket. On one side of the paper she wrote her phone number and on the other there was a line from a limerick. "Don't do today what you can put off until tomorrow."

Linda Eastman, an established photographer on the rock and roll scene, was the daughter of one of New York's finest families. She was on a first name basis with many rock stars. To his friends, musician Michael Bloomfield introduced Linda as the semi-official photographer for Bill Graham's Fillmore East. Her photos of Eric Burdon and the Animals had appeared in **Ebony** magazine, and she was skilled in her craft. A striking, physically attractive woman, Eastman was independent minded and intelligent. This scared off some of the less urbane rockers. Her ability to survive and retain her beauty and humor amidst the rock and roll jungle made her appealing to McCartney.

Before she met Paul, Linda had made Peter Brown's acquaintance and was invited to the press conference for the **Sgt. Pepper** album in May 1967. At this event she mingled in a crowd surrounding Paul, but she wasn't able to capture his attention. Lillian Roxon, the New York rock critic, remembers Linda talking about marrying Paul. Roxon laughed and forgot this playful boast.

During the next year Linda longed to see McCartney but their paths didn't cross. Her father, Lee Eastman, a respected New York attorney, had powerful entertainment connections. He represented music and television stars. His clients included Tommy Dorsey, the Hopalong Cassidy television show and famous American artists. Paul was impressed with Linda's father. He had risen from humble beginnings to a position of power and wealth. The son of Russian Jews, Lee Eastman grew up in the Bronx. He changed his name from Epstein and attended Harvard Law School. In 1935 Lee married Louise Lindner, a Smith graduate. She was the daughter of an Ohio family that had started chain department stores throughout the mid-west. The marriage was a happy one.

Louise Eastman died in a plane crash when Linda was eighteen, and this tragedy took her years to overcome. Lee Eastman's thriving law firm on West 54th street allowed him to bury himself in work. Linda's sisters had gone to Smith, her brother John was at Stanford and she went to Vermont College for two years. Socializing on the Ivy league circuit with

Dartmouth, Harvard and Yale trendies was not too exciting. Linda needed other outlets. "I was a real preppy, a real tweed-bag," she recalled.

On weekends she would flee to the family apartment on Park Avenue or their home in Scarsdale. Linda grew up with the rich and famous. Linda remembers Sammy Kaye playing his music in the living room of their West 54th Street apartment. Her father was an art enthusiast who cultivated friendships with Willem de Kooning, Mark Rothko and Fritz Kline. In time Larry Rivers, Robert Rauschenberg and Hans Hofmann were part of Eastman's salon. "Harold Arlen used to come to our house for dinner and play his new shows," Linda recalled. Despite the impressive array of intellectual talent in her home, Linda grew up a loner. "I stayed in my room a lot or in the stables. I would hang out in the kitchen with the cook," she remembered. None of this was mentioned in the early publicity surrounding her relationship with McCartney. She was described as the rich girl who was after a famous Beatle.

This background unfortunately gave rock journalists and biographers the information to charge that she was arrogant. It is a charge she denies. "Everyone thinks I'm this spoiled Westchester girl, but I'm not." Her close friends agree that she has traditional family values, loves nature and likes to live in the country. "I will never forget the first time I met Linda McCartney," Joe Flannery remarked, "she made me feel like I had known her for years." Paul's close friends unanimously sing her praises.

Once Paul met the Eastman's there was an honest, straight forward quality to the family that McCartney loved. He was impressed by their ability to cut through the corporate jungle and yet continue to maintain family life. While the Eastman's didn't talk business at social gatherings, Paul realized that the family was potentially a powerful ally in his struggle to regain lost Beatle royalties. The Eastman's radiated class, charm, wealth and proper breeding. All of these elements combined to impress McCartney.

Eventually, Linda's brother, John, took over many of Paul's financial problems. Using his prestigious Stanford legal education, John helped McCartney solve many of his business problems. By 1988 **Forbes** listed John Eastman as the seventh best paid corporate lawyer in America. He is described as "a Kennedy type who has a flair for the dramatic." Linda laughs at this characterization as well as the notion that her brother is Paul's puppet. While some of the Eastman's income is derived from McCartney related interests, he has a thriving law practice of his own. It was the Eastman family, though, that helped straighten out McCartney's finances.

It was no secret that the Beatles were in financial difficulties when Paul and Linda met. With a business that catered to musicians and artists, the Eastman law firm was the perfect corporation to represent McCartney. When Linda asked what her father and brother could do to help, Paul replied: "Help me carry on after the Beatles, I suppose." He has carried on admirably. McCartney is now one of the three wealthiest people in the record industry. The Eastman's deserve some of the credit.

Before meeting Paul, Linda had worked for **Town and Country** magazine for $65 a week. Michelle Mazzola, now an editor at **Harper's Bazaar**, recalled that Linda "didn't pull any strings." This seems to be the consensus, and she also created a highly praised portfolio of rock stars. It was the critical and artistic side of Linda that appealed to Paul. She was also health conscious and had a sense of her future. A vegetarian who took excellent care of her health, Linda convinced Paul that he was headed down a one way road to oblivion. It was a sobering message.

When Michael Bloomfield played New York's Fillmore East he spent a lot of time talking with Linda Eastman. Linda loved to listen to Bloomfield talk about recording with James Cotton in New York and Otis Rush in Muscle Shoals. Bloomfield had just left the Paul Butterfield Blues Band and was developing his own sound. The Fillmore East was a natural place for Linda to listen to the blues as she toted her camera to the concerts. Soon the music developed a new side to her personality. As her photography drew critical attention, Linda's self-image improved and she dated a number of musicians. Since the Fillmore East was a hang out for rock and roll musicians, Linda had a ready-made market for her photos.

Many rock stars were eager to purchase Linda's photographs. She was trusted on the rock scene and her photos were snapped up by well-known musicians. Mick Jagger noted the quality of her photos. The Rolling Stones' lead singer praised Eastman's work and asked her to shoot some solo photos. A London session with Stevie Winwood enhanced her reputation. By 1967 Eastman had developed a high profile photography career. But this was only one side of the attractive American.

There was also a strength to Linda Eastman's character. After losing her mother in 1959 and adjusting to her father remarrying, Linda began shaping her own life. While attending the University of Arizona, she married a geology student, Bob See, and they had a daughter, Heather. When the marriage broke up, Linda alternated her time between studying photography at the University of Arizona and working in New York.

While in Arizona, Linda built up her waning self-confidence. On weekends she drove to Nogales, Arizona and crossed the border to drink and dance on the Mexican side. She was not only struck by the poverty and hopelessness of Mexican life but saw beneath it a fierce struggle for survival. This was a feeling that Linda could understand, and she used these images in her own life.

There was a beauty to the bull fights in the Nogales ring and she loved the festive, open air atmosphere in the cantinas. On weeknights she would drive out Tucson's Speedway Avenue to the small seedy bars that featured live music and watch the Beatle sound alike bands that played in the clubs. Linda loved Tucson. The climate was beautiful, the people were relaxed and her art and photography pleased her instructors at the University of Arizona. When Linda returned to New York she was a new woman. "My genes are very in tune with nature. I like the Earth. The Southwest did it to me," Linda reminisced.

Linda Eastman confidently worked on a photography career. When she was hired by **Town and Country** magazine to shoot key photos, there was talk about traveling assignments. Soon Linda was selling her photos regularly to **Rolling Stone** magazine and she began shooting more pictures at functions frequented by the rock music crowd. When Linda informed her dad that she hoped to become a professional photographer, he looked at her quizzically.

In May 1967, Linda flew to London to find work as a photographer. During this time, she was shooting layouts of Steve Winwood and the Animals, she spent her free time in a London club, the Bag of Nails. This trendy disco attracted the royalty of the English rock world. It was at the Bag of Nails that Linda first met Paul McCartney. There was nothing magic that night as she arrived at the club with Chas Chandler, the Animals' bass player. She spent the evening talking to many people. Peter Brown claims that Linda Eastman left the club with Paul and went to the Speakeasy Club. This hindsight doesn't square with the facts. The next day Linda called Peter Brown and wrangled an invitation to the **Sgt. Pepper** press conference. It was at this press gathering that Paul and Linda had a lengthy chat. Paul was intrigued with this young American, and admired her spunky, intelligent manner. Paul's brother, Mike, a bit of a camera bug himself, was impressed with her skilled photography.

The photos that Linda took of Brian Jones of the Rolling Stones intrigued Peter Brown, and he invited her to the Beatles' main office. Brown was struck by Eastman's natural beauty, her stylish clothes, her understated but fashion-conscious makeup and her bubbly personality. He also noticed how aggressive she was with her Nikon camera. Like many Englishmen in the entertainment industry, Brown lacked the vision to understand Eastman. He viewed her as another American groupie.

Linda Eastman realized that she was going to have difficulty penetrating the Beatles' inner-circle. The small group of advisers who set up the Beatles' meetings were like hens clucking at their favorite chicken. Clive Epstein referred to them as "the girls in the office." The most protective was Peter Brown because he envisioned himself as another Brian Epstein. Brown had a bitchy personal nature and was difficult socially. Clive Epstein called Peter Brown the assistant "who stabbed Brian in the back." None of this mattered when Linda attended the **Sgt Pepper** press conference. She shot a number of photos of Paul. At the **Sgt. Pepper** press conference Linda was nervous, so she decided to leave. Before departing Linda tried to find out McCartney's unlisted phone number. Her investigative skills were rewarded when Eastman discovered that the Beatles had unlisted phone numbers that were billed to Harry Pinsker, an accountant for the Beatles CPA firm Bryce-Hammer. Although she called Pinsker, he brushed her off. So she returned to New York.

Her good friend, Lillian Roxon, sent Linda a picture of Paul McCartney and herself standing together. Eastman gazed at the picture and cried. She had missed her chance to get to know one of England's most famous rock stars. During the next year, Linda Eastman brooded about this missed opportunity, she vowed that the next time Paul would recognize her.

When McCartney arrived in New York for the Tonight Show, Linda Eastman was ready to present her best side to McCartney. She had made contact again with Paul and he remembered her fondly from the previous London visit. Paul readily agreed to a meeting. In their early conversations they talked about music, the Fillmore and the new Apple experiment.

Before he appeared on the Tonight Show, Paul arranged to borrow Nat Weiss' apartment. Paul told Linda that the St. Regis Hotel was filled with groupies, photographers and rock fanatics. So they took a cab to Weiss' Manhattan digs and spent a few days there. Weiss was Brian Epstein's New York attorney and a closed-mouth friend. So there was little danger of this meeting appearing in the press. Jane Asher would never know about it. What Paul McCartney didn't count on was falling in love. It was these few days with Linda Eastman that convinced Paul that Jane Asher was not worth his time. She was spoiled, petulant and in love with herself. McCartney appeared like an ornament around her neck.

In contrast Linda Eastman was tired of the rock and roll life. She yearned for a stable family situation. Ironically, this was what McCartney desired. They both rejected the dull celebrations, the presence of excessive ego and the lack of permanent relationships in the rock and roll world. So Linda Eastman took her daughter, Heather, along to spend a few days with Paul McCartney. The rest was magic.

To Linda's delight, McCartney was a natural father. He loved the little blonde girl. They laughed and cavorted in Weiss' apartment and this enhanced their relationship.

McCartney's New York trip was a success. The Beatles were a major topic in the media. Capitol Records touted the coming financial and musical break through of Apple Records and Paul found a woman who shared his values.

Once Paul returned to London, he was struck by Apple's

enormous backlog of mail. His plea for new artists had not gone unrecognized. McCartney realized that he had to spend some time in the studio. The Beatles were scheduled to record for two days at Abbey Road before McCartney could turn his attention to Apple's affairs.

There was also the problem of Jane Asher. He no longer felt comfortable with her. In order to ignore her Paul began looking for another woman. This turned out to be an American, Francie Schwartz. Despite his free wheeling romantic ways, Paul thought constantly about Linda Eastman. In time they would establish a lasting relationship and marry. But during the frenetic summer of 1968, Paul was preparing to save the Beatles financially and musically. He was developing into an executive and musical producer who was destined for great things beyond the Beatles.

Francie Schwartz and Paul McCartney.

7: A GLOBAL AFFAIR, JUNE-JULY, 1968

After Paul McCartney returned to England from his appearance on the Tonight Show, his fervent promotional activity on behalf of Apple and his idyllic interlude with Linda Eastman, he was determined to make the new Beatle album a masterpiece. The New York trip was a positive experience.

While in New York, Paul walked the dirty city streets, ate hot dogs from carts, sampled out of the way restaurants, shopped in Greenwich Village and bought a large supply of records. He loved the bustle of the New York record stores and he walked through these small record collecting havens with ease. Even though he was a famous Beatle, McCartney eluded the media and reveled in the chance to enjoy some personal freedom.

The excitement of New York was a tonic for McCartney. The hustle, the bustle and the impersonal nature of the city appealed to him. He loved the quaint neighborhoods, the business fervor of New Yorkers and the trendy night life. The pugnacious waiters, the diffident store clerks and the unruly passersby were a stark contrast to London.

As a conquering Beatle, McCartney reveled in the attention. The freedom that he longed for in London was glimpsed in New York. He had to get rid of his long time girl friend Jane Asher if he was to develop artistically. Paul needed an excuse to break it off with Jane. She was a sweet woman with a strong feminist touch. Jane had her own career and stood up to McCartney. There was no plan concocted by McCartney to break up the relationship. What happened was that another young woman came into Paul's life.

The young woman was Francie Schwartz. In 1968, the twenty-four year old, Pennsylvania born, New York educated Schwartz was an unlikely candidate to meet one of the Beatles. She worked as a copywriter in New York. She was young and in love with the arts. An average looking girl who aspired to a career as a playwright, Schwartz hung out in and around Greenwich Village. She read the **Village Voice**, frequented the folk and rock clubs, and searched for like minded intellectuals.

At Bleeker and MacDougal Street, the crossroads of Greenwich Village, the commercialization of folk music was evident. The streets were filled with folk singers, the clubs drew large crowds and record executives scouted for new talent. By the time Francie Schwartz frequented the Village it was undergoing a folk-rock phase. From 1965 to 1967 the square folkies no longer appealed to the young, hip college crowd. The change in Bob Dylan's music from folk to electric was the focal point of musical change. Rock and roll had moved into the Village.

By 1968 Greenwich Village was undergoing a transition. It was no longer the hip haven that produced Bob Dylan. As Schwartz walked up MacDougal Street, she was struck by the renovated brownstone apartments and rising rents. Any thoughts of living in Greenwich Village passed as rents escalated.

Like many other young people, Schwartz was fascinated with Bob Dylan. She read about Dylan and listened to his music. She also bought the 1968 issues of **Broadside**, the well known Village folk magazine, featuring articles by A. J. Weberman on Dylan. Weberman brought a new degree of fanaticism to rock and roll reporting. A well-educated Jewish kid from Brooklyn, Weberman called himself a Dylanologist. He collected Bob's garbage, found his unlisted phone number, taped calls to Dylan and announced that he would expose the folk messiah to the world. A record by Weberman of Dylan talking on the phone was played at hip FM radio stations. At KSAN in San Francisco the Dylan-Weberman phone calls expanded into a show on fan fanaticism. If A. J.Weberman could get next to Dylan, Francie Schwartz felt that she had a chance to meet McCartney.

Rock and roll music fascinated Schwartz. The Fillmore Auditorium East was in its heyday and rock stars wandered all over New York. The balmy spring days offered Schwartz the chance to walk through Greenwich Village, and at night she listened to the bands in the clubs. Not only were the rock stars playing a new and vibrant kind of music, but there was an intellectual quality to it. Like many rock and roll devotees, Schwartz believed that the music spoke directly to her.

By chance, on May 15, 1968, Schwartz turned on the Tonight Show and watched Paul and John talk about Apple. Schwartz was mesmerized by the Beatles. Sitting in her small, depressing apartment, she concocted an elaborate fantasy. Francie decided to take a trip to London and meet a Beatle. She thought that Paul was cute and was intrigued by his plea for new talent. When she was fired from her job as an advertising copywriter, it was the excuse she needed to resettle in London.

She asked herself why she was attracted to McCartney. Was it because he was the single Beatle? Was it was because he was tall and handsome in an aquiline way? Was it because he was the intellectual Beatle? These fantasies were harmless ones. Francie's friends didn't laugh at her, but they were skeptical about her dreams.

Francie was short and homely and had accomplished little in life. From the outset, Francie didn't have romance in mind. She yearned for McCartney's intellectual gifts. A week after Paul's appearance on the Tonight Show, Francie turned on her TV set late at night. Instantly, Paul was on the screen. He was smiling. He was serious. The program, Newsfront, was taped prior to McCartney's appearance on the Tonight Show but broadcast a week later. Francie walked over and turned the sound up on the television. Paul was talking politics. She listened intently. He has serious opinions about American politics. She was intrigued and surprised. Like many people of her generation, Schwartz viewed the Newsfront program as an omen. Since the Tonight Show broadcast she believed that McCartney was in her future. It was an unlikely dream but one that was common in the 1960s.

The rise of counterculture journalism, made many previously unknown writers, musicians and artists cult figures. The fame of rock stars and trendy New York intellectuals that Tom Wolfe described in **The Electric Kool Aid Acid Test** intrigued Schwartz. Like many aspiring intellectuals, she believed that Apple would take her work. After all hadn't Paul made a pitch for the talent of the "little people." Schwartz, a self-styled playwright, longed to make a movie. To that end, she wrote a movie script based on a young, long haired musician's life. Schwartz heard this budding talent playing outside of Carnegie Hall one winter night in the rain and sleet. This small, disheveled violinist had a tragic quality that inspired Francie. He not only was a master violinist, but one whose hunched over technique drew curious spectators.

After listening to him play his violin, Schwartz envisioned a tortured soul who longed for stardom. Nothing could have been further from the truth. The young violinist simply loved playing on the street. His career was on the rise and he had a personal manager. A classically trained Julliard style musician, he honed his talent as a street musician. He found it strange that someone would be interested in his life.

The young violinist had a personal quality that attracted Schwartz. She introduced herself and following some banal conversation, Francie persuaded him to have dinner with her at the Russian Tea Room. During the lengthy dinner in this New York restaurant, adjacent to Carnegie Hall, Schwartz admired the violinist's long, curly hair, lithe body and delicate hands. His movements were effete but his violin thundered in New York's dreary streets. Inspired by this scene, Francie raced home and spun out a ten page script. It was this hypothetical film venture that prompted Schwartz to leave for London.

Before she left for England, Schwartz took the screenplay to the violinist's agent. The agent was not only unhappy with it, but he couldn't figure out Schwartz' interest in the fledgling musician. He warned her not to produce the proposed screenplay. In a rage Schwartz flew off to London with her self styled "literary masterpiece."

The London of 1968 was paradise for a young, New York girl. Carnaby street was filled with clothing shops. The West End had the best theater district in the world and local nightclubs featured famous rock and rollers hob-nobbing with the people. It was a perfect time to explore swinging England.

After landing at Heathrow Airport, Schwartz went to

Carnaby Street. It took almost a week to find the right clothes. She had studied pictures of the London birds and she was determined to be one of them. The birds, as the young girls were affectionately known, wore their hair short, affected an A line dress with color coordinated stockings and shoes. They had a look much like a department store mannequin. Breasts were out and a long, lean slender look was in.

With her hair done, coordinated clothes and her squeaky New York accent disguised, Schwartz descended upon Apple with a vengeance. To find out more about the Beatles, Francie visited the Apple shop. Her first trip to this store at 94 Baker Street was not a successful one. She took a cab on a Monday only to find the Apple shop closed. When she tried to enter Apple Music, she was thrown out of the lobby and told not to come back. So Schwartz took another route, she began to hang out at the clubs frequented by London's rock and roll nobility.

She loved the bright lights, the polite conversation and the chance to see the rich and famous. Yet, there was no sign of any of the Beatles. It took some time but Schwartz finally met Paul McCartney's brother, Mike McGear, at the Speakeasy Club. She didn't make an impression upon him despite giving him her favorite roach clip. Paul's brother was sympathetic to the American groupies. A charming, polite young man with impeccable manners, McGear's aloofness kept him from hurting the fan's feelings. He also had a great deal of practice being Paul's brother. For years, McGear sweet-talked fans while pursuing his own career. In 1968 McGear's group, Scaffold, appeared regularly on British television. Scaffold, a satirical trio, performed songs and acted out clever sketches. When Schwartz didn't recognize McGear's success, he smiled and dismissed her. She was obsessed with Paul but unable to locate him.

The London night club scene was a difficult one for Francie Schwartz. She had neither the beauty nor the social skills to fit into the closed British night life. The relaxed club environment was difficult for a New Yorker to understand, and Schwartz appeared as a pushy, gawking outsider. The scouse accent, which separated the Liverpool musicians from others, dominated the clubs. "I went to London for a few days of partying with some of the bands," Bob Wooler remarked, "and I thought that I was back in Liverpool."

When the clubs failed to open doors for her, the petulant and unnecessarily aggressive Schwartz stormed the Apple offices. She realized that chance, savoir faire and a good story might get her inside the Apple empire. So Francie spent some time again redoing her appearance. She also worked on her personality and diction. Finally, during the first few days of June 1968, she took a cab to Apple's Wigmore Street office and ran through the front door. It was the perfect time to storm the Apple bastille.

The old Apple office on Wigmore Street couldn't hold the

Beatles' rapidly expanding business ventures. It was necessary to search out a new headquarters. Since the Apple headquarters was moving, strangers were all over the place and Schwartz passed through the front door unnoticed. She finally had her chance and would make the most of it.

Once inside Apple, Schwartz stopped in her tracks. Standing at the reception desk, Paul was giving instructions to a secretary. Taking a long, hard look at Schwartz, Paul walked over and asked what her business was at Apple. He smiled. Schwartz melted. Just another groupie, Paul thought, who would be sent packing because she didn't have a legitimate reason for being in Apple's foyer. Yet, there was something about Schwartz that Paul liked. He couldn't put his finger upon this elusive quality. Her hair was like every other London girl, her dress was impeccable and she affected the worst English accent that he had ever heard.

Schwartz then surprised McCartney by handing him the screenplay, a picture of herself and a carefully worded letter. She told Paul that she was prepared to meet Apple's artistic challenge. Paul smirked. He was impressed by her diligence. In a playful mood, Paul asked for her telephone number. Schwartz wrote it down and left in ecstasy. As she walked out into Wigmore Street, Paul hollered out the front door. "Come back tomorrow, luv." It was an invitation, she couldn't believe it.

Francie took a cab to her Notting Hill Gate flat. She shared this primitive living space with a young Scottish girl. Van Morrison had lived in the area a few years before Schwartz and her apartment mate regaled her with tales of wild parties. Schwartz had a great deal of time on her hands. Since her girl friend worked, she was alone with her thoughts. Bounding out of the dingy little apartment, Schwartz ran down the street and bought every Beatle record available. When her roommate returned home, she inquired about the records. Both girls laughed heartily when they realized that they didn't own a record player. They talked late into the night about Apple, the Beatles and McCartney. A shrewd girl, Schwartz kept copious notes of her experiences in London around the Beatles and Apple. She planned from the beginning to write about her encounter with McCartney. Eventually, she sold a book and article to **Rolling Stone** magazine. The book, **Body Count**, published under the **Straight Arrow Press** imprint appeared in 1972 with a chapter containing less than flattering references to McCartney. There was also an article in **Rolling Stone** magazine, "Memories of An Apple Girl." She also sold her story to the sensational minded British tabloid, **News of the World**. The bad judgment and poor taste which Schwartz demonstrated in these pieces made them instantly forgettable. Her most vivid memory of McCartney was the size of his penis and his penchant for oral sex. Her notes for a book were disappointing ones. When her book, **Body Count**, appeared the sales were disappointing. The writing was turgid, the stories made little sense and **Rolling Stone**, her publisher, realized that it had made a drastic mistake. The lack of interest in **Body Count** was because the book had only one chapter on McCartney whom Schwartz called "a little Medici prince pampered...on a satin pillow at a very early age." The significance of **Body Count** is that it was the first literary work to take the Beatles' close friends to task. She called the Beatles' Apple staff backstabbers. Tales of intrigue, backbiting and a disregard with what was best for the Beatles made Schwartz' tale appealing to London's sensationalist minded press. While her view of the Beatles was slanted, there were elements of truth in her accusations. She showed that not all was well within the Beatle kingdom.

On another level Francie Schwartz' story offers interesting insights into the groupie mentality. As the women's movement burst out over America and Europe, people like Schwartz were rapidly fading dinosaurs. Her brief stay in London offers a humanistic vision of the depths to which some women went in the 1960s to make a rock star happy.

Schwartz's preparation for Paul was amazingly thorough. The day after meeting McCartney, Francie went to the Sassoon parlor to have her hair done, because she didn't like the way Paul looked at it. Francie told the stylist to give her the Dusty Springfield look. The stylist did it his own way and Schwartz was ready to reenter the Apple offices.

When her hair appointment was finished, Schwartz took a cab to the Apple offices on Wigmore Street. Bounding inside the building she was thrilled that Paul was interested in her screenplay. Perhaps McCartney could rewrite it and Apple would produce the play in the provinces. After a short run in the countryside, it would come to London's West End. This was Francie Schwartz's dream. A play in London's fabled theater district and her opening night escort would be Paul McCartney. It was a wonderful dream, but not a practical one.

Schwartz had outlined every production idea for the movie. The Carnegie Hall location was perfect and she had several well-known American actors in mind for the lead. Apple Films was an avant garde organization and Schwartz imagined that the best English director would be attracted to this project. The problem was that Paul didn't take her seriously.

Francie was crestfallen that Paul was interested in her, not the screenplay. She was stunned when Paul told her that she was to be on a 24 hour dating call. Schwartz found this confusing. After all millions of girls dreamed about McCartney. To be on-call was a plus. Yet, there was a subliminal feminist side to Schwartz that made her shrink momentarily from such a proposal. Reluctantly, she agreed to Paul's suggestion.

When Paul dismissed Francie from his office during one of their early meetings, he told her that he had an important conference with his lawyer. She was confused. Was Paul really interested in her? Taking a cab to Oxford Street, Francie went on a shopping spree. Again clothes, perfume and records from HMV soothed her hurt feelings. She took a cab to Harrods and spent an hour looking at clothes, jewelry and perfume. Anxiety. Tension. Apprehension. Francie felt these emotions. Impulsively, she ran to a telephone and called Apple's offices. To her surprise the secretary put her through to Paul. Suddenly McCartney was not as friendly. He appeared distant.

"Hello, Luv," he mumbled. "Do you need a few quid?" McCartney was testing Schwartz to see if she was after money. To his surprise she was not interested in money. She was perplexed that Paul would ask if she needed money. She curtly refused his overtures.

"Well, luv," Paul chuckled, "you've passed the audition." Schwartz was silent. She didn't know what to say. What audition had she passed? The test she passed was the anti-Gold digger exam. Since Francie didn't want money from Paul, she was let into the inner circle. But there was another quality that appealed to McCartney. He believed that Schwartz had a sense of loyalty and would not speak with the press. It was important to Paul that everyone in the inner circle ignore the press. Or at the very least tell the same stories. There were to be no leaks of unauthorized materials.

After some polite chitchat, Paul informed Francie that he must again leave for a business appointment. He had the rest of the day planned, but McCartney let Francie know that he would be seeing her. She was to wait in her Notting Hill Gate apartment for the Beatle prince. Schwartz felt like a yo-yo and complained to her roommate that she was on a string.

It was late June 1968, before McCartney called. During that month he had a brief fling with American folk singer Julie Felix. At Paul's Mayfair bachelor pad, Felix and McCartney had a number of one night stands. A quiet, unassuming American girl who appeared on British television and sang in small clubs, Felix was intellectually stimulating with a Joni Mitchell voice and an understated personality. When Felix performed on the David Frost television show, McCartney saw her and was entranced. One of Paul's friends phoned Felix and they went out for a few weeks. No details of their rendezvouz appeared in the British press making Paul happy. He loved liaisons that were private.

Fame, fortune and women, Paul drank them all in like fine wine. Eventually, Paul remembered to call Schwartz and pursue the relationship. What stunned Schwartz about McCartney's call was that he acted like they had never been apart. It was Monday, June 3, and Paul called her early in the morning. Groggy when she answered the phone, Schwartz couldn't believe it was Paul. He came right over. "He settled right into a chair with me on his lap," Schwartz recalled. This began a short, but intense, relationship. It also was an emotional roller coaster for

Schwartz. The excitement of Paul's visits paled next to the long wait for the next one. With a giggle, Schwartz remembered "we ran barefoot in the park." Yet, Francie knew that she couldn't depend upon Paul. She was there for his convenience.

All was forgiven, however, when Paul invited Francie to a Beatle recording session. She claims to have been present at one of the "Revolution" sessions. It is probable that Schwartz was in the Abbey Road Studio Three on Monday, June 10, 1968, because of John Lennon's insistence upon bringing Yoko Ono along. If she was there, it was McCartney's way of getting even with John for bringing what he called "a stranger" into the recording session. Francie was excited about the party after the "Revolution" session.

After the recording session, Francie was led to a limousine where the chauffeur opened the door, smiled and remarked: "Hello, mam, we have a surprise for you." Francie was titillated. The excitement was short lived when John, Paul and Yoko jumped out of the limousine at Paul's St. John's Wood home. The three ran into the 7 Cavendish Avenue residence and the chauffeur drove off with a stunned Schwartz. When the chauffeur asked Schwartz where she would like to be dropped off, she was speechless. Francie haltingly told him to go to her Notting Hill Gate flat. Although depressed and disillusioned, Schwartz vowed to keep pursuing her elusive Beatle.

For the next few weeks Paul took Francie to a few parties, out of the way functions and impromptu pub crawls. Each night Paul wandered into his Cavendish Avenue home while the chauffeur dropped Francie at her flat. She yearned to vanish behind the big black gates that separated the St. John's Wood home from the fans outside.

Then without warning Paul left for a business trip to Hollywood. He was concluding a deal with Capitol Records to distribute Apple's product in America. He arranged to have Linda Eastman join him. While staying at the Beverly Hills Hotel with Linda for four days, Paul analyzed his lifestyle.

The small apartment style suites at the Beverly Hills Hotel were conducive to thinking. Each morning Paul got up and wondered out of his suite and walked on the carpeted path past trees and shrubs into the dining room. The Beverly Hills dining room was typically Hollywood. Each table had a person more important than the next, and there was a bustle of industry activity. While McCartney was noticed there was no fuss made over him. Capitol Records furnished him with a two bedroom suite which contained a kitchen and all the amenities of a corporate board chairman. Paul knew he had arrived in the business world. The attention to personal detail that Capitol went to in making McCartney comfortable was a pleasant interlude. He reflected on his life and Linda Eastman became even more important to him.

The warm garden court where Paul and Linda shared their meals was the perfect place to cement a romance. At night Paul and Linda quietly walked into the eight stool bar adjacent to the restaurant for a scotch or two. The bar tender remarked that no one bothered or recognized Paul. Paul sighed. He was relieved and relaxed.

While he was in Los Angeles, Paul arranged to meet American singer Peggy Lee. He had been a fan of Lee's for some time. They met at the Beverly Hills Hotel and Lee struck up a friendship with Linda Eastman. They sat in the flower infested, tree shaded dining room and talked about hit records. Lee's hit tune "Fever" was a McCartney favorite. What impressed Paul was not their discussion of music trends, but Peggy Lee's obvious admiration for his music.

Before they left Los Angeles Paul and Linda went to dinner at Peggy Lee's home. She hosted a party for sixty people who were McCartney fans. As his white limousine pulled up to Lee's Beverly Hills home, Paul was amused that the rich and famous came by to get his autograph. It was satisfying. It was a pleasant dinner and the evening contributed to his euphoria.

Returning to the hotel, Paul wandered down to the small bar for a few more scotches. He talked with the bartender while listening to a few tourist tales. He felt relaxed in Hollywood. Paul was thinking and making some decisions. For half a decade he had been a famous Beatle. Now suddenly Paul was weary of fame and fortune.

McCartney yearned to please the fans, the groupies, the one-night stands, but there was a part of Linda's life and character he envied. Paul hoped to start his own family. He yearned for a tranquil, domestic life. But McCartney still wanted one last fling. So he decided to invite Francie Schwartz to share his house. He would have one last dalliance before he settled in with Linda Eastman.

As Paul planned a rendezvous with Schwartz, she was feeling the strain of their one-sided relationship. Not only had Paul promised her some of his time but he alluded to a relationship. Her feelings were hurt. She wrote McCartney a note threatening to return to New York. Schwartz informed Paul that she had leased a new apartment in Chelsea. If he didn't pay some attention to her, she would sub-lease it and return to America. It was not an idle threat. Schwartz was confused and depressed. After referring to Paul as "Mr. Plump" in her coy message, Francie got McCartney's attention. After his return from Hollywood in late June 1968, Paul appeared unannounced at her Chelsea flat. After a brief fling in the bedroom, McCartney left. He returned eight days later.

Once again Paul appeared at Schwartz' new and trendy Chelsea address, he complained about the Beatles recording sessions. Paul told her that in the midst of cutting key tracks for the new Beatles LP, George had left London for an American vacation. Paul was incensed. He believed that the Beatles came first and was upset. Francie listened quietly. Because he was so depressed with the state of Beatle affairs, Paul took Schwartz to his St. John's Wood home.

The Apple Scruffs were a group of fanatical fans who waited outside Paul's business office and shifted their base to his home at about five in the evening. The scruffs first reaction to Schwartz was a skeptical one. "Paul, where is Jane," one Scruff hollered. "We want him with someone like himself," one scruff remarked. A Texas scruff climbed the fence and walked down the driveway. She looked around and saw Schwartz scowling out a window at her. Paul came out, laughed and escorted the girl out the gate.

Inside Paul's house Francie's fantasies became full blown ones. She imaged herself as Mrs. McCartney. The St. John's Wood home was like a shrine to her. She touched one object after another and inspected every nook and cranny of the spacious home. The magic moment that Schwartz had dreamed about was at hand. It soon turned into a nightmare.

Once McCartney secured the house, he served some wine and talked at great length of Jane Asher. For almost two hours Paul complained about Asher's acting ambitions. He told Schwartz that Jane pressured him to attend the opening of one of her Old Vic plays. She had a prominent role in the production, and the Old Vic's publicity department wanted McCartney's name to enhance the box office appeal. Paul felt used. He wanted Jane to give up her acting. He preferred to go to the opening of John Lennon's play "In His Own Right" but he had promised Jane his support. Emotional. Sensitive. Confused. Schwartz recognized all these traits in McCartney's personality. Paul was calling out for a full-time mate. He was at a transitional point in his life and needed stability.

Schwartz didn't realize that Paul was thinking constantly about Linda Eastman. The memory of his idyllic retreat in Nat Weiss' New York apartment dominated Paul's thoughts. He reminisced about the four glorious days in Hollywood at the luxurious Beverly Hills Hotel. Paul felt that Linda was a soul mate. Yet, here he was in London with a New York girl who was almost a stranger.

For the next few days Schwartz remained at Paul's St. John's Wood home. She quickly became little more than a nanny. During a three week period, Francie Schwartz got as close as any fan could to McCartney, but the results were not pleasant.

Schwartz discovered that Paul's home was untidy, and she made the mistake of cleaning it. This grated on Paul's nerves, but he said nothing. When he awoke late each morning, Francie served him tea. She also cooked, made love and sent out for his marijuana. It didn't take long for Schwartz to tire of this one-sided relationship.

To Paul, she was boring, fawning, and intellectually defunct. Cold. Impersonal. Confused. These were the traits that McCartney used to describe Francie Schwartz. Her personality was not a pleasant one. The scruffs detested Schwartz. They were loyal to Jane Asher and, consequently, extremely rude to Schwartz. When Paul left the house, they hooted little ditties about her New York accent. The few times she left the house it was like running a gauntlet. They hollered at Paul to get rid of her. Since Jane Asher was touring the English provinces with the Old Vic Theater troupe there was little danger that Schwartz would be discovered. Margo Stevens was one of the Apple scruffs who observed Schwartz. Because of her loyalty to Paul, Margo was allowed by the housekeeper, Rosie, to take the dog Martha for a walk. Stevens loved walking Paul's dog, and it was during one of these dog walking tasks that Margo warned Francie that Paul had a different girl every few days. This was an exaggeration. Paul was spending more time working and less with women. Still, a quiet rage built up inside Francie, but she said nothing to Stevens. Schwartz was amazed by the intensity of the Apple Scruffs. They wanted to protect Paul from the wrong people, and they felt that Schwartz was a "predator" and "gold digger." They considered her a meddler. It was not long before Paul agreed with the scruffs.

For a few days Schwartz lashed out at the scruffs. Ashamed of her behavior, Francie was sure that she would hurt her relationship with Paul. She tried to take the scruffs in stride. It was not an easy task. She was after all McCartney's mistress. Where was the respect this position should command? A girl sharing McCartney's house was a signal that he had changed dramatically. Paul was a superb lover. They enjoyed a sex life that was more than just physical release. Yet, something was wrong. McCartney appeared distant. He had mood swings that blocked his emotions from Schwartz. What Francie didn't realize was that she had become the problem. She was not the right person to share Paul's life.

These mood swings had a dramatic impact upon Schwartz. Suddenly life at Paul's home was drudgery. Schwartz screamed that the five cats weren't potty trained and the dog, Martha, needed constant attention. After cleaning the rugs and scooping animal droppings all day, Schwartz was supposed to turn herself into a sex symbol at night. Often Paul came home at three in the morning, drunk and playful. The magic between them wore off quickly. Soon Francie and Paul began bickering and her days were numbered. Paul talked constantly about Linda Eastman. Finally, out of sheer frustration, Francie asked Paul why he didn't go after Linda. Schwartz realized that Paul was in love with the New York photographer.

After two weeks of hearing about Eastman, Francie screamed: "Why the hell aren't the two of you strapping it on...."

Paul stopped dead in his tracks. He couldn't believe his ears. This loutish New York girl was screaming at him. He kept calm. His anger was controlled. He composed himself. Finally, Paul responded: "I need diversion." He now realized that Francie was a problem. His little secret had turned into a possessive, nagging shrew. To get rid of her, Paul put Schwartz to work at Apple's offices. This was a way of paying her off. She was assigned to assist Derek Taylor in the press office, and this sinecure temporarily appeased her. The office staff at Apple found her unpleasant, foul mouthed and rude. She resented the employees who were close to the Beatles and fought with them.

The strange relationship that developed between Paul and Francie was not surprising in the transient rock and roll world. Yet, there were things about Schwartz that appealed to McCartney. She was small and her tiny feet and hands were elegant. There was a mystery to Francie. She fawned over Paul and he basked in her adulation. She talked endlessly about her writing as Paul dozed off. It was a comfortable liaison that required little from McCartney.

Then one night Jane Asher showed up at Paul's house. One of the Apple Scruffs, Margo Stevens, called on the intercom to warn Paul that Jane was walking into the house. It was too late. Paul was in the bedroom with Francie and she was wearing one of his night shirts. Jane viewed the scene and quickly left the house. Not only was Jane Asher an independent woman with her own career, but she possessed a sense of Victorian morality that prompted her to end the long term relationship. In less than an hour, Mrs. Asher called and informed Paul that she would be by to pick up her daughter's belongings. Paul didn't appear hurt. In fact, one scruff thought he acted relieved. Francie Schwartz had served her purpose. The long, stifling relationship with Jane was over, and Paul was free to pursue Linda.

On July 20, 1968, Jane announced on the BBC TV show Dee Time that she had broken her engagement to McCartney. She appeared calm, lacked emotion, and talked about McCartney in an even tempered manner. Paul was unhappy about the breakup. He had genuine affection for Asher. Yet, she had never given herself completely to him. He could never escape the feeling that she was using him. But Paul had so many good times with Jane that he found it difficult to forget her.

In Paul's song writing, Jane Asher's influence was a strong one. In the tune "I'm Looking Through You" on the **Rubber Soul** album, he pined for his old flame. Paul had asked Jane not to leave London. When she did, Schwartz moved in. After Jane had gone to appear in a play in Bristol, McCartney angrily wrote this tune: "Jane went off to Bristol to act. I said, OK then, leave, I'll find someone else." Later Paul admitted this attitude was childish but it demonstrates his stormy relationship with Asher.

Despite the breakup, Jane and Paul did see each other after

the public parting. A strange bond of affection and friendship remained. Alistair Taylor commented on how the breakup hurt both Paul and Jane. As Paul's close friend, Taylor was able to watch McCartney work through this relationship. A few months after the breakup, Jane sounded like a wounded lady. "I know it sounds corny," Asher remarked, "but we still see each other and love each other...." Jane admitted that the relationship simply could not work on a long term basis. Fame had bred differences between Paul and Jane, and they couldn't work out the hurt and heartache that had come between them. Neither Paul nor Jane was ready for a permanent relationship. Paul needed solitude since he was consumed with recording activity and business interests.

By August 1968, McCartney's live-in girl friend Francie Schwartz was sent packing. She left Paul's house bitter and disillusioned. She was soon forgotten in the London scene. This interlude in Paul's life was an important turning point. He had broken his suffocating relationship with Jane and developed a new sense of himself. The new freedom that he felt was possible with Linda Eastman excited Paul, and he prepared to pursue her. He was ready for new adventures.

Francie Schwartz had a psychological impact upon McCartney. Not only did he come to grips with his relationship with Jane, but he faced up to his own loneliness. The result of his time with Schwartz was to push Paul toward Linda.

There was a restlessness in McCartney's life. One that was demonstrated by his search for a new home. At the time he was breaking up with Schwartz, Paul was looking for a place to retreat. He preferred something close to London. Eventually, he purchased a spacious new place in the countryside near Sussex. By seeking out and purchasing country property, Paul was screaming out for peace and contentment.

Earlier on, while Francie was still with Paul, he bought this rambling house in Sussex that he would share with Linda Eastman. Impulsively, Paul called up Alistair Taylor and invited him and his wife, Lesley, to go house hunting with Francie and himself.

"Sure Paul," Alistair remembered answering. A half hour later McCartney showed up at Taylor's house in his Aston Martin DB6. The car was full with Francie Schwartz and Martha the old English sheepdog taking up the back seat. Somehow the Taylor's climbed into the back of Paul's car and they were off on a Saturday afternoon ride to the country.

This late July 1968, trip was not a fruitful one. Paul wasn't able to find a house that he liked. After growing tired of house hunting they took a detour to a tiny village in Kent. While they looked for a country home for McCartney, the locals gawked. Since few showcase homes were available, the afternoon turned out to be a frustrating one. They badly needed some diversion to pep up their spirits.

Heading back to London, Paul suddenly screeched on his brakes. He noticed a sign for a small town, Bean. They took the turn in Paul's Aston Martin DB6 and roared into this small, quaint English village. It was a town of row houses. A dreary place with no past and little future. There was an unkept appearance to the town and the locals walked slowly. Paul and Francie were the only ones who laughed. Paul though that it must be England's Mississippi.

As they turned around to go home, Paul saw a pub. They parked and joined the locals for a few drinks. The barmaid spilled beer all over herself, could it be the famous Beatle?

When Alistair Taylor remarked to Paul that he had been "rumbled again." McCartney replied: "Just look natural. I want to be an ordinary guy. No crowds, no autographs, just a quiet drink." The Bean locals watched and no one said a word. Paul was convinced that it was time to move to a small, out of the way place. The search for a new town dominated the next year of McCartney's life.

McCartney was spending more of his time outside of London, and developing a free spirit. This change in environment had a positive impact upon his creativity. He wrote some of his best songs. There was a sense of order to McCartney's life outside of St. John's Wood. The Cavendish Avenue address was for a carefree young man who wanted the best of the bright lights. Paul had outgrown this life style. He didn't miss the glamour, intrigue and back biting of London and wondered why he had waited so long to leave. While it would be incorrect to give Schwartz all the credit for these changes in Paul's life, she was the catalyst to this new direction.

There was a sense of destiny in Paul's life. He often had experiences which persuaded him to change his ways. One such occurrence took place at his Apple office and it had a profound impact upon his life. These little, seemingly insignificant, incidents were ones that caused Paul to reflect on his future.

In late July 1968, a wind driven sheet of cold air burst into McCartney's Apple office window. A fierce sound, almost supernatural, screeched through the room. Paul considered this strange experience an omen. He looked across his desk at the young blonde secretary seated calmly in front of him. She looked plastic. Maybe Frank Zappa was right, the Dead Girls of London were everywhere. The girl's face haunted Paul. She was lifeless. Not only did she move like a mannequin, but she had a similar personality. Her neatly arched eyebrows, short pug nose, and closely cropped hair made her appear ethereal. McCartney knew it was time to leave London.

8: IN PROGRESS: THE WHITE ALBUM, JUNE-JULY, 1968

During the first week of June 1968, Paul worked intensely on **The Beatles** commonly referred to as the **White Album**. Clive Epstein recalled McCartney's zeal: "Paul was occupied with his own vision, he saw a new era of Beatle music." He believed that the Beatles could somehow overcome their past differences. Because he was in charge of the **White Album**, Paul was diplomatic in all matters. He didn't want to jeopardize the LP's final production and release. "I remember Paul writing 'in progress' on a piece of paper," Epstein remarked. "I didn't understand what he meant, now some years later I think that he hoped to make his mates independent of each other." If Clive Epstein is correct, then, the **White Album** was the beginning of a major breakthrough in the Beatles' affairs. Each member of the band was to play an increasingly larger role. Hence, the wisdom of a double album.

The material for the **White Album** was a combination of Paul in the studio followed by John's deft input. Ringo and George, theoretically, would play a larger role in the production process.

The interaction between Paul and John in the studio inspired McCartney to new creative heights. As Lennon recorded the curious sounds for "Revolution 1," McCartney watched with interest and planned a similar tune. The intense recording activity that characterized the songs in the **White Album** spurred Paul's creativity. He watched Lennon's political songs evolve and moved to emulate them.

"Revolution 1" was Lennon's first serious attempt at a political song which intrigued McCartney. As Lennon worked on "Revolution 1" Pete Shotton, John's old boyhood friend, charged that McCartney displayed hostility to the song. Shotton remarked that Paul's music was "nonpolitical to the core." Paul made little effort to mask his distaste for a few of John's more way out compositions, specifically "Revolution 1." The problems between the two chief Beatles were obvious, but they wanted no more than to continue their tradition of hit records. They also had a strong feeling for the avant garde nature of their music.

A few people close to the Beatles believed that "Revolution 1" was a dangerous song. Paul convinced John to ignore these fears. The press created differences between Paul and John which didn't exist. This was largely due to the continuing fear that John's "we're bigger than Jesus" remark would once again bust loose. Nothing would be tolerated that might damage **White Album** sales. Because of this fear "Revolution 1" was lost. It didn't help that Lennon had three revolution songs- "Revolution," a major hit, and the two **White Album** tunes "Revolution 1," and "Revolution No. 9." There was concern that John was becoming too experimental as these later two songs didn't make much sense.

When "Revolution" was released as the b side to "Hey Jude," no one at Apple believed that it would be a hit. "We thought the timing was wrong for this type of song," Clive Epstein remembered. "I was surprised at its success." Nicky Hopkins who completed a piano overdub on "Revolution" never had any doubts about the song's ultimate success. Mick Jagger, the Rolling Stones' lead singer, was another "Revolution" fan. He first heard the song at his twenty-sixth birthday party at Tony Sanchez's "Vesuvio Club." He toasted the throng and hollered out: "Here's another Beatles hit." This was a magnanimous gesture considering that the Stones' had just played their new album, **Beggar's Banquet**, for the celebrity gathering. Mick Jagger loved the Beatles' experimental nature. Others feared that the Beatles were becoming too psychedelic. "Drugs were ruining the boys," Clive Epstein remarked. "We all thought that they had gone crazy in the studio. There was just too much experimental nonsense."

This fear surfaced during the June 4, 1968, recording session when Lennon asked recording engineer Geoff Emerick to mike his voice from the back of his head. This constant experimentation was part of John's personality. Another engineer in the studio that day, Peter Bown, who was in charge of overdubs, remembers John complaining about the equipment at Abbey Road. "The fucking machine has broken down again," Lennon remarked. Bown quickly changed the headphones that were giving Lennon trouble. This nasty little interchange suggests the pressure upon Lennon to make new music.

As John worked on "Revolution 1," the **White Album** took on a shape and structure different from past Beatles albums. As Jackie Lomax remarked in **Crawdaddy** magazine: "They would play a song in every kind of key they could think of...." The experimental nature of "Revolution 1" and the **White Album** was so broad that George Martin threw up his hands and went on a three month vacation. The reaction to the retooled song simply entitled "Revolution" surprised Lennon. "I should never have put that in about Chairman Mao," John told **Hit Parader** magazine. The controversy over "Revolution" was immediate among those close to the Beatles. "I didn't like the way the boys veered off into politics," Clive Epstein reminisced. The tensions among the Beatles' and their advisers and friends hampered the album's progress. At least this is the explanation of those close to the Beatles' during the production of this LP.

In the American market Lennon's version of "Revolution" was remixed when it was released in 1973 on **The Beatles, 1967-1970** prompting John to label it: "a piece of ice cream." He was infuriated that the revolutionary bite was taken from the song.

After recording the mono and stereo versions of "Revolution," noises were discovered in the stereo tape. It appears that Ringo dropped a drum stick, so the single was released in mono. This incident increased the already high level of tension and made Ringo mad as hell. He had been the drummer too long to put up with petty criticism.

The interruptions during the **White Album** were continual. Chris Thomas, a recording engineer, remembers that musicians were hired and fired in the midst of recording sessions. "Yet when they started playing it was a really great atmosphere."

Not everyone was happy with the studio atmosphere. Peter Bown observed that Ringo was thrust into the background. "Paul would often dub in the drum tracks himself," Bown exclaimed. When Ringo returned to the studio, he was irritated. This is one reason that Ringo became more assertive. He was no longer content to sit back and let Lennon and McCartney dominate the song writing and production process.

Ringo demanded more vocals on the **White Album**. Although Ringo was allowed to sing one song on previous Beatle albums, the **White Album** was the first Beatle LP that he wanted greater input on. He didn't get it. Paul hoped to placate Ringo but he would not be given a greater role.

The London newspapers weren't fully aware of Starr's dissatisfaction. Ringo was tired of taking a backseat to Lennon and McCartney, and he wasn't shy about voicing his unhappiness. Paul wisely kept it within the Beatles family. In June and July, Paul and Ringo fought as did the other Beatles over the **White Album**. It was a bad time as Paul hoped to keep the Beatles together, but his perfectionist nature caused him to holler at Ringo. This criticism had an impact upon Starr.

"I felt I was playing like shit," Ringo recalled, "I had this feeling that nobody loved me," Ringo recalled in a conversation with Max Weinberg. The pressure to create new hits, the business problems and the Beatles' changing personal relationships made it a difficult time.

Paul feared that the Beatles were about to break up. So he stepped in to soothe Ringo's hurt feelings. Why not allow Ringo to sing more than just a song? Paul told John that anything which would make Ringo feel creative and important was essential to continued unity.

It was only natural to give Ringo a song immediately. So on June 5, 1968, the second song for the **White Album** began as "Ringo's Tune." It evolved into the country and western tinged "Don't Pass Me By." Ringo had written the song in India. It was a tune that Starr had experimented with since 1963, but it was not until he had time on his hands at the Maharishi's compound that he finished it. The original title of Ringo's song varied between "Some Kind of Friendly" and "This is Some Friendly." It was a tune which lamented his place in the Beatles' hierarchy. He hoped the lyrics would jog the conscience of his peers. As Ringo sat in the Abbey Road studio he cracked his knuckles, quietly leered at the other Beatles and worked feverishly to establish his own vinyl identity. He was tired of being the outcast Beatle.

Whether or not Ringo wrote "Don't Pass Me By" remains a mystery. Most Beatle insiders credit the tune to McCartney. "I don't think that Ringo wrote much of anything," Clive Epstein remarked. "He didn't have the temperament for it."

There are a number of people close to the Beatles who remember the origins of this tune. "Strange things were happening between Ringo and the other Beatles," Clive Epstein remarked. "They were friends but there were some private differences. I wasn't sure what was going on." Clive put a match to his cigar, blew smoke in my face and continued. "I always thought that the Beatles tried to appease Ringo during the sessions for the **White Album**." When I asked Clive whether or not Paul had written a song to keep Ringo in the group, he smiled and winked. "I can't comment." Bob Wooler also remembered: "I heard the rumors that Paul wanted to write a hit for Ringo to keep the group together. But I was in Liverpool, so it was just a story." Considering how much time Paul spent producing the song, the inescapable conclusion is that he wrote it.

After a day spent recording Ringo's song, the Beatles left the studio. But after five takes they were without a finished product. The following day they resumed work on "Don't Pass Me By," and Paul's earlier bass tracks were altered. Finally, Ringo's song took its final shape. There was a great deal of experimentation recording "Don't Pass Me By." Ringo was simply following the lead of Lennon and McCartney. They all competed with one another for musical variations in the studio.

A strange aspect of "Don't Pass Me By" is that it contained lyrics about a car crash in which someone dies, and these lines helped create the Paul is Dead hysteria. Considering how the Beatles were fighting, there was a subtle irony to this situation.

In the midst of these differences, "Revolution no. 9" evolved from John. The **White Album** lists "Revolution no. 9" as a Beatle tune but it was really Lennon's song. This tune was the result of John meeting the French actress Brigitte Bardot. This abortive meeting with Bardot prompted Lennon to make some tapes of ambient noise. He explained to Clive Epstein that the sounds released tension. This strange melange of sound was used on "Revolution No. 9." Yoko Ono's influence was unmistakable on this tune. She was bringing John into a new artistic direction.

As the June 4-6,1968, recording sessions concluded, Paul was depressed about the Beatles' future. The way to keep them together, McCartney reasoned, was to tour again. As Paul mulled a possible tour, George and Patti and Ringo and Maureen flew to California for a guest appearance in Ravi Shankar's film, **Messenger of the East**. They were not scheduled to return to

London until June 18, and Paul hoped to talk intimately with John about keeping the group together.

The discussions between Paul and John were not fruitful ones. Lennon agreed that business priorities had to be established, but they argued over the future direction of the Beatles' music. Paul was disturbed by Lennon's continual reference to the **I Ching: Book of Changes**. John hired an astrologer who threw the I Ching daily to guide Apple's business activity. "It was a hell of a way to do business," Alistair Taylor remarked, "we had to wait for the throwing of the I Ching to do our business." McCartney felt that it was ludicrous. Undaunted, John brought Caleb the astrologer into the Apple offices each day to begin the financial stargazing. Finally, in a rage, Paul stalked down to Lennon's office. Between closed doors they discussed Caleb the astrologer and Apple business. Lennon's concern about a "spiritual business course" was important to Paul who agreed that he would work out these differences with his long time friend. McCartney hoped to keep the Beatles intact. If John wanted a spiritual business, it was fine.

Before Paul could concentrate upon keeping the Beatles together, he had family business to finish. In early June 1968, Paul and Jane Asher attended his brother's wedding to Angela Fishwick. The wedding was held in Careog, North Wales on a sunny morning on June 7, 1968, and it drew a great deal of public attention. The reason was simple. Paul McCartney was the best man. Mike McGear showed up for the wedding in a white suit he wore with his group, Scaffold. The wedding took place at a small country church and the couple moved into a home thirty minutes from Liverpool. Mike McGear's wedding had a strong impact upon Paul. Since 1964 Paul had been one of London's most eligible bachelors. But few people realized he was tiring of this role. After Paul and Jane returned to London, he continued to work on the new album.

On Monday afternoon, June 10, 1968, a white limousine drove up to Abbey Road and a tired looking McCartney walked into Studio Three. Paul was told that John was busy recording "Revolution 9." Paul was nervous that Ringo and George were out of town. Never before had any of the Beatles left London during a recording session. The boys always rallied behind one another during recording sessions. The old unity was dead, as George and Ringo were not scheduled to return until June 18. After visiting with Ravi Shankar in Los Angeles, Harrison spent some time with his sister and celebrated his brother-in-law's birthday: Gordon Caldwell, Sr., was a warm person who got along well with George. So Harrison let McCartney know that family was more important than the Beatles. This frustrated Paul who believed that the group was at a historical turning point.

The following day a melancholy McCartney showed up at Abbey Road at six in the evening to record "Blackbird." The night before Paul had been up until three in the morning practicing his new song. While Paul was nervous about "Blackbird," he had a feeling it would be a big hit.

McCartney wrote "Blackbird" after reading a haunting newspaper account of American race relations in the **London Times**. When he showed a rough copy of the song to John, there was immediate enthusiasm. John added a line to the song and it was finished. The romantic tone of "Blackbird" was an indication that Paul was in love.

The night before he recorded "Blackbird," Paul opened the windowsill of his St. John's Wood home. He walked to a spot where the scruffs could hear him sing. The moonlight created an eerie shadow as he strummed his guitar. Paul started to hum and gently strum the guitar.

"Is that Paul? a scruff asked

"Quiet," another remarked.

"Paul look over here," a gentle female voice called. Paul turned to see the girls and began singing "Blackbird." The light shifted dramatically and the pale moonlight framed Paul's face. The girls squealed. Paul finished his song and went to bed. The next morning McCartney awoke to the sounds of "Blackbirds." He wasn't sure if they were real or imagined birds. It was a good omen, Paul thought, the song would be a fine one.

As McCartney walked into studio three, he was eager to record "Blackbird." This poignant new song featured a lead vocal double-tracked in spots and a gentle acoustic guitar gave it a commercial sound. Because Lennon had experimented with sound effects on "Revolution no. 9," Paul pulled a blackbird sound from "Volume Seven: Birds of Feather" in the Abbey Road sound effects collection and added it to "Blackbird." The results were magnificent. McCartney's tune became one of the more commercial cuts on the **White Album**.

On Tuesday, June 11, 1968, McCartney returned home at eleven o'clock in the evening to think about the Beatles' future. He was concerned about the lack of musical cohesion. For the next eight days McCartney wrote songs, partied and planned for his twenty-sixth birthday. He talked with Clive Epstein about his life. Since Brian Epstein had died without making a will, Paul told Clive that he had become more concerned about the Beatles' finances. The 7 million pound fortune that Brian left to his mother was dissipated after the debts were paid to NEMS. Paul was not surprised that Brian had borrowed heavily from NEMS. The financial chaos surrounding the Beatles' affairs, Paul reasoned, might undermine their fiscal future.

Paul had a voracious appetite for business, recording sessions and social life. As he neared his twenty-sixth birthday, Paul was at his physical and mental peak. There were changes in his appearance. While in India, Paul's sideburns had grown down to his chin, he had lost weight and his famous smile returned. It had been five years since Beatlemania began in England and Paul was adjusting nicely to fame and fortune. He was maturing into his own person.

McCartney had other concerns. He realized that Brian's younger brother had neither the knowledge of the music business nor the interest in the Beatles' affairs to straighten out their finances. Clive was also genuinely concerned with the boys' welfare and he was an honest man. Yet, he had little business expertise in the music industry.

Since both Brian and his father had died within a six week period, Paul did not intend to challenge Queenie or Clive Epstein's management role. He was a gentleman and would respect Brian's memory. Unfortunately, as Paul was soon to discover, Clive had no idea how to solve the Beatles' business problems. By the summer of 1968, Paul was tired of waiting for a business miracle. When he saw no solution to the Beatles' fiscal problems, he began planning for the future.

Although he was just a week away from turning twenty-six and a multi-millionaire, Paul was depressed over his inability to collect Beatle royalties. So Paul immersed himself in business details. From June 12 through June 19, 1968, he spent virtually every waking hour in his Apple office. Even during his birthday celebration, he continued to work. Paul did invite friends and a few fans into the office for a piece of birthday cake and a glass of champagne. There was an urgency in Paul's behavior. He ignored the distractions available to a famous Beatle to take care of his financial interests.

It was now time for Paul to decide how to promote the Beatles' radically different album. Although it was months before the **White Album** was to be released, McCartney decided to use counterculture newspapers to advertise the LP. Unwittingly, the **Berkeley Barb** changed Paul's attitudes towards the press. At first Paul read the **Barb** for its outrageous ads, letters to the editor and quirky reporting. Soon he was converted to its political ideas. McCartney was uneasy with the direction of the straight media.

By July 1968, Paul believed that that press had to be neutralized. The new Beatle LP was different from past efforts. He worried that the reaction of London newspapers and perhaps even the rock publications would hurt the sales. An article in the **Berkeley Barb** advocated guerrilla public relations to control the press. This idea appealed to McCartney. Soon Paul implemented his own strategy, thereby breaking Brian Epstein's careful media path. McCartney's approach to the press would be even more successful and provide him with excellent coverage.

The members of the London press who attacked Paul were not granted interviews. He no longer freely cooperated with reporters. Paul was determined to control the press. He called some journalists "venal jackals" and mentioned that he would grant interviews only to the "cooperative media." This began a policy that remained in effect for the next two decades. The Apple scruffs laughed as Paul told the press one thing and did another. They were amazed at how many reputable journalists agreed to restrictions in order to interview McCartney.

The press had been a source of irritation for McCartney since the early days of Beatlemania. For years Paul had cooperated with reporters, but he was chagrined by continued irresponsible news stories. Because of the press, Paul changed his approach to the music business. Interviews were set up in a room that McCartney selected. Questions were carefully screened. A cordial, friendly atmosphere, replete with food and drink, made it easy to divert the reviewer's questions. Serious writers were put off. English journalist Ray Coleman complained at a Beatlefest about McCartney's unwillingness to meet the press. Other journalists, notably Chet Flippo, suggests that "Paul reveals little of himself in interviews...." The charge that he hides behind his music is one made by a wide range of journalists.

When Chris Welch conceived his book **Paul McCartney: The Definitive Biography**, he wrote to MPL and asked for McCartney's cooperation. He heard nothing for a long time. Then he sent samples of his carefully researched and tightly written book to McCartney's office. As Welch recalled: "...the messages I kept getting back were-he didn't like books about himself." Welch hoped that his work would appeal to McCartney. Undaunted, he finished the small biography and it appeared to excellent reviews. Paul never acknowledged it.

Much like Welch, New York journalist Chet Flippo began **Yesterday: The Unauthorized Biography of Paul McCartney** by writing to McCartney Productions Limited. In an erudite and fair minded letter, Flippo made a strong case for a biography that "didn't play to the McCartney myths." Flippo was rebuffed. "The press," McCartney remarked, "could never be trusted."

In a hilarious article, "High-Octane Lunches and Paul McCartney Biographies," which appeared in Flippo's **Everybody Was King Fu Dancing: Chronicles of The Lionized and the Notorious**, he writes: "Maybe it was the $24.95 steak that did it, or maybe it was the profusion of two-fisted, man-sized, drink-em-up beef-tails that fueled our high-octane lunch which inclined me to agree to the editor's suggestion: 'Do an unauthorized bio of Paul McCartney." An excellent book followed, but it was one that failed to gain McCartney's cooperation. Flippo was agitated by Paul's attitude.

Flippo's revenge was apparent in his book. Like many journalists, he couldn't resist making fun of McCartney. He related the tale of how a senior executive from MPL was summoned to McCartney's High Park Farm in Scotland and given the task of mixing a special feed for the senior sheep. It was a silly little tale that enraged McCartney, because it reflected on his modest lifestyle. As the Flippo book suggested, the McCartney's and their four children live out of the public eye.

There were tales that Flippo missed. The most persistent is that Linda McCartney complained for years about not having a proper washer and dryer. The story may be myth but the locals chuckled at McCartney's notoriously parsimonious attitudes. Paul simply couldn't spend a nickel. Hadn't his mother washed her clothes by hand? No one is sure of the veracity of these tales, but they offer some interesting insights into the McCartney legend.

McCartney's wealth is another matter. More than two decades after the turbulent Apple experiment and **White Album** period, Paul remains show businesses richest singer-songwriter. The incongruity of his wealth and average living standard continues to puzzle the media. Paul's view is that it is not the media's business.

The McCartney's life on the High Park Farm began taking shape in the summer of 1968. There was a dramatic change in Paul's life. He had tired of fame and fortune and desired to create a new order. Fame was a burden. His steps were dogged continually by journalists, fans and businessmen. Weary. Frustrated. Crabby. Mercurial. These were the words used by Paul's close friends to describe him five years after Beatlemania invaded England. He was a man of extreme highs and lows. Paul was a character with contradictions.

In late July 1968, Paul's friends found these contradictions a manifestation of fame and fortune. At one moment Paul was a happy, jovial person and the next minute he would worry about minor details in a recording session or a business meeting. Clive Epstein recalls: "Paul was obsessed with success and this made for alternately happy and sad moods." As the **White Album** continued its slow, uneven progress to fulfillment, Paul was "very happy with the way things were going," according to Alistair Taylor. "The breakup with Asher caused McCartney serious mood swings." So he took to calling Alistair late at night. For a couple of weeks after the breakup Paul called Taylor nightly. They met or Alistair came to Paul's house for a few drinks. At these bull sessions, Paul complained that he was sick of the night clubs. He also couldn't forget Jane.

"With a bottle of scotch and a bottle of coke at our elbows we sat talking through the night," Taylor recalled. They listened to music and Paul would combat his depression by writing new songs. It was a creative period for McCartney who used the breakup to move into new musical and business directions. It was at these bull sessions that McCartney's creative imagination ran rampant. A good example occurred one night after a frustrating recording session at Abbey Road. Rather than walking or driving home, Paul called for a cab. As Taylor and McCartney rode home, Paul invited his friend in for a drink. The ride home was generally a silent one, but once inside the St. John's Wood mansion, the conversation took a serious direction. Paul's frustration was apparent. He started out lightly before getting to more serious matters.

"Alistair, I think, I've found a new bird," McCartney declared one night. Taylor was excited. He pressed McCartney for information.

"The Wigmore office is the clue," Paul laughed.

"What in the hell are you talking about?" Taylor responded.

"Mary Hopkins, you idiot," Paul screamed.

"Huh, I'm missing something," Taylor mumbled.

"Yes," Paul smiled, "she's Apple's next recording star." Taylor got up from his chair walked over to pour a drink and relax from Paul's ubiquitous tale.

Paul continued to confess his feelings. He told Alistair that the sight of Derek Taylor's desk enraged him. It contained every new gimmick, electronic device and cute office product available. It had the look of an office where little was accomplished except for eating and drinking. The carefully laid out pencils, the squared away pads of paper and the proliferation of meaningless memos made for little more than busy work.

Paul felt that he had established a sinecure which funnelled money into hell. He loved the Apple Corporation, but, in private moments, McCartney had his doubts about the enterprise.

Despite his misgivings, Paul continued to pour out his heart to Alistair Taylor. Unlike the others at Apple, Taylor had genuine concern for McCartney. Taylor made it clear that he would help Paul advance Apple; this was an emotional catharsis that made McCartney feel whole again. His vision for Apple was still alive. It was the new artists that Paul would bring into the mainstream of the Apple empire.

As a result of this conversation, Mary Hopkins, a new Apple Records star, came to live with Alistair and Lesley Taylor. "I invited her to come and stay with us until she was settled into the London life," Taylor remembered. It was Paul who urged that the Taylor's take care of Apple's newest artist. It was typical of McCartney to take an interest in fledgling Apple artists.

During Paul's trying times Alistair Taylor was given a chance to witness how McCartney composed his songs. While the other Beatles were writing new tunes, Taylor watched Paul work in the studio, at home and at the office. As Taylor suggested: "...Paul is the one whose skills leaves me with the most wonder." Then Taylor described the ease with which Paul wrote songs.

"Paul is one of those rare craftsmen who make their skill appear so easy that is seems the most natural thing imaginable," Taylor wrote. Because of his close relationship with Paul, Taylor was able to hear many of these new songs. One night as they left Abbey Road Studio at 3:00 A.M., Paul was in a jovial and relaxed mood. Alistair was happy to see his friend in a spirited frame of mind.

Later that night Paul invited Alistair over for a nightcap. Taylor readily agreed. Paul was in a creative trance and talked like a poet barking at the sky. Taylor was intrigued by McCartney's mood swings. He was always happier when he was working on a new tune. When Taylor was present, it seemed that Paul could compose rapidly.

As McCartney and Taylor walked from Abbey Road Studio to Cavendish avenue the unpredictable London weather reflected the turmoil surrounding Paul's life. The pale London moon hung over the sky and an unusually warm breeze swirled through the streets. There was an eerie sense. Nature seemed to take over the London night. Taylor thought this mood was a perfect one for Paul's new song.

Walking into the front yard of his Cavendish Avenue home, Paul stood on his disheveled lawn and began singing a song about a blackbird with a broken wing. "Several yards away two fans stood...silent," Taylor remarked. It was a magic moment. The creative process was one that never stopped with Paul and he used the evening moon and the Apple scruffs to enhance his song writing. Paul failed to tell Taylor that he had already previewed the song for an attentive group of Apple Scruffs.

Alistair Taylor witnessed another unique song writing display by McCartney. During the summer of 1968 Paul was unusually preoccupied with Mary Hopkins' career. The beautiful young blonde folk singer from Pontardawe in Wales was brought to Apple, because of British model Twiggy. One night as Twiggy watched television, she spotted Hopkins on a TV talent show, Opportunity Knocks. Twiggy called Paul and Hopkins was signed to an Apple recording contract. As he worked with Hopkins, McCartney tried to teach her his song writing method. They worked diligently on a number of tunes, but Paul was frustrated by his inability to communicate his technique to Hopkins. So he took matters into his own hands and provided a crash course in song styling.

One day at Abbey Road Studio, Paul sat Mary Hopkins at a piano. He told her that he would write a song in a matter of minutes. But before he wrote the tune, Paul talked about language, imagery and syntax in rock music. Hopkins looked at him blankly. She had no idea what he was talking about. Not only was Mary Hopkins surprised by the breadth and depth of Paul's song writing, but she was amazed at his use of language. She had never considered words "friends" as Paul fondly referred to them. The ease with which Paul wrote a song impressed Hopkins and those who witnessed this demonstration. But she was hopelessly out of touch with Paul intellectually.

Throughout June and July 1968, the **White Album** was foremost in Paul's mind. The volatile changes in his personal life contributed to a new burst of creativity. Taking care of business was another facet of the new McCartney. Apple was a potential source of great profits and Paul was determined to make it work.

For much of McCartney's life he had thrived on adversity. The summer of 1968 convinced him that it was time to forge on with new goals. Paul had grown into a reasoned and mature man. The sordid little affairs and the tightening up of loose ends in his life made the next few months among the most creative in McCartney's life.

9: INTENSITY IN THE STUDIO: AUGUST, 1968

There was a renewed intensity to the Beatles' music during August 1968. It was as if they had to prove their worth again. During August, the Beatles' **White Album** was nearing completion and this was the reason that they spent twenty days that month in the recording studio. The missionary zeal to the recordings, the sophisticated nature of the remixes and the exciting direction of Beatles music was a reflection of how serious Paul was about the new LP. There was an attention to detail that not only made the **White Album** an extraordinary piece of work but indicated that the Beatles had moved beyond producer George Martin's control. There were also changes in their attitude toward management and the music business.

The loss of Brian Epstein was still a critical blow to the group. He was the glue that had held them together. The ego battles that emerged after Brian's death slowly splintered the group. There was a vacuum in the Beatles' management and no one was sure how to fill it. In deference to Brian and his mother Queenie, the boys allowed Clive Epstein to step temporarily into the management fold. For years Clive had been on the periphery of the Beatles' lives. He had little knowledge of the music business and the Beatles disliked him. Clive had a grating personality and insisted on being addressed as "Mr. Epstein." The Beatles couldn't put up with this type of behavior.

By August 1968, Clive tried to help the Beatles, because he believed that they were entering a critical period of their career. One that combined musical change with business-management reorganization. Clive was troubled by the murky business environment. "I never felt comfortable around the London music types," Clive remarked. "But I knew that something had to be done to salvage the business end of the Beatles career. He urged Paul and John to make changes in the Beatles' business structure. This suggestion appealed to Paul but John was uncertain about the Beatles' business future. Lennon didn't like Clive Epstein whom he believed was unsuited for the record business.

Although the Beatles' were guaranteed millions of pounds from the success of Apple Records, there was too much squabbling over the distribution of money. Since the **Sgt. Pepper** album there had been one money argument after another and these disputes were followed by artistic differences. The Beatles had committed one million pounds of their assets to the Apple enterprise with about 800,000 pounds going for set up expenses. When Apple began the four Beatles agreed to be personally responsible for the Apple debt. By August 1968 this was an unpopular idea. Apple had lost 80,000 pounds a week in recent months. The losses were labelled "start up or operating expenses." It was the last free lunch in London and no one was happy. Paul feared that the end of the Apple dream was near. Yet, he plodded on trying to create a business empire. Many believed that the Beatles should admit their defeat and move on.

The expenses associated with the Apple experiment were enormous ones. A puppet show in Brighton was an example of their penchant for strange schemes. Magic Alex's laboratory on Boston Street was a money drain. The number of promotional records and other free items staggered the imagination. Peter Shotton allegedly drove off an Apple Jaguar and kept it for his personal use. When Stephen Maltz, an Apple accountant, pointed out the ludicrous nature of Apple spending, he was forced to resign.

While vacationing in London during the summer of 1968 a junior college history professor walked into the Apple offices and was given an entire collection of Beatle records. When asked if he could take some memorabilia, the Secretary smiled and went to the bathroom. A number of Beatle collector items were stuffed in a bag and the following year the young professor's apartment in Douglas, Arizona was adorned with the precious Beatle artifacts. Somehow the cost accounting didn't report this incident in the Beatles' financial structure. The Beatles desperately needed to have the appearance of a regular business.

To create an aura of credibility Lord Beeching, a figure famous in Great Britain business circles, was approached about heading the Apple Corps. Beeching remarked that he had saved the British Railways but Apple was too far gone for financial restructuring. When the chairman of Lazard's bank, Lord Poole offered to help the Beatles redo their business structure, Paul thanked him but declined his help.

The reason was a simple one. Most conventional businessmen didn't know how to do business in the rock music subculture. To complicate matters, George and Ringo complained that they weren't making the money that Lennon and McCartney did from their song writing and publishing. As Marc Eliot suggests in his pathbreaking book, **Rockonomics: The Money Behind The Music**, "George Harrison, the first Beatle to record solo, in 1968, did so for a very simple reason. In order for him to make the kind of money that Lennon and McCartney earned...."

The Beatles found it difficult to make business decisions. They didn't seem to have a firm grasp of their economic problems. It appears that McCartney had some idea of the degree of organizational chaos, but he failed to solve Apple's problems. "I was frustrated with the Beatles lack of business knowledge," Clive Epstein remarked, "they found it difficult to find and spend their own money."

No one fully realized the fiscal difficulties. The reason was that the Beatles were selling millions of dollars worth of record, but they found it difficult to collect their money. The media reported huge sums of money flowing into the Apple coffers, but there never seemed to be enough money to pay the bills.

Paul couldn't understand how the Beatles could have sold 250 million record albums and singles and not be able to have the money to pay the bills. One of the reasons for this failure was the Beatles Boutique. It opened amidst a great deal of fanfare but closed shortly thereafter. The last day of business the boutique simply gave away what was left.

The immediate and total failure of the boutique, the film branch and the art operation drained millions of pounds from the Beatles' records. It was a giant economic drain that the Beatles filled with hit records. The publicity machine, however, talked about nothing but profits. After all weren't the Beatles still a million selling record act?

Because of Apple Records apparent success, the press took a renewed interest in the Fabulous Four. Much of this media attention revolved around Paul McCartney and his business-musical contribution to the Beatles. As a result of this publicity, the remaining Beatles became increasingly hostile to McCartney. Few Beatle insiders will talk about this period, but the tales of shouting and shoving matches are legendary.

In August 1968, Paul faced a series of new challenges. There had been enough time since Brian Epstein's death to sort out the Beatles business affairs, but they were no closer to solving their financial problems. Bad business advice had cost them large sums of money. Fiscal problems also produced strain within the group. Eventually, these tensions escalated into open warfare. Misunderstanding had been a problem for McCartney since his early days with the Beatles, but the stress surrounding this period was more intense than usual

Because he was frantically trying to keep the Beatles together, no one asked McCartney if he was happy with his mates. In August 1968, Paul told one Apple employee that he was considering ending his association with the Beatles. The years of discord and personal differences had taken their toll on McCartney. He couldn't stand the way the Beatles were breaking apart.

No one is sure when Paul began thinking about a law suit. However, those close to Paul pinpoint August 1968 as the beginning of the end. "I think that McCartney was ready to give it all up," Clive Epstein remarked. "I didn't realize that he was about to sue his mates." Clive wouldn't answer any questions about motivation, but he does remember that the 1968 summer was the end of the Beatles. At least that was Epstein's opinion fifteen years later. In less than three years McCartney filed his suit to end the group.

It was not be until March 1971, that McCartney versus Lennon, Harrison, Starkey and Apple Corps. Ltd. reached the

High Court and Mr. Justice Stamp informed the British citizenry that the Beatles were finished. The intensity of Paul's hatred for his mates has manifested itself publicly over the years. The most obvious incident was the Rock and Roll Hall of Fame third annual induction ceremony on January 20, 1988.

The press hinted that McCartney would make the trip to the Grand Ballroom of New York's Waldorf-Astoria for the $300 a plate black-tie rock bash. The afternoon of the banquet Paul had his New York public relations firm, Rogers and Cowan, issue a press release. It stated: "After twenty years, the Beatles still have some business differences which I had hoped would have been settled...they haven't been, so I would feel like a complete hypocrite waving and smiling with them at a fake reunion."

In 1988, in a privately taped interview with his lawyer, Paul looked back upon the Apple years with bitterness. On this tape McCartney castigates Ringo Starr for a lack of business awareness and Linda makes fun of George Harrison's speech patterns. "They still think they're the fucking Jackson 5," Paul remarked about his band mates. No one close to the Beatles was surprised by McCartney's comments.

When Tony Sheridan read about the Beatles dissolving in Hamburg in 1971, he was far from surprised by the court action. "Paul was uneasy with the Beatles," Tony reminisced, "and he never got on that well with John Lennon." Sheridan, like most early Beatles associates, blamed their problems upon fame and fortune. "If the Beatles hadn't become a million dollar act," Sheridan concluded, "they would have broken up much sooner."

From the earliest days of English Beatlemania in 1963 the group had lived in a fishbowl atmosphere. Sheridan remembers the years from 1960 to 1962 when the Beatles' put together their music. There were disagreements, but the lack of commercial success de-emphasized these differences. "When the Beatles had a hit record they were doomed," Tony Sheridan recalled, "from that point on they had to fight for survival."

In late 1962, as "Love Me Do" became a minor English hit, the infighting began in earnest. Although they had enormous success in England in 1962-1963 there were strong differences over their musical direction. The differences between John and Paul were already pronounced, and the selection of concert and recording tunes was a problem. The bickering, petty in-fighting and egomaniacal tirades hurt the band. Bob Wooler remembered: "John and Paul never got on with each other." Clive Epstein reinforced this notion: "The boys all had different ideas about the Beatles future and they squabbled constantly." Brian Epstein skillfully kept these conflicts from the press.

When the American triumph came in 1964, John and Paul temporarily reconciled their song writing differences. Fame, fortune and power healed many of the early wounds. They realized that a united front was important to their continued success. Over the next few years poor business deals, a changing public sentiment and the Beatles' new sophistication renewed many of the old petty feelings.

In Paul's case there were many reasons for renewed resentment. He believed that Lennon received more public acclaim for his tunes and that no one recognized how he had recreated the music into a commercially acceptable product. Paul kept a low profile but resented the work that he put in daily at the Apple office. It was a thankless task each day at Apple to try to sort out the Beatles' tangled affairs.

The years in the spotlight had cost Paul a great deal. McCartney's personal life was miserable. He felt lost amidst his fame. This lack of security resulted from his impersonal relationships. For years these female conquests had caused Paul anxiety. His private doubts were enormous. However, he had learned long ago to put on a smiling and strong public face.

On August 1, 1968, in the midst of these self doubts, McCartney drove to the Trident Studio on Wardour Street for a recording session. From five o'clock until eight in the evening the Beatles completed "Hey Jude." For three days before the recording session, Paul had tinkered with the song. He worked on its arrangement, the music and the vocal structure. As a result, this recording session was marked by efficiency and precision. There is a simplistic sense of Chuck Berry's guitar riffs in "Hey Jude." There is also a theme to the song that both Lennon and McCartney identified as part of their lives, and "Hey Jude's" lyrics reflected their differences. It was such an evocative song that Lennon was torn apart by it. Paul's lyrics evoked unpleasant images from the past. Ones that John hoped to forget. So Lennon was torn apart by the song. On one hand he loved it musically, while on the other hand he was upset over its personal nature. The tension within the Beatles' affairs was dramatized at two minutes and fifty-nine seconds of the completed version of "Hey Jude" when a swear word showed up on the song.

One observer recalls George Harrison leaving the studio and screaming an obscenity at engineer Barry Sheffield. Only the practiced patience and guidance of producer George Martin prevented this session from disintegrating into complete chaos.

The words to "Hey Jude" were special to McCartney. "You're waiting for someone to perform with," Paul wrote. He explained the lyrics to "Hey Jude" as the musical poetry which could release the Beatles' from the doldrums that had overtaken their lives.

The musical impact that McCartney had upon "Hey Jude" was significant to the songs' success. As Paul overdubbed his bass guitar and lead vocals on the tune, the other Beatles added a background vocal chorus. By using 36 instruments on "Hey Jude" a complex sound was developed. This bit of last minute experimentation not only added a commercial touch to the song, but it indicated Paul's experimental genius. Trident Studio was not suited to a large number of musicians. Consequently, Chris Thomas, George Martin's assistant, suggested that the trombones be placed in the front of the studio so "that they didn't poke anyone in the back." The use of the trombones in the orchestral overdub added a new dimension to "Hey Jude" and made it a stronger song.

Unwittingly, Paul had written a song so special that it would break his song writing link forever with John Lennon. What surprised Paul was how much praise John gave him when he presented a rough version of "Hey Jude." "It's great," John exclaimed. Paul couldn't believe his ears. He had finally written a tune that Lennon didn't want to alter.

There was a sense of accomplishment for Paul after "Hey Jude" was completed. He spent the next few days relaxing. It was time for reflection. Paul spent many hours in his Regency style house. In his living room the French windows led out to a patio. He loved to look out into his yard and speculated on the future. There were two paintings by Rene Magritte that hung on the wall next to a Peter Blake painting that adorned the **Sgt. Pepper** album sleeve. It was an eclectic room and Paul loved it. A beautiful Takis sculpture decorated one side of the room next to an Indian sarod. The carpet was thick and pleasant, and the ambiance was a long way from the bleak Liverpool years. After being home for a few days, Paul was again ready to work on some new projects.

At noon on August 7, 1968, Paul entered the closed down Apple Boutique. He looked at the disheveled shop and realized that his dreams were in disarray. Paul had once believed that his musical success would carry over into the business world. The Apple Boutique reminded him how precarious this business venture was for a musician. Grabbing a cigarette and a glass of scotch Paul reminisced about the past. He fondly recalled John Lennon's friendship. Paul wondered what had happened. Was it just fame and fortune that was splitting the Beatles? Was it the unyielding press criticism that was tearing the group apart? These questions floated through Paul's mind, and he smiled remembering the good times. The years in Hamburg drinking with Tony Sheridan, making love to young German girls and eating and drinking until the wee hours of the morning in the small Reeperbahn cafes were pleasant memories. This was the nostalgic inspiration that McCartney needed to write a new song.

As Paul sat down at an empty Apple Boutique desk, he thought about the last few weeks. He had written one of his best songs about John's son Julian. The young man was an inspiration as Paul recalled the joy, the anticipation and the sense of the future that his birth brought. It was a magic moment. Paul had written "Hey Jude" to celebrate this event. The pet name that McCartney used for Julian was Jules. Soon when a song appropriately entitled "Hey Jules" began taking shape, Paul used it to express his deep feeling for the young boy. A few weeks later

McCartney changed the song to "Hey Jude" because he feared that John might somehow become offended. These thoughts raced through Paul's mind as he stared at the Apple Boutique's mess and clutter. Things had gone so poorly between Paul and John that McCartney did not want to take a chance on ending the friendship.

The pressures that had been building for years in the Beatles' life led Paul into his most creative period. He also had other reasons to feel elated. He was constantly in demand to write tunes for other singers. During August 1968, Paul stood up to the enormous pressure of completing the songs for the **White Album.** If the Beatles weren't in the studio recording, they were mixing a tune or figuring out the next song. A review of key recording dates in August and an examination of the forces pressuring the Beatles suggests why this was their last real album.

Some of the musicians who worked on "Hey Jude" recalled the tension and acrimony that rose to the surface during the lengthy sessions. From five in the afternoon until three in the morning there was activity in the Trident Studios. As one musician suggested there was a short break at about seven-thirty and then and from eight o'clock until eleven that evening; then the Beatles worked on the musical build up used to close "Hey Jude." It was an arduous task as thirty-six instruments blended into the closing riff. The Trident Studio was so small that the musicians were cranky and ill at ease. The sweaty musicians were calmed by working with the Beatles and the environment was surprisingly calm considering the working conditions. Yet, there was a schizoid atmosphere. At one moment the Beatles were serious musicians and minutes later they fought like undisciplined children.

Many musicians at this session laughed about their myriad duties. Besides playing their instruments they were asked to contribute a hand clapping refrain for "Hey Jude." Only one musician walked out. He complained that McCartney was "a millionaire and a bloody cheap bastard." Whether or not any other musicians felt that way is unknown. This particular session player, who requested anonymity, suggested that McCartney demanded too much from the musicians. "He was a bloody hypocrite, telling us that we were being paid top dollar. We never got more than scale." This opinion is a minority one. Generally, the musicians who worked with McCartney praised his musical skill and intellectual integrity. However, they all agree that he was tight with a dollar.

As the musicians worked in the studio that night they were surprised to hear John Lennon complain about an interview with Paul McCartney in the **London Daily Mail**. The musicians read it with eager anticipation. The story revolved around the Apple Boutique and painted Paul as a farsighted businessman. John laughed that the boutique was a disaster. Someone hollered out that the other Beatles were responsible for these problems.

The **London Daily Mail** article created new problems. The tensions surrounding the Beatles were enormous ones. The combination of business and musical problems did not bode well for the future. Paul and George finally broke this stalemate by hollering at each other. When Paul shouted that he was carrying George musically, the youngest Beatle stomped off vowing to quit the group. This argument was quickly forgotten, but Paul was upset about the continued friction within the group.

The next day Paul and George got together to patch up their differences. Early in the morning Harrison took a cab to McCartney's home. After an ample breakfast they had a long and pleasant chat. The subject was the Beatles future. Whatever the outcome, the acrimonious incident of the previous night was forgotten. Both Paul and George indicated that the media pressure over the Apple business venture was straining their long friendship.

After his meeting with George, Paul rang up Trident Studio to ask about the stereo mixing for "Hey Jude." It was just after two o'clock and George Martin and Barry Sheffield were beginning three stereo remixes for "Hey Jude." Paul wanted to stay home because of the London press. Everywhere he went they shadowed him.

The media's explanation of Paul's private life continued in the August 3 issue of **Disc**. An article on McCartney's dating habits was included with the usual tidbits about the music scene. On British television the celebration of Paul McCartney's creativity continued with the TC comedy series, "Thingumybob," which featured a McCartney written theme song played by Apple's Black Dyke Mills Band. Despite the media attention, it was necessary to complete the **White Album**.

On Tuesday, August 6, 1968, the Trident studio was abuzz with activity at five thirty in the evening as George Martin began the first mono remix of "Hey Jude." There was anticipation in the air. Everyone felt that this was a special Beatle song. In a highly unusual procedure, George Martin made the mono mix of "Hey Jude" from the best available stereo mix. Martin didn't believe that the original eight-track tape was strong enough for a proper mono mix. During the next two nights a more acceptable mono mix of "Hey Jude" was created at Abbey Road. This incident suggests the power and skill of George Martin in shaping the Beatles' music.

Because of the problems that McCartney and Harrison had in the studio, Paul suggested that George take over a session. Both George and Ringo were eager to expand their singing and song writing, and Harrison eagerly welcomed this suggestion.

When George Harrison showed up at Abbey Road Studio no. 2 on August 7, 1968, he was struck by the intensity of Paul's working habits. Perhaps Paul was making up for their fight.

George wondered if Paul was intent upon helping him record his own song. The chemistry in their relationship was volatile but George was struck by how friendly and confident Paul was in the studio. It caught on and Harrison began fervently working on his own music.

As George Harrison concentrated upon recording "Not Guilty," mono mixes for "Hey Jude" and "Revolution" were completed. No one realized that as George Harrison began cutting "Not Guilty" that it would turn into one of the most extended songs in the Beatles' history. This marathon tune began innocently that night with forty-six takes. The first eighteen takes were the song's introduction and from takes nineteen through forty-six there were only five completed songs. Not surprisingly the song continued into the next night. Then it was mysteriously shelved. It would not be released on a Beatle album. "Not Guilty" eventually showed up on George Harrison's 1979 solo LP, **Dark Horse**.

This was a period of trial and tribulation for Harrison. One of the songs that George composed during this period, "Here Comes The Sun," reflected his unhappiness. It was written because he believed that "Apple was getting to be like school." He saw himself as a student who was forced to go to work each day. He was training to become a businessman. The regimentation, the continual presence of "the suits" and McCartney's intense preoccupation with the almighty pound made this an uneasy time. As Harrison remembered, he felt ill at ease with all the signing of accounts. The "sign this" and "sign that" mentality that permeated Apple prompted Harrison to withdraw from business activity. In his autobiographical tome, **I, Me, Mine**, George explains his disgust with Apple. One day George played hooky from Apple and wrote "Something" while sunning himself in Eric Clapton's garden. This was an act of defiance. Paul demanded that the Beatles adhere to business matters. The pressure to create new music was enormous and Harrison dealt with it through relaxation, meditation and the confidence he had built into his personality.

The other Beatles weren't able to see that George had grown into a creative artist. In later years Harrison remarked: "Both John and Paul didn't read me right, they didn't realize how serious I was about my music." Eventually, John and Paul acknowledged George's musical growth, but in 1968 they treated him like the younger brother. It didn't make for a smooth relationship.

When the Beatles reported to Abbey Road on Thursday, August 8, 1968, there was a feeling that too much time was being spent in the studio. More than one engineer believed that the use of both Trident Studio and Abbey Road was creating musical problems. The Beatles were producing records that had a wide variety of sounds. A record might sound one way at Trident and the same tune would contain a much different tone at Abbey Road.

Ken Scott pointed out the differences between the Trident Studio version of "Hey Jude" and the Abbey Road recording. Scott suggested that the Trident Studio version of "Hey Jude" sounded awful. He was amazed how George Martin's mix had altered the tune. Scott believed that the original version of "Hey Jude" was technically inept, and he alleged that McCartney had a negative impact upon the tune. As Scott sat in the Abbey Road Studio no. 2 telling George Martin that he thought "Hey Jude" sounded terrible in its original form, Paul walked in and lit a cigarette. Taking a sip from a cup of tea, McCartney looked quizzically at Scott and Martin. With a sly smile, Martin turned to Paul and said: "Ken thinks "Hey Jude" sounds awful."

"Does he," McCartney replied.

"Yes," George Martin continued. "We need to straighten out the sound."

"I will personally handle it," Paul concluded. McCartney looked pained. The long hours in the studio and constant pressure from the media was taking its toll. He was tired of other people's opinions. After all, who in the hell was Ken Scott? Paul contained his rage. For years every hanger on, assistant engineer and would be production assistant had ventured their opinion. Paul simply smiled and ignored Scott. Whether Ken Scott's opinion changed Paul's mind is open to question but he remixed "Hey Jude." The battles in the studio were escalating, because too many voices were heard regarding Beatle affairs.

Over the years, Ken Scott's self serving comments have obscured that McCartney intended all along to add some subtle production changes to "Hey Jude." Once the meddlesome interference with "Hey Jude" ended the Beatles were free to get on with George Harrison's music.

There were signs of the tension lifting between the boys. On August 13, 1968, the Beatles showed up in the studio and Paul came to the session in George's white Mercedes. They were again friendly. The Beatles were determined to make this a fun session. John Lennon broke the tension by recording "Yer Blues." This humorous put down of the British blues scene appealed to everyone, and Paul loved John's imagery in this irreverent tune.

The Beatles used this night to engage in some impromptu jamming. This helped to ease the hurt feelings and strained egos. The next night Paul took a break from the recording process.

As the band assembled on August 15, 1968, at seven in the evening, it was Paul McCartney's turn to introduce a new song. He had written a tune "Rocky Raccoon" which Paul sang along with George Martin on piano. As the session began George Harrison in a light hearted frame of mind remarked: "take one." The engineer Ken Scott chuckled and accused George of taking over his duties. Mirth. Humor. Camaraderie. These elements had returned to the Abbey Road studio.

Surprisingly, Paul was uncertain about the lyrics. He

stumbled over the phrases and appeared unsure of the cadence. Between takes Paul stated: "I don't quite know the words to that verse yet!" The other Beatles and George Martin laughed heartily. It took just nine takes to get the song right. George Martin's honky-tonk piano, John's harmonica, and backing vocals by John, Paul and George created an inspiring song.

There was pressure to complete the songs for the **White Album**. Consequently, "Rocky Raccoon" was remixed for mono in one quick take and Paul took a copy home. The demands for new music took its toll on George Harrison. He decided to take his family and Mal Evans to Greece for a short holiday. Dissension was once again in the air.

On Tuesday, August 20, 1968, Paul, John and Ringo arrived at Abbey Road at five in the evening. John and Ringo quickly vanished into a studio to complete "Yer Blues" and supervise the mono mix of "Revolution 9." Paul went into another studio to complete "Mother Nature's Son." The engineer remembered that Paul wanted a different drum sound. So they placed a set of drums down the hall with mikes at the end of the hallway. During the production of "Mother Nature's Son," Paul overdubbed the timpani, another acoustic guitar and brass instruments. The result was a wonderful sound that revealed all of McCartney's complex studio skill.

As Paul worked on "Mother Nature's Son" there was a feeling that something special was being produced. Ken Scott and John Smith were engineers who remembered this unique session. Then suddenly without warning John and Ringo invaded Paul's studio. There was a great deal of tension and a stiffening in McCartney's personality. Something was wrong, but the Beatles weren't sharing their secrets. After John and Ringo left, Paul returned to his studio work and the tension subsided. The message was clear to anyone in the studio, the Beatles were in trouble as a cooperative recording group.

The next day Paul got out of bed and called George. No one was home. Then McCartney remembered that George was coming home that afternoon. Paul left his house and took a walk. He needed time to think. George was due that night at Abbey Road. Like clockwork at seven thirty Harrison walked into the studio. A lengthy session that lasted almost twelve hours created "Sexy Sadie." This song was started on July 19 and finally completed during this marathon session.

When Paul went home from this session, he was determined to bring some order to the Beatles' music. Paul wrote a lengthy memo to the other Beatles. One Beatle took this memo too seriously. The next night, August 22, 1968, Ringo Starr quit the Beatles. It was obvious that the boys couldn't work together. When the Beatles sent engineers Ken Scott and John Smith out for dinner all hell erupted. Shouting was heard from the studio. A bottle was broken.

"I remember Ringo being uptight about something," engineer Ken Scott remarked, "I don't remember what...I was told that he's quit the band." The band was completing the first five takes of "Back in the U.S.S.R." when the controversy took place. Paul filled in as the drummer on "Back in the U.S.S.R." And there was apparently little concern over Ringo's departure. When he returned a few days later, Mal Evans placed flowers all over Ringo's drum set. No one seemed to notice or care.

When Ringo returned the Beatles recorded as though they had never been apart. The Friday, August 23, 1968, session produced a well recorded version of "Back In The U.S.S.R." There was also work to do at Apple. The release of new Apple singles and the need for publicity slowed the Beatles' recording. While work went on in the studio, Paul spent four days at the Apple offices, cleaning up personal business. Mal Evans was sent to check out copies of Beatle tracks that Paul wanted to listen to at home.

On Friday, August 30, 1968, the Beatles first Apple release "Hey Jude" was sent out to record stores. HMV had a special section for the new Apple single. The length of "Hey Jude" intrigued the critics and the song immediately became one of the Beatles' best selling tracks with eight million copies sold worldwide.

Paul's vision of Apple's future was a bright one, and he felt good about the August 1968 period. It was one in which McCartney's solo skill was demonstrated and his business aptitude was impressive. The time was ripe for the Beatles to continue their musical stardom and combine it with business success. There was no limit to the future and Paul believed that Apple would be successful.

Although Paul was exhausted, he continued to work as a feverish pitch. Yet, there were clouds on the horizon. The twenty days that the Beatles spent in the studio during August 1968, led to a great deal of infighting, ego manipulation and petty behavior. The Beatles were in trouble. No one knew it because the press continued to play out the myth of happiness, togetherness and family. Nothing was further from the truth.

10: PAUL IN CONTROL: SEPTEMBER-OCTOBER, 1968

By September, 1968, Paul not only dominated the Beatles' music, but he was thinking of new ways to promote their records. He polished new tunes for the **White Album**, while planning a concert film to promote "Hey Jude." The differences between John and Paul had escalated because of Lennon's belief that "Hey Jude" was a soft song. John didn't want to make a film of it. It didn't take long for Paul to convince John that a promotional film clip would sell a lot of records. This disagreement was typical of the Beatles in late 1968. They would fight like cats and dogs and then suddenly agree on a debated point.

When "Hey Jude" was released in England on August 26, 1968, it took only two weeks to reach no. 1 on the **Melody Maker** and **New Musical Express** charts. In the next four years "Hey Jude" sold in excess of seven million records. As the Beatles' most commercial song it was also a no. 1 hit in Holland, Ireland, Belgium, West Germany, Denmark, Malaysia, Singapore, New Zealand, Norway and Sweden. Ironically, "Hey Jude's" success led to the Beatles squabbling over money, music and the future. It was not a pleasant situation. It was not easy for Lennon to allow "Revolution" to appear on the b side, but John did it. The reason was simple. He felt that he owed this to Paul because of his work on the **White Album**.

A few years later, Paul confessed to **Rolling Stone** that he wasn't sure that "Hey Jude" would be a hit. Because of his fears about its potential commercial appeal, Paul convinced John to make "Hey Jude" the A side of the record. John agreed, indicating his willingness to cooperate with Paul. The incident that brought John and Paul together was one that owed its success to Yoko Ono's compromising hand.

In order to convince John to make "Hey Jude" the A side of a Beatles release, Paul played a demo tape for John and Yoko. When he finished the scene was an emotional one. Some years later, John remarked in a **Playboy** interview that "Hey Jude" is a damn good set of lyrics, and I made no contribution to that." John changed his mind and recognized Paul's song writing talent. Clive Epstein believed that the Beatles had broken their Liverpool bonds when John made this remark. "There were some tense musical moments during the "Hey Jude" sessions as the Beatles were often at each others throats," Epstein remarked. Much of this tension was due to media pressure. London newspapers hinted at McCartney's differences with the other Beatles. The most overblown bits of publicity centered around Paul's relationship with George.

While Paul was rehearsing "Hey Jude," he told George not to play his guitar. George blanched. This made for some tense moments. George was playing better than ever and showed signs of a new musical maturity. Some observers believed that his talent was equal to McCartney's.

While the London newspapers picked up these differences, they failed to report that Paul worked intensely with George on his song writing and recording. Many of Harrison's early solo records depended upon studio tricks and writing techniques that Paul imparted to the youngest Beatle. Paul had planted creative seeds in Harrison's music.

The experimental nature of McCartney's music bothered people close to the Beatles. Although Bob Dylan had broken the time honored pattern of three-minute singles, George Martin worried that Beatles songs were becoming much too long. The length of "Hey Jude," George Martin argued, seven minutes and eleven seconds was too long, and he complained that four minutes of the song was a fadeout. He believed that it was a waste of time. All of this was forgotten when "Hey Jude" became a mammoth hit. Its sales ensured a promotional video.

On September 4, 1968, a large group of fans stood outside McCartney's St. John's Wood home as he prepared to leave for Twickenham studio to film the spot for "Hey Jude." When McCartney's limousine arrived, Nat Weiss was sitting in it. As the limousine wound its way slowly to Twickenham studios, McCartney and Weiss talked about the future. Their discussion centered around Apple's fiscal problems and Paul's prospective solo career. McCartney believed that a solo album would solve his artistic and financial concerns. There was a festive atmosphere in the limousine as McCartney talked about his plans. He had a solo career on his mind but few people realized it.

Once they reached London's Victoria Station a group of more than 60 Beatles fans anxiously awaited the chance to board a bus for Twickenham Studio. A brief announcement offered the fans a chance to participate in the "Hey Jude" promo film. One fan carried a sign reading: "We love you Paul." Another had a hat filled with John's pictures. There were signs of affection for each of the Beatles and a sense of anticipation among the young girls. As the girls prepared to descend upon Twickenham Studio, a London celebrity interviewer eagerly anticipated the days events.

British television personality David Frost was enroute to Twickenham Studio to introduce the Beatle film clip. Frost was anxious to complete this assignment for his weekend television show. The David Frost Show was a popular Sunday night feature in England, and a Beatles promo video was important to its ratings. Not only was Frost aware of the personal differences between the Beatles, but he was nervous about the videos quality. He had heard stories of the Beatles drug induced behavior. Although he had seen this type of behavior, Frost was apprehensive. The London entertainment establishment had filled Frost with gossip and innuendo. Much to his credit he ignored these scurrilous tales. Yet, he worried. Frost was aware that Ringo Starr had left the Beatles. He breathed easily when he saw Ringo in Twickenham Studio. The press had not reported accurately the dissension within the Beatles camp, but Frost believed that the latent animosity could explode into open conflict. He approached John and quizzed him about the Beatles' problems. It took Lennon only a few minutes to set Frost straight. Internal differences, Lennon lectured Frost, would not be made public. He invited Frost to sit down and watch the taping. Paul walked over and told Frost that the Beatles wouldn't air their dirty laundry publicly.

As the Beatles assembled at Twickenham Studios they warmed up with an old folk song "Tom Dooley." For the next five hours the Beatles worked on the film clip of "Hey Jude" in front of sixty fans. As midnight approached the fans began leaving Twickenham Studio and David Frost fidgeted eagerly waiting for his interview.

After the "Hey Jude" film and the Frost interview was completed everyone left Twickenham in a state of exhaustion. The Beatles were more cohesive than the press and gossip mongers had suggested. They could still make excellent music despite the infighting.

The day after the "Hey Jude" promo film, the Beatles were back in the Abbey Road Studio. At seven o'clock in the evening Paul showed up to add piano and organ sounds to George Harrison's "While My Guitar Gently Weeps." After this recording session the Beatles stayed around the studio to talk about their new Apple releases. Eric Clapton was the inspiration for this extended bull session. He was given a ride into London earlier in the day by George Harrison and when George asked Clapton to add some guitar riffs to "While My Guitar Gently Weeps," he agreed. While Paul provided background harmonies, George finished the song.

Early in the day Apple released a number of singles by new artists. Among these were the Paul McCartney produced single by the Black Dyke Mills Band, "Thingumybob," and Jackie Lomax's "Sour Milk Sea" backed with "The Eagle Laughs at You." These records were lost in the excitement surrounding the Beatles' new release.

"Hey Jude" entered the number 1 slot on the **Melody Maker** chart while Apple releases by other artists floundered. Seeming oblivious to "Hey Jude's" success, Paul showed up each day at the Apple offices and puttered with pet projects. He was worried about Apple's lack of business success and general corporate disorganization. McCartney had reason to worry. Press barbs flew continually and there were numerous media investigators snooping into the Beatles' affairs. Ray Coleman, who edited **Disc** and **Music Echo**, was one journalist who covered the Beatles fairly. Not only did Coleman respect the Beatles individual privacy, but he placed Apple's business problems within the context of the times. Few, if any, rock groups controlled their own destiny. Coleman applauded the Beatles' Apple experiment and defended their business direction. Despite his obvious affection for the Beatles, Coleman was an independent-minded journalist who criticized some of their avant-garde musical experiments.

It was Ray Coleman who subtly suggested the existence of Paul's differences with Brian Epstein. Not only did McCartney question Epstein's business tactics, but he complained about the direction of the Beatles' career. When Epstein was asked who the most difficult Beatle was, he answered: "Paul McCartney." The six years of Epstein's management did produce some positive business lessons that McCartney used in the Apple venture. Coleman's book, **The Man Who Made The Beatles: An Intimate Biography of Brian Epstein**, published in 1989, offers a view of Paul McCartney, Brian Epstein and the other Beatles which explains their success. They would fight like cats and dogs over an issue and then agree on a plan or policy. In the end, they pursued what was best for the group, but they came almost to the point of fist fights before they agreed on an issue.

Most other English reporters heavily criticized the Beatles. They failed to report that compromise did take place. Jeremy Pascall of **Rave** and **Nineteen** magazine was a conscientious critic with a penchant for demanding the truth. The London newspapers were the worst critics. They employed sensational journalism that bore little resemblance to reality. The **London Daily Mail** was the most ruthless Apple critic. Another newspaper the **London Evening News** went so far as to suggest that the Rolling Stones were more responsible and business minded than the Beatles. Even the **Liverpool Daily Post** speculated on the problems that living in London had created for the four boys from Liverpool. Philip Palmer, of the **Record Retailer**, allegedly approached Derek Taylor with a request to learn the key to the Beatles' financial success. **Record Retailer** and **Time Out** were magazines that allegedly demanded ads from Apple to guarantee positive coverage. The litany of press abuses extended to the **London Daily Mirror**, the **London Evening Standard** and the **London Daily Telegraph**. There was a race on to see how much scandal, pithy personal details and drug rumors could be dug up on the Beatles. The truth had little, if any, bearing upon this reporting. It was no wonder that Paul refused to cooperate with the press.

As things fell apart in late 1968 the Beatles missed the public relations expertise that Brian Epstein had provided. Although Brian had his shortcomings and made many mistakes, there was a flair to Epstein's management. He had helped the Beatles earn enormous sums of money. Too much emphasis has been placed upon Brian's faults and not enough on his accomplishments. Many of Brian's closest friends cried out about the abusive publicity which obscured his financial dealings. Alistair Taylor, the General Manager at NEMS after Epstein's death, stayed on with the Beatles only because of Clive Epstein's insistence. "I knew that I could trust Alistair," Clive remarked. The reason for this trust was a simple one. Taylor had worked with Brian in the record department at the NEMS Department Store in Liverpool, and he was in a position to understand the jostling for power that was destroying Apple. As Clive pointed out not all those who worked for Brian were loyal employees. "I am sick over Peter Brown's book, **The Love You Make**," Clive remarked in 1983. But there were others whom Clive praised, among these was Alistair Taylor. "Since the 1960s I have come to appreciate Alistair's integrity and business skill," Epstein concluded.

But by September, 1968, Taylor was unhappy. As a member of Apple's Executive Board, Taylor met regularly with the other officers and the Beatles. It was a tense and difficult situation. Taylor insists that Brian approved of the Apple experiment. But Epstein never realized how difficult it would be for the Beatles to carry it out. "I don't think Brian understood how varied and complex the Beatles' affairs were," Taylor remarked.

As Taylor sat in the Apple offices he was reminded of Brian's dictum. "Novices in any business will have difficulty." This phrase was uttered by Brian as a warning of future problems. A simple item like purchasing IBM typewriters was difficult. One day Alistair Taylor walked across Wigmore Street to the IBM sales office to purchase five typewriters. Not only did the sales person on the floor ignore Taylor, but he found it difficult to believe that this scruffily dressed young man could afford such equipment. It was only after Taylor presented his card as Apple's General Manager that he was given proper service. This attitude was one that plagued the Apple Corporation throughout its brief business career. The haughty, stuffy British merchants found it difficult to do business with these young upstarts. So Apple didn't receive the business communities cooperation and this doomed a noble experiment.

Another member of the Apple Executive Board, Derek Taylor, recalled that local businesses didn't welcome the Apple Corporation. "Many of the shopkeepers," Taylor wrote, were "silly snobbish...obsequious people...." This sentiment was echoed by many people at Apple. At the Wigmore Street Apple office there were business people dressed in fashionable suits who looked askance at the millionaire counterculture types who ran the corporation.

In the midst of this business revolution, Paul continued to write songs. In September, 1968, Alistair Taylor watched Paul write a song "Martha." Although it had little to do with his

English sheepdog, Paul used the dog's name as the song title. It was amusing for Taylor as Paul's dog chased another dog around the front yard of McCartney's St. John's Wood home and he quickly dashed off a hit record. It took Paul less than an hour to write the song. Paul's song writing was a relaxing break from Apple's tedious day to day business atmosphere.

One night Paul and Alistair had an experience that was on the edge of reality. Paul called his friend and asked him to come up to his Cavendish Avenue home in St. John's Wood. When Taylor arrived a distraught McCartney was eager to drink and talk. They stayed up most of the night laughing and reminiscing about old times. As dawn broke, Paul suggested that they take his dog, Martha, for a long walk. They commandeered one of Paul's luxury cars and drove to the London Zoo. After parking they began climbing a steep hill. The area, known as Primrose Hill, prompted Paul to remark that the hill had a mystical quality to it. Paul suggested that they scurry up the hill for a better view of the city. A skeptical Taylor walked slowly up Primrose Hill and was treated to a spectacular sight. It was a panoramic view that included Westminister Abbey, St. Paul's, the Post Office Tower and in the distance Surrey and Kent sparkled in the orange morning sunlight. The sounds from the zoo and the soft noises of the birds made Primrose Hill special. There was a quality that relaxed McCartney and Taylor.

As McCartney and Taylor walked with Martha tagging along on a leash they talked at length about the future. Suddenly Paul remembered that he needed to go home. It was time to go to work. As they turned to leave a man appeared at their side. He introduced himself as John and quickly left Primrose Hill. Neither Paul nor Alistair had seen the man walk up the hill. Paul interpreted the visit as an omen. It was a positive sign that the Apple experiment would provide artistic freedom and financial stability.

The Beatles' music continued to be the dominant force in McCartney's life. He spent hours planning his new songs. The song writing process was an instant one for Paul, as he coaxed new meaning out his tunes. As Paul wrote the songs for the **White Album**, he also created elaborate musical pieces for a solo album. There was a creative tension to McCartney during this period. All was not roses at Apple as Paul tried to shape a million pound corporation into a legitimate business venture. His only solace was in the recording studio. There he could hide out from the day to day business problems and the tensions surrounding his life.

Paul was relieved that there were numerous Beatle recording sessions scheduled for September, 1968. Despite their business and personal problems, the Beatles continued to work on the **White Album**.

On September 9, 1968, Paul walked over the Abbey Road Studio No. 2 at six-thirty in the evening anxious to complete some new music. These sessions were a tonic to McCartney. They inspired him to write new tunes. "The line between lunacy and genius," Paul once remarked, "is in a song line." After Paul uttered these words to a close friend in the Abbey Road parking lot, he walked into the building eager to record. Neil Aspinall and Mal Evans were in the studio waiting for Paul. As was his usual practice, Paul was the first Beatle in the Abbey Road studio. He was eager to play his new song. It was a tune inspired by a rock music newspaper. Because he had time on his hands prior to the recording sessions, McCartney read voluminously and often came up with songs.

Paul had read an interview in **Melody Maker** with the Who's Peter Townshend and was intrigued by the musical ideas he generated. Pete talked about one of the Who's songs and called it "the loudest, the most raucous rock 'n' roll, the dirtiest thing they'd ever done." The concept of nasty rock and roll intrigued Paul, and he loved the challenge that Townshend threw out to the rock and roll establishment. Perhaps everything was too pop. It was time for the major groups to challenge the prevailing song writing and production standards. The Beatles would record the same type of song. So McCartney wrote what he called "the nastiest, sweatiest rock number...." he had ever experienced and entitled it "Helter Skelter." On July 18, 1968, "Helter Skelter" was put in the can, but the best of the cuts was twenty-seven minutes long. So McCartney had to go back into the studio. A nine minute song was reaching the limits and a twenty seven minute piece was unthinkable.

The September 9, 1968, session didn't get off to a good start when McCartney walked into the studio and spotted producer Chris Thomas sitting in the corner. In his fashionable suitcoat and trendy Carnaby street tie, Thomas cut a splashy figure. Paul looked at him and remarked:

"What are you doing here?"

"Didn't George tell you?" Thomas blurted out. "

"No," Paul screamed.

"Well, George has suggested I come down and help ya out," Thomas stammered.

"Well, if you wanna produce us, you can produce us. If you don't...we might just tell you to fuck off," McCartney screamed. Paul was furious because the Beatles were producing their own music and McCartney didn't want anyone meddling in their affairs. After he calmed down, Paul changed his mind and allowed Thomas to produce.

Despite McCartney's initial misgivings, Chris Thomas provided a steady hand in the studio. He had a calming effect upon the musicians. By arranging the studio in a way the Beatles approved of, he helped to coax some of the best music from the Fabulous Four. In the industry Thomas was well thought of and eventually did some producing for Badfinger. In later years he worked with the Sex Pistols and Paul hired him to co-produce the **Back To The Egg** LP. Thomas was a recording professional and this won McCartney's loyalty. As they worked in the studio, Thomas helped to mold "Helter Skelter" into an acceptable tune. Eventually, takes four through twenty one of "Helter Skelter" were used with some additional overdubs to complete the song. It took two nights of recording to put this peculiar tune into the proper context. The two evenings in the Abbey Road studio recording "Helter Skelter" were strange ones. The Beatles used a number of musical innovations. They allowed Mal Evans to play a horrible sounding trumpet as John plunked on an out of tune bass guitar. Much like John's excursion into craziness in "Revolution No. 9," Paul used "Helter Skelter" to validate his musical weirdness.

The zaniness in the studio during the "Helter Skelter" sessions was climaxed by George lighting fire to an ashtray and running around the studio with it. Harrison pretended that he was Arthur Brown, whose hit "Fire" provided the excuse for this charade. When an alternate cut of "Helter Skelter" was released on the **Beatles Rarities** LP, it contained laughter, a different drum ending and exaggerated beeping sounds.

After a week in which the Beatles recorded Lennon's "Glass Onion," Paul went back into the studio to cut "I Will." In a marathon sixty-seven take session, Paul completed a song that was much like "I'll Follow The Sun." There were only three Beatles in the studio for this tune. George was not present. The following day on Tuesday, September 17, 1968 the final version of "I Will" was completed and a mono mix of "Helter Skelter" was finished.

On September 18, 1968, the Beatles recorded "Birthday" in a session where there was still a song writing magic between Lennon and McCartney. A rock and roll movie on British television was the catalyst to an evening of recording magic. When Paul showed up at 5:00 in the afternoon at Abbey Road, producer Chris Thomas mentioned that **The Girl Can't Help It** was on BBC-2 from 9:05 to 10:40 that evening. It was the first English telecast of the classic American rock and roll movie featuring Little Richard, the Platters, Gene Vincent, Fats Domino and Eddie Cochran. When the other Beatles arrived Paul was playing the "Birthday" riff and he finished writing the song quickly in the studio that night. "Birthday" was written quickly by Paul and was influenced by Little Richard's music. Pattie Harrison and Yoko Ono were in the studio and added backing vocals. By take 22 Paul had the master for one of the Beatles' best rock songs. In a little more than three hours the Beatles had worked together as efficiently as in the past. Yet things were not the same. They just seemed that way. By 8:30 the basic tracks for "Birthday" were laid down and the Beatles walked to Paul's house to watch the movie. But John had some ideas about "Birthday" and he urged

McCartney to make a number of changes. Some of Lennon's suggestions were included but the majority were disgarded. In a **Playboy** interview, John called the song "a piece of garbage." No one revealed the extent of John and Paul's disagreement over "Birthday," but the pop tone of McCartney's songs bothered Lennon.

After the movie the Beatles returned to Abbey Road and at four-thirty in the morning "Birthday" was laid to rest. This long evening was an important one for the Beatles. They envisioned the end of their new album.

During the last few days of September, McCartney worked feverishly on Apple business affairs. Since the Beatles were finishing the **White Album**, it was necessary for Paul to wear two hats-one for business and the other for music.

On September 21, 1968, Mary Hopkin's "Those Were The Days," produced by Paul McCartney, entered the American **Billboard** singles chart at number 132. It remained on the American chart for twelve weeks and rose to number 2. Because of Hopkins' success and the continued sales of Beatle records, the **New York Times** called Apple Records an American success story. This publicity alerted the media to McCartney's production skills and garnered him a great deal of attention. In England, Hopkins' song spent 21 weeks on the charts and was a number one hit.

The average employee at Apple was a star struck groupie with a penchant for alcohol, drugs and sex. Not a bad choice in the 1960s. However, it was one unlikely to produce large corporate profits. The work ethic was not a major concern to Apple employees. Considering the atmosphere, it was amazing that the creative juices flowed so freely. It was one of McCartney's most significant intellectual periods. "Paul wrote furiously and surprised me with this ability to transcend the Apple circus," Clive Epstein remarked.

As September, 1968 drew to a close, McCartney was pleased with the Beatles' progress. An interview in the September 14th **Melody Maker** indicated how happy Paul was with the two million copies of "Hey Jude" that had been sold. During this interview Linda Eastman was at Paul's side in the Abbey Road Studio. She had the appearance of a steady girlfriend.

On Tuesday, October 1, 1968, Paul arrived at the Trident Studio to record "Honey Pie." With an English music hall sound as his backdrop, Paul blended delicate lyrics with saxophones and clarinets to recall the 1920s. It took only one cut to complete "Honey Pie." While there may have been rehearsal sessions, the Beatles were eager to finish the song. "The boys were up and down due to the Apple business," Clive Epstein remarked, "and I think that they were feeling the pressure to complete the new album." Paul was concerned about the quality of songs for the **White Album**, so he furiously rewrote one tune after another.

Three days later, he showed up at Trident Studio once

again with another unique song. "Martha My Dear" appears to be an affectionate tribute to McCartney's sheepdog. It was a song he had written during one of his forays with the Apple staff. Mark Lewisohn's pathbreaking book, **The Beatles Recording Sessions: The Official Abbey Road Studio Session Notes, 1962-1970** suggests that the song was not about Paul's dog. As Lewisohn points out, Paul "may have got the title from his canine friend but that was where the association ended." Like many of McCartney's songs it was a reflection on his changing life. The positive signs of artistic growth, the media publicity surrounding the records McCartney produced for Apple, and the prospect of cleaning up Beatle business affairs made this song a personal catharsis. Paul also continued to take great pride in writing and producing songs for other artists.

On October 5, 1968, "Those Were The Days" rose to the number 1 spot on the **Melody Maker** singles chart. Four days later Mary Hokpins appeared on the David Frost show performing "House of the Rising Sun." This appearance was highlighted by a Paul McCartney introduction. Since the Frost show was one of England's most popular, her appearance helped Apple record sales enormously

After the show Paul and David Frost spent an hour talking about the Apple business venture. McCartney was confident that the experiment would work, and he predicted that the company would alter the direction of the rock music industry. If they were successful business wise, McCartney reasoned, it would open up new financial and artistic avenues for rock musicians.

Shortly after the David Frost Show, Paul went back into the studio and played a demo version of "Why Don't We Do It In The Road?" Ken Townsend, the Abbey Road engineer, listened to the song. He suggested it was a tune that showcased McCartney's unique writing talent. It took only a few minutes for Paul and Ringo to tape the song on a four-track machine. As he recorded the song, Paul remarked to Townsend: "I want to do one quiet verse, one loud verse, that's it really." The result was a high pitched vocal and after five takes the song was finished. John remarked to **Playboy** that Paul completed the song himself in another room away from the other Beatles. "That's how it was getting in those days," Lennon reminisced. He was hurt by Paul's instant recording and saw it as a bad omen.

Paul defended his actions. "There's only one incident I can think of which John has publicly mentioned," McCartney remarked in 1981. "It was when I went off with Ringo and did "Why Don't We Do It In The Road?" "He did the same thing with 'Revolution No. 9," Paul remarked of Lennon. What these differences suggest is how strained the Beatles partnership had become by late 1968.

When this session was completed, Paul went into the Abbey Road library and made a copy of the July 18 recording of

"Helter Skelter" for his private collection. The tension and controversy surrounding the Beatles' career created a great deal of personal pressure and Paul often taped songs to relieve this anxiety. He maintains an extensive collection of Beatles materials but is very quiet about what is in his private archives. There was a feeling of accomplishment for Paul as he stored the memories of the Beatles' triumphs.

Other rewards helped Paul cope with the turmoil surrounding the Beatles. Among these was his continued productivity as an Apple producer. On October 11, 1968, Apple released the Bonzo Dog Bands "I'm The Urban Spaceman." The band formed in 1965 consisted a group of ex-art students who played for sheer fun and had no idea that they would pursue a musical career. After a cameo part in the Beatle film **Magical Mystery Tour**, the band became a London favorite. They began performing at Raymond's, a strip club in seedy Soho where the Bonzo Dog Band played to avant garde followers and developed a cult following. They also generated a great deal of newspaper publicity. When the groups leader, Neil Innes, approached McCartney with the song "I'm The Urban Spaceman," Apple agreed to record it.

When he first met with Innes, McCartney was struck by the Bonzo Dog Band's iconoclasm. Once he listened to their music, Paul realized that they were in the best tradition of the English music hall. In their music McCartney envisioned the freedom and the nonsensical lyricism that had appealed to the English since Lewis Carroll.

Because McCartney produced "I'm The Urban Spaceman," the single attracted a great deal of attention. The initial publicity over the Bonzo Dog Band was due to Paul playing on the song as Apollo C. Vermouth. This little tidbit of information was leaked to the press and the publicity over Paul playing ukulele generated chart action. The song reached number 5 on the British charts but failed to achieve American success. The following year the Bonzo Dog Band album was released in the United States with McCartney's name on the album jacket. It failed to sell.

As Paul enjoyed these triumphs, Jane Asher emerged in the press spotlight. She resented the media attention focused upon her ex-Beatle lover. For years she had competed with Paul as an entertainment figure. She believed that her talent and calling was equal to McCartney's and over the years Jane grew to resent his enormous media presence. So she decided to make his life miserable. She would call attention to him through the media.

As Paul was moving in new personal and musical directions, an interview with Jane Asher appeared in the **London Evening Standard**. She complained about Paul's lifestyle and intimated that he was not all he seemed to be. Using innuendo, cute little phrases and a hostile tone, Asher attacked her former lover with a ferocious intensity. She displayed a hatred that bordered on the pathological. There was no reaction from McCartney, but he was hurt by her willingness to rub his nose in the publicity trough. It made it much easier for McCartney to forget Asher. She had violated the cardinal rule that Paul had set up among his friends. Never speak to the press about personal matters.

Paul continued to immerse himself in the music. The **White Album** was reaching a critical stage. It was nearing completion, so the time had come to publicize it. The Beatles were testy with one another. The pressure over the lengthy recording sessions was evident and the Beatles needed a break. Circumstances arose which brought McCartney happily back into the recording studio and reduced the distractions threatening the group.

On October 14, 1968, Ringo Starr flew to Sardinia for a two week vacation. The **White Album** was almost complete. There was some final recording, mixing and overdubbing to finish it. Then George flew to Los Angeles. This left only Paul and John to work with George Martin on the final cuts.

A twenty four hour recording session on October 16-17, tied up many of the **White Album's** loose ends. It had taken five months to cut thirty-two songs. As the **White Album** prepared to be shipped, there was a great deal of anticipation over it. There were other worries for McCartney as the Apple Corporation continued its business activity.

In late October, 1968, Paul spent a great deal of time on the telephone at home and at the Apple office answering questions about Mary Hopkins' career. Her records were selling briskly in Italy, Spain and France. She was scheduled for an appearance on the American Ed Sullivan television show. Sullivan's Sunday night program was the premiere show spot for rock and roll records. If Hopkins did well on the Sullivan show, she was assured of continued American success. Paul did everything he could to prepare her for the brief segment on this popular TV institution. Not only was Hopkins' dress and grooming carefully reviewed but Paul urged her to unwind a bit on stage. She was stiff and flappable in front of live audiences and Paul worked with her on her stage presence. Paul also found some time for social life.

In the midst of these successes, McCartney found his greatest joy in his relationship with Linda Eastman. They had been close for some time. Finally, she told Paul that she would clean up her business in New York and move to London. The couple planned to live together. On October 31, 1968, Linda boarded an airplane in New York bound for London and four and a half months later, she married Paul McCartney.

There have been too many articles analyzing why Paul and Linda got married. The answer is a simple one. He wanted a family. There were other considerations. Linda came from an achievement oriented family. She was an independent woman who understood Paul's needs. Her continued support of his music was one of the reasons for the surge in McCartney's productivity. For the first time in his life he had a woman who believed in his talent and was not interested in competing with him.

Paul was optimistic about the future. He had hopes for the **White Album**. It represented the experimental approach to rock and roll music that he had advocated since the early 1960s. At home in St. John's Wood he talked for hours about the new album.

There was a retrospective nature to McCartney's conversations in October, 1968 as he recalled the success of the **Sgt. Pepper** album. Sitting in his living room, looking at the two paintings by Rene Magritte which hung on one wall, Paul talked at length about William Burroughs. The American author had appeared on the **Sgt. Pepper** album sleeve. For years Paul had been intrigued by Burroughs' iconoclastic prose. Poets, beat writers and experimental artists were part of McCartney's consciousness. He was searching for his own creative personality through these figures.

For the month prior to the release of the **White Album**, Paul took a working vacation. He showed up each day at the Apple office with an energy and enthusiasm that inspired his co-workers. "I think Mr. McCartney saw something in the future," one office staffer remarked. "It was a time in Paul's life," Bob Wooler remarked, "in which everything was going well. He asked me to come to London and work for him."

Paul was in love. His music was critically acclaimed. He believed that the new Beatle album would be their best to date. So the natural buoyancy and enthusiasm which Paul used to greet the press was rooted in success. There was another plateau for the Beatles to reach and McCartney envisioned himself as the leader in this rush to new heights.

The recording sessions that created the **White Album** were over and the Beatles were prepared to release it. No one realized the impact that the **White Album** would have upon the Beatles' career. The prospect of two Beatles discs on one album excited the fans. Few Beatle fans were surprised when the **White Album** became the best selling double album in history. It was not until 1977 when **Saturday Night Fever** eclipsed it, that the **White Album** was overtaken by the disco craze. It was also the first Beatles album to feature guest musicians in large numbers. Eric Clapton, Jackie Lomax, Nicky Hopkins and Dave Mason were among the best known musicians. The controversy surrounding Ringo Starr's unhappiness with the group was one of the most titillating aspects of the Beatles career. Peter Brown alleges that Ringo was frozen out of the group during the recording sessions. Others close to Apple Records blame London newspapers for blowing minor disagreements out of proportion. The problems with Ringo's ego were what caused the conflict. No one would praise Ringo's efforts, and he became testy and temperamental.

One of the Apple Scruffs remembers Ringo playing cards in a corner with Neil Aspinall and Mal Evans. "He no longer felt that he was a productive Beatle," Clive Epstein remarked. "The rest of the boys were developing their own musical identity and Ringo was plodding along with the same songs." Once the **White Album** began to sell, Ringo changed his mind. He was convinced that the Beatles would not have been successful without his drums. Despite their differences, the Beatles remained close when attacked by someone else. "I don't think the boys fought as much as the press speculated," Bob Wooler remarked. "They knew they were good; fame simply drove them apart."

Looking back upon the **White Album** in a 1985 **Musician** magazine interview, McCartney remarked: "The **White Album** was the tension album. There was a lot of friction." Paul also pointed out that the Beatles were becoming a bit too experimental. He worried that this might hurt sales. They were becoming too esoteric. "You can still make good music without going forward," Paul remarked. "Some people want us to go on until we vanish up our own B sides."

11: FROM THE WHITE ALBUM TO GET BACK, NOVEMBER-DECEMBER, 1968

On November 22, 1968 the Beatles' **White Album** was released. The speculation over its commercial future prompted critics to pounce upon it with nasty reviews. Inside the fold out album cover there were four small pictures of the Beatles and a large poster with pictures on one side and lyrics on the other. Newspaper critics pilloried the LP for its non-commercial look. But fans coveted it and the album instantly sold in the millions. McCartney was vindicated, because he had fought for the album concept.

Released with the simple title: **The Beatles**, the **White Album**, as it was dubbed, was a departure from the past. This guaranteed the Beatles a great deal of publicity and focused attention upon the music. "We wanted the **White Album** to be a look into our private song writing kingdom," McCartney remarked.

The album containing thirty songs was an eclectic mishmash. The tunes were not collaborations and there was little teamwork among the Beatles. It was the first public indication that the Beatles were in trouble. Clive Epstein remembered that when they returned from India, the Beatles presented George Martin with thirty-two new songs. Martin was horrified by many of the tunes. He believed that there were only a few commercial songs. There was barely enough material for a single album, Martin argued, and he tried to discourage a double LP. Martin argued that the material was not strong enough for a double album. There were other problems for Martin with the Beatles.

He was unhappy with their interest in LSD and American politics. One day Lennon took Martin aside and explained that LSD gave the Beatles' music color, small objects appeared huge in the recording studio and figures glowed and pulsated. Martin stared at Lennon and was speechless.

Paul was the last Beatle to use LSD and he praised the drug to London newspapers. The expanding creativity characterizing the Beatles' music, McCartney told one interviewer, was due to the drug. It opened his mind to new ideas and brought out images which had remained submerged for years. One important change in Paul was that he became more political. But it was a quiet, highly private, form of politics. Only a few close friends observed this new found political sophistication in Paul.

In the months prior to the release of the **White Album**, McCartney displayed an unusually strong interest in American politics. It was a private interest in which only a few of Paul's close friends were included. He talked daily to Barry Miles and often asked Alistair Taylor his opinion on the political condition. Paul feared that the Summer of Love and the peace dreams of his generation were about to end up in a violent confrontation with established authority. But he expressed these concerns only in private discussions.

What Paul witnessed in the political arena depressed him. The overwhelming vote for Richard Nixon in the 1968 American presidential election was a defeat for rock and roll music. If the parents couldn't halt the music, they could vote for the man who criticized rock and roll and vowed to stop its impact. Paul could see that it was a mistake to become too political. Yet, he was curious about American politics. The Beatle tours from 1964 through 1966 had whetted McCartney's political appetite.

He found it interesting that the British press charged that the American CIA was engaging in domestic surveillance. A small group of American radicals had befriended the Beatles and Paul listened in wide eyed amazement as Abbie Hoffman warned of the CIA's clandestine methods. Dr. Timothy Leary, the LSD guru, babbled on about the decline of American civil rights, and Paul identified with these radical arguments. He also read **The Economist**, a British economic and foreign policy journal, which argued that there was little real freedom in America. This helped McCartney to understand the machinations of the American right.

The protesting mobs who had badgered the Beatles during John Lennon's "we are bigger than Jesus" period prompted Paul to rethink his political ideas.

Although McCartney was intellectually sympathetic to radical causes, he was stung by the criticism that he was not political. Rather than becoming more political, Paul withdrew into his music and life. He had an inclination toward the political world but realized that it was a no-win situation. So McCartney read, thought, wrote and planned his future.

He finally had some time to pursue long neglected intellectual interests. Among the new books in McCartney's life was Tom Wolfe's **The Electric Kool-Aid Acid Test**. When this book was published to critical acclaim it established Wolfe as a journalist who had offered a popular view of the counterculture that was friendly and intelligent. Not only did this book discuss the wonders of LSD but it lead McCartney to read Thomas De Quincey's **Confessions of an English Opium Eater**. The De Quincy book, published in 1882, was widely read in England.

But it was making music which occupied Paul's time. The newly charged Beatle music was the catalyst to a great deal of bitterness within the group. Not only were Lennon and McCartney not co-writing songs, but George was emerging as a major composing talent. This did not sit well with neither Paul McCartney nor John Lennon. They had always looked upon Harrison as the young upstart member of the group.

While the Beatles had never been a harmonious group, there was very little negative publicity surrounding this phase of their career. The publicity machine ground out a fairy tale version of the Beatles' career that had little basis in fact. George Martin watched in astonishment as the Beatles fought with one another and complained about each others songs. George Harrison and Ringo Starr were so enraged by the problems with the **White Album** that they temporarily quit the group.

There were serious reservations from George Martin about the quality of the music. "I really didn't think that a lot of the songs were worthy of release," Martin explained, "and I told them so." The Beatles were polite to Martin, but they failed to heed his advice. Since many of the songs on the **White Album** were solo tunes by individual Beatles, there was a great deal of bickering over the final mixes. "The rot had already set in," George Harrison remarked. When the **White Album** sold two million copies during its first week of release, the criticism surrounding the large number of songs on the LP ended.

By numbering individual copies of the **White Album**, McCartney argued, the Beatles created a collectable. It was also McCartney who opposed the original title: **A Doll's House**. This title was John Lennon's idea for a tribute to Henrik Ibsen's 19th century literary masterpiece. McCartney challenged Lennon's assertion that the Beatles become more intellectual. In a heated argument McCartney accused Lennon of going beyond the Beatles' music. He pleaded with John to consider the fans. All they wanted was the music. Paul urged Lennon to wait for the critics reaction. John dismissed Paul's arguments. Within days, however, Lennon and McCartney patched up their differences. The **White Album's** success helped to end these acrimonious exchanges.

At least a dozen major reviewers praised the glossy-white laminated album jacket and the notion to include thirty songs in the LP. Simon Frith called the **White Album** a form of "low pop art." Tony Palmer, a critic for the **London Observer**, lectured British readers on the seriousness of Lennon-McCartney songs. Palmer pointed out that the English public didn't take the work of the Liverpool songwriters seriously, and he equated the **White Album** with the work of Schubert. "The last vestiges of cultural snobbery and bourgeois prejudice," Palmer wrote, "ended resistance to the Beatles' music." The general public ignored this tedious proselytizing by rock music critics and simply bought the album.

The debate over the LP cover, the two albums of music and the press reports of bickering within the Beatles' organization helped to sell the **White Album**. The Beatles were at a personal and musical crossroads, and there were signs of change.

The **White Album** was released just five years after the groups first English LP **With The Beatles**. No one noticed or celebrated this ironic twist. Nor did anyone point out the clear distinction between the Lennon and McCartney songs. The division within the Beatles was deep and the rupture would never be healed. The complex studio histrionics of the **Sgt. Pepper's Lonely Hearts Club** album were not evident in the **White Album**.

Equally significant was the influence that other albums had upon the Beatles. In 1966, Bob Dylan's **Blonde on Blonde** LP served as a model for McCartney's approach to the **White Album**. After listening to Dylan's eclectic double album, McCartney conceived a similar Beatle product. The idea germinated for more than a year and the Dylan songs never left Paul's head. There was nothing more than a foldout picture of Dylan on the cover of the album and the inside of **Blonde on Blonde** contained nine pictures. The only printing was on the spine: **BOB DYLAN BLONDE ON BLONDE**. McCartney was so intrigued by this album cover and Dylan's music that he listened to it for more than a year. One day he walked into the HMV record store on Oxford street and bought all the remaining copies. McCartney used these LPs to influence the other Beatles as well as people close to the group. Paul believed that Dylan's use of key studio musicians like Charlie McCoy, Al Kooper, Kenneth Buttrey and Hargus Robbin strengthened his music. Not to mention giving it a stronger commercial appeal. For some time Paul talked about using session musicians on Beatle recordings and now realized that Dylan's creativity was due in part to these session artists.

It was Dylan's musical diversity that inspired McCartney to experiment in the studio. There were other artists who brought new musical ideas to McCartney's mind. The appearance of Jimi Hendrix's **Electric Ladyland** album helped the Beatles' **White Album**, because the Hendrix material created a commercial market for lengthy, musically unconnected LPs. George Martin shuddered over the **White Album's** lack of a coherent theme, and complained about the disorganized presence of the songs. Paul countered Martin by suggesting that the **White Album** reflected musical ideas. He also informed Martin that he didn't give a damn it the LP sold or not. The Beatles were going to do their own music as they pleased.

At least a portion of the avant garde feeling of the **White Album** could be traced to Yoko Ono. Not only was Yoko a catalyst to Lennon's thirteen songs on the album but a creative force in the studio. She challenged the Beatles at every production turn, often creating irrevocable bad feelings, but she drove them to a higher level of musical perfection.

The well-chronicled 1968 romance between John and Yoko often ignores the influence that Yoko had on Lennon's song writing. While John and Yoko lived together in the small, cluttered apartment that Ringo Starr owned on London's fashionable Montague Square, they were beginning a new intellectual life. This would show in the songs that John wrote for the **White Album**. Things were changing rapidly within the Beatle kingdom.

The cover design for the new LP was not that of a traditional rock album. When Richard Hamilton designed the **White Album** he realized that the Beatles were moving beyond commercial considerations. Hamilton believed that a pure white jacket with a plain cover would represent an example of "esoteric art publications." EMI was initially horrified by the idea. How could anyone sell a Beatle album without an identifying mark? EMI changed its mind when the albums were numbered. By numbering the album in a seemingly awkward manner, the fans were led to believe that a hand numbering machine completed the job. This gave the LP a personal touch. A private little Beatle album for every fan. It was a merchandisers dream.

As the Beatles released the **White Album**, they remembered the nasty time that Frank Zappa had given the Beatles during a 1967 visit to London. While in London Frank criticized the Beatles' commercial success. John Peel, a pirate station DJ and a columnist for the underground **International Times**, found Zappa a bore. He also criticized Frank for an excessive amount of self-promotion and a mania for control. Zappa brought a film intended to hype the new album **We're Only In It For the Money**. The album cover, a hilarious parody of the Beatles' **Sgt. Pepper's Lonely Hearts Club Band** album, did not sit well with the Beatles.

Just before the Mothers of Invention released **We're Only In It For the Money**, Zappa called McCartney to request permission for the parody cover. McCartney didn't explode with rage, he simply let Frank know his discontent. A one-dimensional thinker, Zappa didn't realize that in McCartney's subtlety there was a quiet rage. When Paul informed Zappa that business managers took care of these details, it was McCartney's way of letting Zappa know that he had gone too far. Capitol Records then delayed the release of Zappa's record. This created nasty feelings and led to Zappa digging at the Beatles on subsequent European tours. So the Beatles used the **White Album** to strike back at Frank Zappa's **We're Only In It For the Money**. They produced an album which sold on its musical merits and not on cute publicity and rock and roll muckraking. Frank Zappa had appeared on the cover of England's trend setting **Melody Maker** music newspaper; this prompted McCartney to point out that Zappa could not stand on his music alone.

When Zappa released his Mothers of Invention album **We're Only In It For the Money**, not only were the Beatles offended but many musicians saw it as another example of Zappa's self-promotion schemes. Among rock musicians Zappa had a reputation for stingy financial arrangements. Frank loved to provide a house for the musicians, a car to drive around and free time in the studio. Frank kept most of the money. As Jeff Simmons remarked: "Frank knew we were into rock and roll and he provided the lifestyle." Zappa played the role of hip musician to the hilt and his criticism of the Beatles was a stronger mirror of his own unquenchable thirst for profit. Zappa realized that being hip meant staying ahead of the worlds greatest rock and roll band. Frank couldn't do it musically, so he became an eclectic sociologist. He failed on all accounts, but privately Zappa recognized how bohemian the Beatles were in their new musical identity. The roots of Zappa's criticism was the result of the Beatles educational background.

The art school education of many English bands bothered American rockers like Frank Zappa It was Lennon's wit that Zappa resented. Frank believed that he had a monopoly upon parody and irony. When Lennon went one step beyond Zappa's cute, but infantile, criticism the American rocker never forgave the Beatles.

The Beatles were changing. The old image of a self-contained, but controlled, rock band was a thing of the past. Suddenly the Beatles were a new band with a wandering talent. No longer did the Beatles sing safe commercial songs, but they were innovative and creative. After the **Sgt. Pepper's Lonely Hearts Club Band** album the hostility from American bands was enormous. The San Francisco based Jefferson Airplane complained that the Beatles were too complex. The reason for the Airplane's criticism was the stunning variety of songs on the **White Album**. During one of the Jefferson Airplane's frequent Fillmore appearances, they talked about the new Beatles with awe. No one could figure out where the Beatles got their musical ideas.

After an exhausting set at the Fillmore, Grace Slick, lead singer for the Jefferson Airplane, lit a cigarette and talked about the Beatles. "I thought that they were cute. Then I met Paul and found out there was substance to him. (Loud laughter). No pun intended, I mean he had a hell of a mind." Like many rock and rollers, Slick now took the Beatles seriously. The Grateful Dead's guitarist vocalist, Jerry Garcia, had a similar view. "I don't think the critics saw the Beatles as a new band in 1968," Garcia remarked, "they still did cute songs but there was now a purpose to their music."

The American critics failed to realize that there was an English minstrel tone to the **White Album**. The Beatles unwittingly parodied the street corner musician. Lennon's contributions were strongly in this vein. In "Dear Prudence" and "Cry Baby Cry" Lennon uses images of his new life with Yoko Ono. As Lennon told **Playboy**, Yoko inspired him to reach into a new musical direction. "It wasn't that she inspired the songs," Lennon remarked, "she inspired me." As John grew in new musical directions, the fans reasoned that he was breaking with the other Beatles. Nothing was further from the truth. John simply became a different person: one who saw a world outside the Beatles music.

Paul loved the new musical freedom. Unwittingly, Paul encouraged a new direction for Lennon's writing. Many of the songs on the **White Album** sketched a detailed story of recent Beatle events. Lennon's "Dear Prudence" was a simple song about trying to lure Mia Farrow's sister out into the sun at the Maharishi's retreat. As John looked into the Beatle past he wrote "Glass Onion" with its sly references to other Beatle tunes. He was free of the Beatles and "Glass Onion" indicated that he was wandering off in new directions.

The usual interpretation of Lennon's songs on the **White Album** is that they were snide and showed contempt for the Beatles. The reality is that John was writing new music and Paul was a strong supporter of Lennon's creativity. In particular, Paul was taken by "Julia," because of its sensitive picture of Lennon's mother. Since Paul had lost his mother at a young age, he played the master tape over and over again. He cried when he heard the final cut. There was still a strong bond between the two chief Beatles and nothing could break it.

This was one of the tragedies of the **White Album**. The Beatles could still make music but they did it apart from each other. Despite the tensions inherent in this situation, John and Paul were still friends. Not close ones, but they tolerated each other.

Of the dozen songs that Paul wrote for the **White Album**, some offer insight into his growth as a singer-songwriter. "Back In The USSR" is an attempt to recreate a Beach Boys type sound. In the recording studio John played a six string bass and George added a bass guitar. The high energy harmony of the Beatles indicated that not all was lost musically. On "Ob-La-Di, Ob-La-Da" Paul sang lead with John and George providing the chorus. Not only did Paul play the piano but he arranged the tune. It became an instant hit in England with the Marmalade and The Bedrocks recording cover versions that appeared briefly on the **New Musical Express** Top 30.

When Paul wrote "Ob-La-Di, Ob-La-Da," he was inspired by a band of the same name. The London-based rock group was short on talent but long on fun. Paul went to see them in a small club on Eel Pie Island and again during a Sunday jam session at the Camden Town flea market. What Paul thought was fun, was in reality a disaster to the other Beatles. So they looked askance at McCartney's tune "Ob-La-Di, Ob-La-Da," and the internal bickering continued to undermine the Beatles' unity.

From July 3 through July 15, the Beatles' worked on "Ob-La-Di, Ob-La-Da," and for almost two weeks there was constant turmoil over the song. After hiring session musicians for the tune, the Beatles rejected the final product. Richard Lush, an engineer at Abbey Road told Mark Lewisohn: "They'd do it one night and you'd think that's it. But then they'd come in the next day and do it again in a different key or with a different feel."

Ringo Starr was the first to object. This occurred after a marathon ten hour recording session. John was stoned and George didn't communicate. Everyone at these sessions agrees that the Beatles were no longer a functioning group. They couldn't stay together with so much tension and disagreement in the air. Paul was also becoming too dominant. He had usurped so many duties, powers, prerogatives and directions that the band no longer could make collective decisions.

There were a number of impressive songs written and performed entirely by Paul on the **White Album**. "Wild Honey Pie" was a tune where Paul sang as well as played guitar, bass and drums. On "Martha My Dear" Paul used the same technique. "Blackbird" continued the use of a double-tracked song with Paul playing an acoustic guitar with a blackbird singing in the background. On this song Paul taps out a drum beat on a table top.

There were songs written with collaborators. "Rocky Raccoon" was a McCartney song composed with John and Donovan while in India. The original title "Rocky Sassoon" was changed during the recording session. George played lead guitar and bass while Paul sang and added his own lead guitar and bass lines. When "Rocky Raccoon" was recorded at EMI on August 15, 1968 there was a festive studio atmosphere inspiring George Martin to add a honky tonk piano to the tune. It took all night to record "Rocky Raccoon." The song celebrated Paul, John and Donovan sitting on the roof of one of the Maharishi's buildings playing their guitars. The inspiration for this tune came to Paul during this moment of solace. Donovan added lyrics and John inspiration.

In the recording studio Paul often came up with songwriting ideas. Sometimes it took months for these songs to develop. A good example of this type of tune occurred at 3 A.M. on August 9, 1968, when Paul recorded "Mother Nature's Son." The other Beatles had returned home and the studio was empty. With an acoustic guitar Paul sang intensely about his experiences in India. The following month on September 16, 1968, Paul went into the EMI studio and recorded "I Will" with an acoustic guitar and bongo backing as Lennon played skulls. Two days later, Paul and John wrote "Birthday" and recorded it with Yoko Ono, Patti Harrison and others providing the chorus. It was a light hearted moment which suggests that the tensions were not as great as many have suggested.

Paul personally believed that "Helter Skelter" was one of the strangest songs on the **White Album**. After Paul wrote the song he confessed that he had read a review of a Pink Floyd record in a London newspaper. Consequently, he decided to record a song that was "Helter Skelter" in its tone and direction. As Paul sang lead, he brought in Mal Evans to play the trumpet and recorded the song on a new eight track machine. The story behind "Helter Skelter" was lost in the later declaration that Charles Manson was inspired to kill Sharon Tate by it.

Paul was ecstatic that when the **White Album** was released, it was a success with the fans and an enigma to the critics. In England the Beatles failed to place a record from the **White Album** on the single charts, but the LP still shipped gold. The **Billboard** Hot 100 charted the non-**White Album** song "Revolution" at the no. 12 position. The other songs from the **White Album** didn't make the charts. On the **Billboard** album listing the **White Album** went to number 1 in December, 1968 and was a charted LP for 144 weeks. With the exception of the **Sgt. Pepper's Lonely Hearts Club Band**, which remained 168 weeks on the Billboard listing, the **White Album** was the Beatles' most popular LP.

The day after the **White Album** was released the Beatles received bad news from the head of Bryce-Hamner, their accounting firm. Chairman Henry Pinsker announced that he was resigning his position as fiscal adviser to the Apple Corporation. In a pompous gesture, Pinsker thanked the Beatles for their business and then alluded to their financial difficulties. The Beatles were astonished that Pinsker delivered a series of well-publicized remarks about their lack of moral character. He spoke out against John and Yoko's affair and he talked at length about the Beatles' negative public image. It was the direction of the music, not the financial difficulties, which prompted Bryce-Hammer to end their business relationship with the Beatles.

The publicity over the **White Album** and the controversy surrounding the Beatle's accounting firm obscured McCartney's musical efforts. The day after the **White Album** was released the Bonzo Dog Bands song "I'm The Urban Spaceman" entered the **Melody Maker** chart at number 29.

On December 1, 1968, the Beatles announced that they were postponing plans for a concert until after Christmas. A publicity release confirmed rumors that the Beatles intended to return to live performances. Without consulting his mates, Paul rented the Roundhouse for an impromptu London concert. He hoped that this show would prompt the band to go back on the road. The publicity release had just the opposite impact. John, George and Ringo had no intention of touring. The other Beatles let Paul know unequivocally that they would not return to live concerts. To underscore their point, John was dispatched to tell Paul that they would not play the December 15th concert date. The other Beatles were upset that Paul rented the Roundhouse in London for a concert. They felt that he was usurping power. By not playing the concert they let Paul know the depth of their feelings. George and Ringo continually told Paul that they had solo projects in mind. Harrison had a movie soundtrack completed and was surprised when McCartney congratulated him on it.

When Harrison's soundtrack for the **Wonderwall** film was released on December 2, 1968, in America, McCartney was both happy and sad. He wished George well on his solo effort but Paul knew that the LP might hurt the Beatles' unity. The next day the U.S. charts reported that "Hey Jude" was number 2 and Mary Hopkins' "Those Were the Days" was number number 10 on the **Billboard** album chart. At the same time the **Sgt. Pepper** LP was no. 74 and **Magical Mystery Tour** no. 91 on the American album listing. This success inspired McCartney. He believed that it would guarantee Apple's corporate future.

During the 1968 Christmas season, McCartney continued to work on new Apple records. For years the Beatles had sent out a recorded Christmas greeting to the members of their British fan club. This tradition had begun in 1963 as a token of appreciation for the Beatles extraordinary fan support. By 1968, however, the Beatles were unable to get together to record a Christmas jingle. No one could figure out why the 1968 Beatle Christmas song was called "Happy Christmas." This strange tune concluded with a special soloist, Tiny Tim, singing "Nowhere Man." For all practical purpose the 1968 Christmas record was the last significant holiday message. The next year the Beatles' last Christmas single was a jumbled mess that had little to do with the holiday season.

As Christmas 1968 approached the Beatles were through as a rock and roll band. At twenty-eight Lennon was moving in new artistic and commercial directions. For some time Yoko Ono had opened up new vistas to Lennon's expanding intellect. As a result the founding Beatle left McCartney to move into his own distinct cultural milieu. George Harrison and Ringo Starr were tired of their limited role in the Beatles, and they yearned to make their own music.

During the three weeks prior to the Apple Christmas party, there was a great deal of activity in McCartney's life. Carlos Mendes, a Portuguese singer, recorded Paul's "Penina," and plans were made to break the record in the European market. On December 6, 1968, the **White Album** was certified as a gold record by the R.I.A.A. and the same day Apple released James Taylor's LP in the United Kingdom with McCartney playing bass on "Carolina In My Mind."

The **New Musical Express** awards for the best British and World Group was announced on December 6, 1968, and "Hey Jude" was voted the best single. The **White Album** was number 24 as the trendy British music weeklies recognized new artists. On the eve of the **NME** awards the English press realized that one Beatle had a new love interest.

The British tabloids discovered Linda Eastman during the first week of December, 1968. As London newspapers speculated on her forthcoming role in Paul's life, Jane Asher was mentioned in the past tense. Prior to the Christmas holiday, the Beatles' authorized biographer, Hunter Davies, left England for a Portuguese vacation. After completing the first intelligent biography of the Beatles, Davies took his wife and two small children to Gozo in Malta and then to Portugal for a well deserved rest.

As Hunter Davies relaxed in a rented house in Praia da Luz in the Algarve, he was awakened by a loud banging on the door. Stumbling to the cottages front door, Davies opened it to find a young man screaming:

"Wake up Hunter Davies, you bugger."

"I looked blurily out my front door," Davies remarked, "I was surprised to see a young man with a young woman and a five or six year old girl."

Davies realized that it was Paul McCartney. He remembered leaving his address with Derek Taylor in the event of an emergency. On a whim, Paul hired a private plane and dropped in on the Davies.' Neil Aspinall planned the trip and it suggested the closeness that McCartney had developed with Davies. It was a warm moment, Davies could tell that there was a mission in Paul's life and that he was happy. He not only bubbled over about the artistic accomplishments of the Apple Corporation but he talked enthusiastically about the Beatles future.

As McCartney and Davies talked, their conversation centered around the new girl in his life, Linda Eastman. Not only did Eastman come from a prominent New York family, but she was intimately acquainted with the rock scene. Unlike Jane Asher, Eastman was warm and lacked pretension. She had the ability to fit into any setting and she turned her charms upon the Davies' with considerable skill.

After giving Hunter Davies some whiskey as a Christmas present, Paul presented Linda Eastman to the Davies. It was not long before they all were at ease. The day after Paul and Linda arrived the local press asked McCartney to hold a press conference. He complied. When word of Paul McCartney's stay in Portugal spread, local citizens arrived with gifts of food and invitations to parties and restaurants. Paul was pleased by these affectionate gestures as he began an idyllic vacation.

For the next ten days Paul and Linda enjoyed a holiday with the Davies. As the McCartney-Eastman romance blossomed, Davies remembered that Paul was very good with children. There was no doubt that McCartney wanted a family. Heather Eastman was a gorgeous little girl whom Paul doted upon, and this was an important aspect of the developing romance. They were destined to marry and sixteen years later when Davies revised his Beatles biography, he offered some interesting insights into the McCartney marriage: "after sixteen years...they appear pretty secure."

As Hunter Davies suggested, Linda gave Paul the encouragement and support that he needed during the trying Apple years. She also nurtured his creative growth throughout the early Wings period. The family stability and sense of accomplishment fostered Paul's continued growth as a creative artist.

During his visit with McCartney, Davies listened to Paul talk about the **White Album**. McCartney's concern for the Beatles future struck Davies as unusual. Not only was Paul still a Beatle, but he was upset about the in-fighting and the business problems.

The seriousness of the Beatles' problems surfaced during the holiday season. On December 23, 1968, the annual Beatle Christmas party was held at the Apple Building on Savile Row in London. The party commenced in Peter Brown's elegant first floor office. Brown moved around the room with social skill and considerable charm. He effusively greeted the guests and acted like nothing was wrong in the Beatles' kingdom. The party was announced as an annual children's celebration, but this was forgotten in the mania to get close to the Beatles. After the children watched a magician and gaped at John and Yoko dressed as mother and father Christmas, there was a party for the adults.

With its expensive furnishings and elegant decor, Brown's office was an example of conspicuous consumption. At the end of the evening knives were stuck in the furniture and momentos and artifacts were taken. A felt marker was used to draw on the walls and girls phone numbers were written everywhere. Marcie "38D" Johnson left her phone number from London and Boston residences. Someone made a joke that Marcie must be related to the turkey. With great laughter the crowd massacred a 42 pound turkey and drank brandy, cognac and beer until the wee hours of the morning. The pungent smell of marijuana filled the air and Carol Paddon, a Secretary in the Press Office, fought off the advances of two California Hell's Angels. As John and Yoko sat on the floor laughing and staring at each other, there was a frenzy among the guests. As tension developed during the festivities, there were fist fights. Many people were staring at the wall. They were not only obviously stoned but not having much fun.

Soon the two California Hell's Angels, Frisco Pete and Billy Tumbleweed, began making fun of Lennon's beard. As they poked fun at John he looked on in terror. They were nasty, large, menacing types who had no Beatle hero worship. Because of their behavior Alan Smith, a rock music writer, began berating Frisco Pete.

"You're a filthy animal," Smith hollered.

"What, ju say?" Pete responded.

"Leave Mr. Lennon alone," Smith screamed.

Frisco Pete hit Smith in the eye and a trickle of blood ran down his horrified face. Smith fell onto Lennon and the party atmosphere disappeared. As Smith lapsed into child-like tears, John fled the room.

"I'm no longer a Beatle," John screamed running for his car.

"You miserable asshole," Frisco Pete cried out.

"You English queers need to learn a lesson," Billy

Tumbleweed screamed.

The two Hell's Angels left the building amidst a stunned silence. Heavy breathing was followed by people shuffling out into the street. The party was over. Without warning, Smith lapsed into violent sobbing and curled up into a ball, Lennon left the room screaming: "Fuck the Beatles."

There were other reasons why this party was a disaster. The most important one was that the guests were largely strangers, hangers on and the celebrity minded. The doorman at Apple, Jimmy Clark, watched the sullen faces enter Apple Corp. with their fine clothes and he speculated on why everything was falling apart. A large, but gentle, young man, Clark was astonished to find that George Harrison had invited the San Francisco chapter of the Hell's Angels to the Apple Christmas party. Only two Angels, Frisco Pete and Billy Tumbleweed, arrived in London for the celebration. Apple paid for their airfare and even shipped their motorcycles to England. They showed up at Peter Brown's office with a bevy of young girls.

The 1968 Christmas party was not only full of strangers but of bad feelings. The San Francisco Hells Angels and the large contingent of hippies who followed in their wake argued continually with Peter Brown and Derek Taylor. Harrison was amused, and he suggested that Apple do everything to make the Angels and their guests comfortable. At the Christmas party there was a long silence when Derek Taylor announced that John and Yoko had a special Christmas message.

After a period of uncomfortable silence, a tape recorder was turned on and large studio quality speakers blasted the sound of a baby's heartbeat growing weaker and weaker until it died. Few people understood this message for peace as Frisco Pete quietly lit a joint. Billy Tumbleweed looked bewildered and scratched the swastika on his arm. Few party guests knew what to make of the Lennon's Christmas message.

As the Beatles prepared for the 1968 New Year's Eve party there was a sense of foreboding. There was some satisfaction from the sales of the **White Album**. By December 28, 1968, the **White Album** entered the number 1 position on the **Billboard** album chart and remained there for nine of the next ten weeks. Another indication that the Beatles' record sales were expanding was evident when "Back in the U.S.S.R." entered the Polish radio charts at number 16 and "The Continuing Story of Bungalow Bill" appeared at number 17. Rozglasnia Harcerska, the official voice of Polish radio, introduced another Beatle song "While My Guitar Gently Weeps" and it rose to number 10. The Beatles' success behind the Iron Curtain was testimony to their universal appeal.

The Beatles' musical success failed to slow their disintegration. They could no longer talk with each other. There were frequent shouting matches and the tension over Apple's business affairs opened up old wounds and created new hatreds.

For years the Beatles were like a marriage Now it was time for a divorce.

In order to make the coming New Year's Eve celebration special, Paul decided to do some quick shopping at Harrods' Department Store. This London specialty store offered exotic imported food and Paul spent more than an hour picking up everything from smoked oysters to funny-shaped American crackers. Food, wine and a few well placed joints, McCartney reasoned, would bring the others back to their senses.

As Paul prepared for the Beatles' annual gathering at Cilla Black's expensively furnished Portland Place apartment there was trouble in the air. Paul hoped that from Black's comfortable terrace the Beatles and their Apple cohorts could renew old friendships and toast new business successes. Each year the party ambiance had been friendly and warm. But this changed by 1968. There was a nasty, testy atmosphere that ruined the party.

The annual Beatles New Year's Eve party had a tradition of sending the "darkest" member of the group into the street to find a piece of bread and coal. This symbolized food and warmth. In 1967 Ringo was sent out into the cold, snowy London streets amid laughter and merriment. In 1968 there was no longer a festive atmosphere. So the tradition was abandoned. It was an ominous sign. The people invited to the party had changed. Cynthia Lennon was missing. Brian Epstein was dead. John and Yoko didn't show up. Ringo's marriage to Maureen was in trouble and Jane Asher had another party. The newest addition, Linda Eastman, was nervous around the rock and roll royalty. George Harrison and Pattie were fighting, so the party offered little excitement. At midnight Pattie Harrison was heard crying in the bathroom. Depressed with the party, Paul walked out the front door and looked pensively out into the dark night.

A cloud hung over Portland Place and McCartney couldn't see the sky. He stood in the cold air thinking. The pressure of the **White Album** had taken its toll, but there was still an air of anticipation about the future.

In the midst of this atmosphere Paul McCartney dreamed of taking the Beatles back on tour. He reasoned that a carefully planned series of concerts would rejuvenate the band. For a month Paul badgered his colleagues to perform a live concert.

Once again Ringo Starr quit the Beatles for a week. Ringo soon returned and passed off his behavior as a temporary fit of depression. Despite their personal differences the Beatles remained the darlings of key music critics. William Mann, writing in the **London Times**, remarked that the **White Album** represented "thirty tracks (that) contain plenty to be studied, enjoyed, gradually appreciated more fully...." This review encouraged McCartney's scheme to bring the Beatles back out on the concert trail.

In order the reassemble the Beatles as a concert act, Paul

persuaded his Liverpool cohorts to record at Stage One of Twickenham Studios. Located just outside London this studio was remote, but comfortable, and it would allow the Beatles to play a live, in concert set.

At noon on January 2, 1969, the Beatles began filtering into the enormous recording complex. They had previously recorded scenes for the movies **A Hard Day's Night** and **Help!** at this studio. So they felt a sense of nostalgic relief once inside the facility.

As Paul McCartney got out of bed the morning of January 2, 1969, he was nervous about the recording date. His disagreements with Ringo Starr during the previous year had almost driven the Beatles hirsute drummer out of the group.

During the past year in the recording studio, Paul had berated George Harrison for failing to understand McCartney's musical direction. George had told Paul to "bug off." These tiffs frustrated McCartney, because he had genuine feeling for both Ringo and George. The pressure of making hits records had taken its toll and Paul found it difficult to get along with his long time mates.

These thoughts weighed upon Paul's mind as he prepared to drive to the recording studio. One morning as Paul ate his cornflakes he was struck by the possibility of failure. His past behavior had caused problems. He needed time to think. So Paul walked out of his St. John's Wood home and caught a public bus to the Twickenham Studio. It was not to save money, as some rock critics have suggested, Paul simply needed time to figure out the dynamics of this Beatle recording session. When Paul arrived at the studio he was half an hour late. The other Beatles were glumly eating toast and cornflakes while drinking tea. They looked uneasy. Yoko Ono hung onto John, George was quiet and Ringo appeared distant. No one knew what to expect.

As the catalyst to this recording session, Paul McCartney was the first to speak about the music. He wanted the Beatles to think not only about a new album but a film and a tour as well. If the Beatles didn't want to tour, Paul reasoned, perhaps they could produce a documentary film which would recall their past triumphs. Paul ached to get back on the road. He believed that the Beatles had lost contact with their audience. As a technician was adjusting the sound level, Paul and John began talking. Soon there were heated words and a loud thud. John kicked at the side of the drum set. Mal Evans ran up to avert a fist fight.

"You asshole," Paul screamed at John, "you fucking asshole." As Paul walked away there was silence. George lit a cigarette. Ringo slumped in a chair. Yoko walked nervously over to John and put her arm around him. The session appeared doomed. Mal Evans broke the tension by singing and dancing. This was one of his favorite pastimes to lighten the atmosphere. It worked. A calm set in and the boys were ready to get back to the task at hand. They were in the studio to tape some songs for a possible television show. The title, **Get Back**, would show that the documentary film was to bring the Beatles back to their musical roots. The director, Michael Lindsay Hogg, tried to persuade the Beatles to film **Get Back** in an exotic location. The sights and geography of Africa were appealing to Lindsay-Hogg, but this suggestion fell upon deaf ears. The Beatles were tired. The only place that would film and record was at Twickenham Studio.

Once the sessions began for **Get Back** there was hostility, tension and suspicion surrounding the project. For the next two weeks the Beatles arrived at the large, cold stage very early in the morning, and the band simply couldn't record in the morning hours. The two 16-mm movie cameras filmed everything and soon the natural buoyancy of the Beatles vanished.

The end of the Beatles was near. It would take some time for the success of the **White Album** to pass, then, trouble would once again set in. The problems with Apple's finances, the sharp personality conflicts, and the changes in the music business hastened the Beatles' demise.

12: THE FIRST NAIL IN THE BEATLE COFFIN, JANUARY-FEBRUARY, 1969

Paul McCartney was exhausted after the release of the **White Album**. It was a project that had not been a pleasant one for him. There were signs that the group was falling apart. When the Beatles aired their complaints to the press, every remark was duly reported. The impending air of controversy was greater than the arguments. To the casual observer it appeared that the Beatles' had broken apart. Yet, once the **White Album** was in the record stores, Paul approached John, George and Ringo about returning to the live concert stage.

Paul beieved that the **White Album** was a portent of things to come. He told Clive Epstein that despite the problems surrounding the **White Album** the Beatles were on the verge of a new career direction. Clive was astonished.

"I always thought that Paul had a fantasy about the Beatles returning to the concert arena," Epstein remarked. "They were through as a live concert act because of internal differences." Through the early months of 1969, Clive attempted to dissuade McCartney from the notion of touring. "Paul wouldn't listen to me," Clive explained. "The boys were unhappy with him and they had no interest in going out on the road."

As Clive indicated, a concert tour did excite the other Beatles. They made it clear to McCartney that touring was no longer a realistic possibility. So why did Paul persist? The answer to this question is an elusive one. Perhaps the Beatles had talked about performing somewhere in person. The idea of one giant concert a year had been bandied about from time to time. "I'll never forget the Beatles kidding each other about that special concert," Bob Wooler remembered. No one knew that the Beatles' concert days were long gone. "I waited in Germany for the Beatles to return," Tony Sheridan commented. "I didn't realize that they were through as a concert act."

McCartney's close friends speculated that he was lost without a live audience. So he began devising a plan to return to the concert stage. Even one live performance would be enough to mollify McCartney's ego. When he was alone with his friends, Paul talked about the rush he received while on stage. "Paul needed a new medium for his art," Clive Epstein remarked. "It was clear that a movie was McCartney's direction."

So it was McCartney who reasoned that a film was the answer. It could be a limited live performance, and the film could be released to theaters as well as television. Paul hoped to induce the other Beatles to rethink going on tour with a critically acclaimed movie.

The December 1968, holiday season temporarily derailed McCartney's plans. It was not until after the annual Apple Christmas celebration that Paul talked about new Beatle music. This behavior was a part of McCartney's personality. He needed to write new songs and make music. This was increasingly difficult to do without live concerts. So he began reflecting on the past. Suddenly the last Beatle concert took on a renewed importance. It was something that Paul couldn't get out of his mind.

Paul let Clive Epstein know how unhappy he was about the prospects of the Beatles never touring again. He was obsessed with the notion of touring. It was increasingly obvious that the other Beatles did not want to return to the concert arena.

Suddenly Paul feel helpless in the Beatles' affairs. He began to brood about the Beatles' last San Francisco show. This concert took on an air of importance that transcended the other events in the Beatles' illustrious history. McCartney forgot the circumstances which created the Beatles' last concert.

On August 31 1966, when Paul walked off stage after the performance at San Francisco's Candlestick Park, he didn't have an unusual feeling. It seemed like just another night in concert. "The Beatles were bored," Bill Osterloh, a San Francisco police lieutenant, remembered, "they seemed tired of performing." This opinion was echoed by many close to the Beatles. The Candlestick Park show became a symbol for McCartney. One that reminded him that the Beatles had missed a golden opportunity by not going out on tour. He had argued for almost three years that the Beatles were cutting their financial throats by not touring.

In January 1969, Paul cornered Clive Epstein and talked about the San Francisco show. "Paul was obsessed with a return to the stage," Clive remembered. Perhaps a concert film would bring the Beatles magic back. During the first week of January, Paul carefully collected tapes, old records and other reminders of the past. To facilitate a Beatle tour, Paul brought out souvenirs of a happier time.

Paul also allowed himself some personal indulgence. One of McCartney's favorite artists was an American blues singer Jimmy McCracklin. In 1958 McCracklin's hit, "The Walk," had inspired McCartney's early song writing. But it was a recent McCracklin song that Paul brought to the Beatles' attention. McCracklin's tune, "Get Back," which was released in 1967, failed to make the American charts, but it was a marvelous rock and roll song. McCartney loved its infectious chorus. The staccato cries of "Get Back" inspired Paul. Listening to McCracklin's "Get Back" there is no mistaking the cadence, lyrical similarities and tone to the Beatles' song of the same title. Even though they are different songs, McCracklin's influence was a pervasive one. McCartney's "Get Back" was written after listening intently to McCracklin's tune.

"I listened to "Get Back' by the Beatles and knew my song

had influenced it," McCracklin remarked. "Those boys had done my song 'The Walk' and I could hear my chorus line in 'Get Back." McCracklin added that he was proud to be associated with the Beatles' music.

During the first week of January 1969, Paul continually played tapes from the old days. But it was McCracklin's record, "Get Back," that intrigued the Beatles. "I don't think Paul could have brought out a better record," John Lennon remarked to Clive Epstein, "it made us think about getting a little closer musically once again."

It was in this atmosphere that the Beatles began practicing in the Twickenham Studio on the project entitled "Get Back" which resulted in the film **Let It Be**. The proposed Beatle film used the working title "Get Back" to excite the Beatles and bring them back to their roots. The project was full of promise but from the beginning there was a foreboding feeling..

Paul was excited over the prospect of a live show. From the first day the Beatles gathered the project was in trouble. McCartney did everything he could to make it an exciting venture.

To make the project work, Paul appealed to Lennon's vanity. He told John during the early stages of the **Let It Be** sessions that they could make music like in the old days. But they could do this only if Lennon agreed to return to live performing. Paul admitted that he needed John's help and this was a boost to Lennon's confidence.

Everyone was surprised to learn that Lennon hoped to return to live performances. The problem was that he hoped to do so as a solo artist. John was through as a Beatle. He liked the concert stage and missed the audiences. He also had some recent performing experiences which once again whetted his appetite for the concert stage. John had appeared in the Rolling Stones' abortive film **Rock 'n' Roll Circus** and also was part of the "Alchemical Wedding" a Christmas event sponsored by the British Underground. Both of these live performances intensified John's resolve to go back on the road.

The changes in the rock music business and the rise of a new cultural milieu was apparent in 1969. It was the last stand of the hippie sub-culture with concerts at Woodstock and Bob Dylan appearing before half a million people on the Isle of Wight. There was an excitement in the air, and, to many observers, the Beatles were no longer as important to the scene.

They had suddenly become passive statesmen in the rock revolution. The question of age, generation gap and musical content plagued the Beatles. McCartney recognized the changes in the music scene and argued that film was the future rock and roll medium. No one listened to Paul or seemed to care. Long before MTV, McCartney's commercial sense told him that film and television were the wave of the future.

What did result from this early January 1969 filming was

a continued rift between George Harrison and McCartney. Sometime during the first week of filming at the mammoth Twickenham Studio something went wrong. Since the Beatles were required to report early in the morning to this desolate and uncomfortable sound stage there was constant friction. The tea was cold, the help grumpy and the working conditions abysmal. No one seemed to realize that they were working with the famous Beatles. This attitude galled George because he was often the first to arrive. He spent his time trying to keep warm and his bodily needs were ignored.   He stood largely unnoticed in a corner. Harrison fumed and fussed and no one cared.

These slights, real and imagined, were intensified by McCartney's role in creating the Beatle movie. Paul was everywhere during the filming. Sitting at the grand piano at Twickenham film studio, he looked more like a media mogul, Harrison thought, than a pop star.   During the lengthy filming schedule Harrison was hostile to the changes McCartney brought to the Beatles.

Not only did Paul have ideas about the music, the lighting, and the stage presence of the band, but he also instructed the other Beatles on how to perform the songs. As George sat quietly in a corner watching McCartney take over the band, he tried his best to keep quiet. There was a nauseous feeling in his stomach and he felt ill. Harrison worried about his health. The strain of being a Beatle was too great. He was ready for life in the countryside.

The cameras whirred as Paul worked on correcting Lennon's off key vocals on "Across the Universe." When Paul and John sang the "Two of Us" there was a sign of approval radiating from McCartney.   Then Paul moved in to help Harrison on **I, Me, Mine** and the tension in the studio built. As Harrison remarked in his autobiography, **I, Me, Mine,** "We had been away from each other after having had a very difficult time recording the **White Album** and...I couldn't stand it." Harrison continued: "it's not fun anymore." What George needed was an excuse to quit the Beatles. He got it shortly after this incident.

Innocently, one night in the studio Paul began instructing George on how to play the guitar. This action in the Twickenham Studio weighed heavily on Harrison. McCartney had gone too far. He was not only directing every move, but he failed to show Harrison the proper respect. The boys had too much free time on their hands and they were unhappy with more than just the music. It was at this point that Harrison began reviewing his underdog role with the Beatles and he considered pursuing other options. But George needed time to think.

So on a cold winter night on January 9 1969, Harrison went home and vowed to quit the Beatles. He sat at home and contemplated his years with the Beatles. The early concert era was a pleasant one, but it was followed by three years of nightmares. George still liked to perform the old songs. They had played some Chuck Berry, Elvis Presley and Little Richard tunes in the Twickenham studio and Paul always had a tape handy with roots rock songs on it. This gave George a schizoid feeling. His loyalties were divided between the old and the new Beatles.

The next morning George showed up at Twickenham Studio vowing to quite the group. He was fed up with McCartney's control, the demand to return to touring and the constant interference from the media. It was time to retire to the country and grow flowers. The cold weather, awful food and constant harassment from the groupies drove Harrison crazy.

Finally, during a lunch break on January 10, George announced that he was quitting the Beatles. His frenetic state of mind combined with McCartney's "musical meddling" created a nasty and divisive atmosphere. No one recognized Harrison's obvious unhappiness. Each Beatle was into his own little world. Harrison's remark shattered the illusion that the Beatles were a tight performing and recording unit. Harrison's announcement took the Beatles by surprise.

After it there was a dead silence. Ringo had already quit the group but he returned in a day. The night that Harrison decided to quit the group he drove home to Esher dejected. He was physically and emotionally exhausted and he immediately reconsidered his decision to quit the Beatles. The psychological toll that the 1960s had taken on George Harrison was obvious to Clive Epstein. "He had aged and he was unhappy, but he was a team player," Epstein recalled. The reason that Harrison continued on with the Beatles was his loyalty to the **White Album**. The new album was important to George, if for no other reason than his songs on it. So George quit the Beatles for one day. He returned with little explanation.

One of the reasons that Harrison was so disenchanted was McCartney's precise attitudes in the studio. "I don't think that Paul and George were on the same wavelength," Clive Epstein remarked. Whatever the problem, the Beatles were being torn apart. The rift was subtle but one that was apparent in all aspects of their music. There were other factors tearing the boys apart. The Apple management structure was a continual source of irritation.

When an audit was taken of the Apple Corporation for 1969-1970 it revealed that there were twenty areas where Capitol and EMI had "inaccurately accounted" for promotion, sales and manufacturing costs. Eventually, this report by the accounting firm of Satin, Tenenbaum, Eichler and Zimmerman revealed that there were $19 million dollars in unpaid Beatle royalties. McCartney suspected this was the case in early 1969, but he was more concerned about the business structure at Apple.

The Beatles' hired help was either uniformly excellent as in the case of Apple General Manager Alistair Taylor or disastrous as in the case of Alex Mardas. For years Magic Alex had promised all sorts of marvelous sound inventions. During the filming of **Let It Be** he failed to deliver a special sound mixer. His Swiss manufactured sound system was no more than talk. The machines that would take rock music into a new phase were on the drawing board but Magic Alex couldn't produce them.

It was at this point that Paul complained about the failed promises of the Greek sound wizard. Magic Alex frustrated Harrison and infuriated McCartney. One day at Abbey Road, they had a friendly shouting match about Magic Alex's shortcomings. The controversy over Magic Alex intensified the constant bickering and led John Lennon to holler at the other Beatles for not standing behind their long time friend.

The problem was not just Magic Alex, but the large number of sycophants who hung around the Twickenham Studio. They helped to doom the project as did the janitor who inadvertently turned on the air conditioning while the Beatles were recording.

The attempt to bring back the old days even stretched to a studio version of "Maggie Mae." This was a Liverpool sailor song that was popular in local pubs. The tune was one that John had performed in 1957 at the Woolton celebration and Paul hoped that it would spark nostalgic musical images. It appeared to do just the opposite. Lennon was now more determined than ever to quit the Beatles.

George Martin remembers that the Beatles bickered constantly during the filming. There were tensions resulting from too many takes in the studio. This seemed to stretch the music and make it generally uninspired. The attempt to recapture the old magic brought a drudgery and staleness to the Beatles.

As things became disjointed and emotional, Paul began singing a new song with the working title "Loretta." McCartney was afraid that someone would recognize that Jimmy McCracklin's tune was the inspiration for "Loretta," so he asked everyone not to mention the blues tune. Once McCartney rewrote the song, it became his own personalized "Get Back." McCracklin's song was obscure and wasn't a hit in the American market. But even this magnificent tune wasn't enough to bring the Beatles back together. After the film crew completed twenty-eight hours of footage they left the shambles of the Twickenham Studio unaware that the Beatles were an act destined for self destruction. This movie was the first nail in the Beatles coffin. Others would follow.

The one hundred odd tracks that the Beatles recorded during the **Let It Be** sessions were inspired, insipid and uneven. Clive Epstein called these sessions brilliance backed with a careless musical direction. A perfect ending to a legendary musical career. Paul was depressed with the results. John argued they could release any of it and have a hit. George wasn't so sure. Ringo didn't care. The game was coming to an end.

By January 16 1969, the Beatles completed their last

rehearsal session at Twickenham Studio. After a three day weekend the cameras and recording equipment were moved to Central London. The Beatles had a new recording facility in the basement of their Apple headquarters at 3 Savile Row near the tourist infested Piccadilly Circus. Paul still liked to think of this period as one where the Beatles performed as nature intended. That is Paul didn't want any form of electronic gadgetry. It took all day on January 20 to set up the cameras and sound equipment.

On Wednesday, January 22 1969, the Beatles finally overcame the long delay by bringing down some equipment from the Abbey Road studio. When Magic Alex's electronic innovations didn't materialize, the Beatles began to record. Young Alan Parsons, a teenage audiophile, was sent to Abbey Road to borrow equipment. Parsons remembers Magic Alex's sound machine as a large and unworkable monstrosity that failed to record anything without a hum. The true worth of Magic Alex's electronic gadgetry was demonstrated when he sold it to a local pawn show. For all practical purposes this was the end of Magic Alex Mardas.

George Martin was nervous about the recording sessions. The material recorded at the Twickenham Studio was not professionally taped and the songs were little more than rough rehearsals. Because of his strong feeling for the boys, Martin often stayed away from the filming. He viewed the movie, **Let It Be**, as an unfortunate foray blending film and music.

Just as everything fell apart George Harrison showed up one day with American organist Billy Preston. Not only did Preston sit in on the **Get Back** recordings, but he signed a recording contract with Apple Records. The musical excitement and infectious humor that Preston brought to the studio saved the day.

The Wednesday January 22, session was one that McCartney loved. Paul taped an instrumental entitled "Rocker" and completed a cover version of the Drifters' 1960 hit "Save the Last Dance For Me." Another McCartney warm up tune was a version of Canned Heat's "Going Up the Country." Not only did Paul love going back into the studio, but he laid down an excellent version of "I've Got A Feeling."

After a night of rest Paul returned to the studio and worked on "Get Back." It was decided that this would be the title song for the new album. In a light mood Paul used some interesting lyrics in the original "Get Back." He sang "don't dig no Pakistanis taking all the people's jobs, get back to where you once belonged." Amidst a great deal of joking the Beatles rehearsed the song using these lyrics. When the tune appeared on bootleg releases, it caused a minor furor. No racism was intended. It was simply Paul's way of having fun.

The tenth take of "Get Back" was marked the best one on the studio recording box. As Mark Lewisohn has shown the Beatles returned to a pre-1965 recording technique during these sessions and the results were magnificent ones.

McCartney's studio magic continued on Friday January 24, when he recorded "On Our Way Home." It was later retitled "Two of Us" and became a key song on the album and in the movie. Paul wrote the song for his wife, Linda, and omitted the bass guitar during the recording session. Paul loved this tune and sang it twice in the film **Let It Be**. Because of his roots background, McCartney recorded a song entitled "Teddy Boy" to recall the old days. There was a hilarity to "Teddy Boy" that inspired the fragile voiced McCartney.

While he recorded "Teddy Boy," Paul had great fun. He completed three versions of the song as well as two break downs during the recording process. This song bored John because of its corny inflection of past Liverpool times. Lennon was thinking about the future, not the past, and he was clearly irritated by McCartney. The song remains unreleased by the Beatles but Paul re-recorded it for his first solo album.

From this cold Friday session in January the McCartney-Lennon tune "I've Got A Feeling" was considered a strong one and suitable for commercial release. This song was one of the few collaborations between the two chief Beatles during this period. It wasn't enough to save the group. There were, however, some moments of harmony and a spirit of cooperation that prompted the Beatles to continue their sessions.

The Beatles' eagerly recorded for the rest of the weekend. The Saturday, January 25 session was an unusually productive one for McCartney. He completed a take of the "Two of Us" in which he shared vocals with John. Another version of "Let It Be" was recorded which was the best cut of this McCartney inspired Beatle standard.

Suddenly the Beatles were a tight group. On Sunday June 26, the old magic appeared to return. Paul benefited from this atmosphere as he taped the ballad "The Long and Winding Road." This song was one that McCartney loved, and he was furious when Allen Klein gave the tapes of the recording sessions to Phil Spector for remixing. When Spector added an orchestra with violins, a harp and a female chorus, McCartney protested. In 1973 in an interview with Peter Gambaccini, Paul stated: "I'm not struck by the violins and ladies' voices on 'The Long and Winding Road." McCartney was so upset with Spector that he worked up a new version of the song for the 1975-1976 Wings tour.

Another version of "Let It Be" was cut as the Beatles continued to search for the right commercial track for this exquisite song. On Monday January 27, the Beatles continued to record "Let It Be" and found themselves with 14 separate tracks of this tune. So it continued with such silly introductions as John's parody line "Sweet Loretta Fart she thought she was a cleaner but she was a frying pan." This play on words was typical of John Lennon's humor. It was also juvenile fun which hid the tremendous pressures tearing the group apart. No one laughed at John. In fact, Paul called him childish. George went to the bathroom and Ringo had a smoke. It was not a pleasant time.

For the next three days the Beatles continued to work in the studio. The recording sessions produced excellent results and the **Get Back** material came together nicely. Few people in the studio could understand why the music was so strong. Perhaps conflict did create great art. There were other reasons for this creativity. The Beatles were using ideas from their past songs. A montage of old Beatle tunes was used by the group to achieve commercial success.

In order to reestablish their live concert capabilities, the Beatles decided to perform a noontime concert on a London business building. On January 26 1969, the idea for a rooftop concert emerged during a Sunday drinking session that got out of hand. The most convenient site was the roof at the new Apple Studio at 3 Savile Row in downtown London. The Thursday, January 30, rooftop show was a 42 minute concert which made for great footage in the **Let It Be** movie. A typically cold London day brought out a large lunch time crowd. The noise and the commotion was not new to the Beatles' Savile Row offices and the locals were looking for a good time. They found the Beatles shivering on the Apple office rooftop performing a loud concert which drew complaints from the neighbors.

It was Paul who said: "Why don't we play the songs in front of a few people?" The sound men and engineers suddenly found themselves on the roof of the Apple building with equipment, musicians and a large group of hangers on. It was a strange sight. "I couldn't figure out what the boys were doing," Clive Epstein stated, "perhaps they wanted to recapture the old magic."

No one hoped to do this more than McCartney. He reasoned that some songs would be better performed in a concert setting. He had a favorite tune that he believed the Apple rooftop could rescue. The song that Paul selected was "I've Got a Feeling." Because he had written half of it with John, Paul hoped that it would bring them together again. He rehearsed it for four days prior to the Apple rooftop concert. While Paul's version of "I've Got A Feeling" was a splendid one, it wasn't the highlight of the rooftop concert. Once again Paul had misjudged John's feeling about the Beatles' music.

The closing tribute to the project saw McCartney attempting to perform "Get Back" while the police marched onto the roof. In support of Paul, Maureen Starr screamed encouragement and Paul ends the session by muttering "Thanks Mo." It was a fitting tribute to a strange day. When the **Let It Be** album was released a studio version of the title song from the January 27 session was spliced together with the closing comments that McCartney made during the rooftop performance. It gave the song a wonderful feeling. One that showed the spontaneity of the **Get Back** project. Alan Parsons, the young recording engineer, remarked: "To see the Beatles playing together and getting an instant feedback from the people around them, five cameras on the roof, cameras across the road, in the road, it was just unbelievable,....a magic, magic day."

When the Beatles assembled on Friday, January 31 1969, at the Savile Row studio they cut the final songs for the **Let It Be** album. Paul was concerned about which versions of "The Long and Winding Road" and the "Two of Us" would be used on the album. Watching the Beatles in the movie **Let It Be** there is no doubt that McCartney was in charge and concerned about his music.

As Ray Coleman suggested: "At the beginning of 1969 the Beatles were beginning to crumble." The disintegration began in February when the Beatles found it difficult to work together in the studio. Although they would record the **Abbey Road** album later in 1969, for all practical purposes the group had disbanded.

Alistair Taylor, the Beatles Mr. Fix It, was one of the more astute observers of the **Get Back** sessions. "The recording studio in the basement was an enormous drain on resources," Taylor wrote. As Apple's General Manager Taylor saw the handwriting on the wall. It spelled bankruptcy. "We actually went through a period when nobody was allowed to do any business until John's soothsayer had thrown the I Ching!" With this observation Taylor left Apple and the Beatles. It was a wise decision. They were through as a recording group.

When the film **Let It Be** appeared in the spring of 1970 it documented the end of the Beatles. It was a month after the official breakup of the group, but it suggested that January, 1969 was the first nail in the Beatles coffin. It would take more than a year to end the group as a performing and recording unit.

13: ANOTHER NAIL IN THE BEATLE COFFIN, LATE FEBRUARY-MAY, 1969

In London the spring mornings are often unpredictable. The fog creates a lazy atmosphere and the city limps along. On March 12, 1969, a cool, lifeless day greeted the businessmen scurrying to work. There was little need to hurry as winter had not yet shed its coat. The dreary weather made it difficult for news people to find a good story. The Beatles were always a possibility on a slow news day. The press was busy as Paul McCartney was about to get married.

The previous day the Apple press office announced McCartney's wedding. Paul's brother, Mike, was in Birmingham appearing with his group, Scaffold, when he learned of the impending nuptials. After performing in two local night clubs, Mike returned to his hotel room. Paul called. They talked at length about the wedding. Mike wished his brother well and warned him to beware of the press.

Because of McCartney's distaste for the media, Apple Scruffs were the main source of press speculation on McCartney's impending marriage. Local newsmen descended upon the St. John's Wood home on Cavendish Avenue, and a circus atmosphere prevailed in this normally staid neighborhood. Once McCartney's wedding was announced, hundreds of Apple Scruffs descended upon London.

One of Paul's scruffs, Jill, was down from Birmingham getting her hair done when she heard about the marriage. She ran out of the hair styling parlor, got into her mini and drove to Paul's St. John's Wood home. Like many scruffs, Jill imagined that she had a personal relationship with McCartney. When she arrived outside Paul's house there were little knots of girls crying in the street. One scruff, Margo, offered Jill a room and they cried late into the night.

Another scruff from San Francisco, Barbara, painted her face with glo-in-the-dark paint and vowed never to remove it. She was joined by Brenda from Kansas who had a Paul McCartney tattoo on her left breast. It was a strange sight as the fans milled around McCartney's home in obvious hysteria.

Unaware of the adulation and weeping, Paul McCartney and Linda Eastman hurried to Marylebone Registry to get married. What did the marriage mean? That question was on the lips of the Apple scruffs as they paraded in front of McCartney's house. Everyone speculated. Few had answers. McCartney was the only Beatle who had remained single for a lengthy time. Paul believed that this helped his chances for a more stable marriage. In an interview some years later, Paul recalled the general decline in English family values in the 1960s, and his own need for a more tranquil lifestyle.

It was not surprising that on his wedding day the press speculated on the reasons for the other Beatles not attending the ceremony. The day prior to Paul's wedding a series of strange excuses emanated from Apple's press office. It was an attempt to explain why McCartney's life long musical mates would not attend the wedding. The answers were ludicrous ones. John and Yoko begged off because they were finishing an album, **Unfinished Music No. 2: Life With The Lions**. George Harrison lamely commented that he had some work at do at the office. Ringo Starr had chores around the house that his wife had scheduled. None of these explanations were convincing, and they suggest the depth of hostility among the Beatles toward McCartney.

What made Paul furious was that the London press reported that Patti Harrison had driven to Ozzie Clark's Design emporium to pick up a new dress for a "Pisces" party that she was attending. This party was to be graced by the presence of Princess Margaret and Lord Snowdon and would attract the cream of London society. This angered Paul, because he realized that his mates didn't care about his impending marriage.

After Patti Harrison paid for her dress and walked outside she found a note on her car windshield. The scribbled card read: "Call Me." Inside the cigarette pack that the note was attached to there was a small piece of hashish. Patti simply put it in her pocket. She took the dress home and after a bath the doorbell rang. It was the police.

Detective Sergeant Norman Pilcher, a sly smile on his face, stood at the door with a drug sniffing dog named Yogi. After a quick search, Pilcher found the drugs and the Harrison's were booked. Sgt. Pilcher called a press and informed the media that he was saving the Harrison's from "harder drugs. If Pilcher was a savoir, Harrison's friends remarked, he was not too smart, because he overlooked more than 37 pounds of various drugs. This controversy upstaged Paul's marriage.

To McCartney this incident was meaningless. He was more concerned with the slow, methodical rain that interfered with the wedding. Mike McGear was late for the ceremony, further delaying the wedding. This interim allowed the press to interview the "McCartney widows" as the press called the scruffs. It was a new low in British journalism as one reporter viewed with another to find a new angle.

Once inside the Marlebone Registry, Mal Evans made small talk while Peter Brown looked disapprovingly out a small window at the score of young girls standing in the street. Mike McGear was concerned about his hair and combed it incessantly. He looked out onto the street and remarked that the scruffs looked plain, simple and distraught. They had every reason to be unhappy. The last bachelor Beatle was about to become a married man.

As Paul and Linda's wedding ceremony concluded, the English press went on a rampage. They looked for anything that would cast a disparaging light upon McCartney. They failed to find any new or interesting scandals. Eventually, London newspapers found a girl who was the symbol of the McCartney widows. The young lady, Jill Pritchard, was featured on the front page of a leading London newspaper and she became the symbol of the grieving young fans. Pritchard was a hairdresser, a fan and someone who knew almost nothing about the Beatles. Her airheaded comments brought snickers and failed to sell newspapers. The St. John's Wood church, as the Apple scruffs referred to Paul's house, was never the same after the wedding. For Paul the wedding offered solace, peace of mind and a chance to focus his attention upon the pressing business and musical needs of the Beatles.

Paul envisioned a future that was tranquil. The problems with the Apple business venture, the increasing business animosity amongst the Beatles, and the grating hostility that was smoldering over the Northern Songs fiasco frustrated McCartney. He had a mercurial temper that could explode into a rage. The tension from dealing with the Beatles' complicated business affairs took its toll upon Paul.

In a conversation with Mal Evans, Paul exploded and talked at length about the long running battle with the Beatles' music publishing company. The differences over the Northern Songs contract and Paul's penchant for business analysis prompted him to tear the agreement apart.

When he gave Mal Evans his opinion on the deal, Paul displayed a sense of outrage. Not only did McCartney feel that It was not a pleasant story, but talking about this fiscal debacle brought back memories of his youthful Liverpool poverty.

Paul remembered the incident like it was yesterday. Once the Beatles went into the recording studio they needed a publishing agreement. When Brian Epstein brought the Beatles to London to record "Love Me Do," George Martin suggested that they ring up Dick James to work out a music publishing deal.

From the time that he first saw James, McCartney didn't like him. He was from the old school of song pluggers. Personally, James was a cigar chomping, balding entrepreneur who had little knowledge of rock and roll music. There was a slick tone to his speech. However, he was no fool. James was a shrewd man who had the ability to turn out contracts that made him a rich man. James was rapidly becoming a power in the London publishing industry. His contract with the then unknown Beatles brought James into the mainstream of music publishing world.

As he recalled these events, McCartney remembered in detail how anxious Brian was to make the deal with Dick James.

In a late night conversation at his Apple office, Paul recalled those days.

He remembered that Brian Epstein arrived a half an hour early for his appointment with Dick James. It was winter and Brian worried about London's traffic delays. Dick James explained that a company he would call Northern Songs, out of respect to Liverpool, was to be the publishing arm for John Lennon and Paul McCartney. James had no idea about the magnitude of the two chief Beatles songwriting. So James suggested that a separate company would allow him to manage the Beatles' songs and he considered a 50-50 split to be fair.

Eventually, Northern Songs was incorporated as a public stock on the London Stock Exchange. When it was set up as the Beatles' song publishing company, the idea was to provide a vehicle for the Beatles to write and publish their own songs. This ended the need for song writers, pluggers and musical arrangers. In London on Denmark street the professional songwriters shuttered as the songwriting and musical styling of a new generation ended the dependence upon the chain-smoking professional songwriter. By signing new rock acts like the Beatles, James was suddenly in the forefront rock music publishing business.

While he was an honest man, there was very little that Dick James did which made the Beatles happy. He wore the wrong suit. He was too Jewish. He was too old. He was too conservative. For almost six years the Beatles complained about James. It was a tragedy because the publishing controversy was another nail in the Beatles' coffin.

The reason for the Northern Songs deal was a simple one. The Beatles could avoid paying taxes through this intricate business plan. Dick James also convinced Brian Epstein that Northern Songs was a sound investment. After James worked out the business details, the Beatles entered their first corporate nightmare.

James persuaded John and Paul to incorporate Northern Songs. He failed to warn them that they would lose control of their product. Taking advantage of Lennon and McCartney's lack of sophistication in songwriting and publishing matters, James convinced them to give up 50% of their earnings from songwriting in return for James business expertise and a tax deduction. It was poor advice and reeked of self interest. The terms of the Northern Songs agreement stipulated that John and Paul each receive 20% of the company stock with Brian Epstein retaining 10% in lieu of his management fee. James was a lothario with a vision of millions of pounds in his pocket.

It was a vision that ultimately became a reality. Soon James was a multi-millionaire from Lennon-McCartney publishing royalties. The headquarters of Dick James Music at 71-75 New Oxford Street was located above the Midland Bank.

This symbolic location was not lost on McCartney.

As Paul explained to Mal Evans in his Apple office, he was tired of hearing James tell the press that the Beatles saved millions in taxes through the Northern Songs arrangement. The anger and resentment toward the Northern Songs set up was evident in McCartney's public comments.

Once he formed Northern Songs, James took advantage of his position with the Beatles. Soon every young songwriter in England was knocking on James's door, and potentially lucrative publishing concerns like the Hollies' Gralto company, Gerry Marsden's Pacermusic, and Spencer Davis Music hired James to handle their material. McCartney believed James' success was due to the Beatles, and he argued that Northern Songs was lining its pockets because of James' association with the Beatles.

McCartney was never able to influence Brian Epstein. It was as if Dick James was a vision of the rock and roll songwriting future. When Brian and Dick met for the first the, James enthralled the young LIverpudlian with the tale of his rags to riches life.

In conversations with Paul, Brian loved to recount James' life. At fourteen James left school to become a singer, but he was destined to fail as a dance band crooner. A bright young man, James recognized the opportunities in publishing songs. With a fine ear for hit songs and a flair with the pen, James was successful. The year before he offered the Northern Songs agreement to the Beatles, James formed his own publishing company.

When James began his publishing venture in 1962 he relied upon his sixteen year old son, Stephen, for musical advice. It was Stephen James who convinced his dad that the Beatles "Love Me Do" was more than just a good record. When James met Brian Epstein he listened to an unreleased pressing of "Please Please Me." James was so impressed that he decided to make the Beatles a publishing deal.

The Northern Songs agreement eventually was the cause of much of the Beatles infighting. It was a festering sore. The mere mention of Northern Songs sent McCartney into a rage. He realized too late that the Beatles had signed away one of their most important assets---the right to collect mechanical rights and publishing royalties on their songs. By March, 1969, Paul McCartney couldn't stand the Northern Songs arrangement. So he broke the time honored code of silence and made nasty comments about James. In retaliation for McCartney's barbs, James announced that he was selling Northern Songs to ATV for ten million pounds. Anger spewed from the Beatles. Paul and John were incensed over the sale of their songs. They no longer controlled the most popular rock music of the 1960s. It was a frustrating and demeaning situation.

As the Beatles business affairs simmered, John Lennon

chartered a plane to Gibraltar. On March 20, 1969, John and Yoko Ono were married in a circus like atmosphere. While the wedding was private, there was intense media interest. Then John and Yoko flew to Amsterdam to check into the Hilton Hotel, where they staged a bed-in for peace. The media descended upon the hotel like locust. As John and Yoko peered from a bed their images were on television all over the world. Newspaper coverage was equally intense and helped to divert attention from the Beatles' financial affairs.

John and Yoko's brief honeymoon was upset by an article in the **London Times** which announced that Dick James was selling his remaining interest in Northern Songs to Lew Grade at ATV. Although James stock declined to 23% of Northern Songs total stock offering, Paul McCartney was furious about the ten million pound price tag.

The 159 tunes that made up the Northern Songs catalog were the personal property of John and Paul. The songs represented the entire history of the Beatles' work. Dick James didn't even have the courtesy, Paul screamed, to ask them if they would like to buy back their songs. Sir Lew Grade further incensed Paul with gratuitous comments about the commercial future of key songs. Two decades later Michael Jackson would own the songs and Nike would sell tennis shoes to the strains of "Revolution."

The hard feelings between James and the Beatles surfaced once again when John and Paul refused to extend their agreement with Northern Songs. When James appeared to watch the Beatles film the **Let It Be** promo at Twickenham Studios, they asked him to leave.

The reason for this action was due to comments that James made in 1968. These snide remarks not only infuriated Paul McCartney, but he informed close friends that James was using the Beatles. He was neither the tax savoir nor the business genius that the press described. Not only did James complain that the quality of Beatle music had declined, but he attacked John Lennon's lifestyle. Despite these differences with John, McCartney was infuriated. He felt like a pawn in a musical game. Anyone who came near Paul heard vitriolic comments about Dick James. Yet, the English press continued to print the myths that the Beatles were happy with their publishing agreement. Why this charade continued is a mystery.

In an unusually giddy mood James complained to the press that "the boys," as he called the Beatles, were embracing the wrong ideas and this somehow had eroded their music. Snide comments about their flirtation with the Maharishi, world peace, an avant garde lifestyle and the Apple business caused McCartney to break with Dick James. The "little song hustler," as Paul referred to James, had not only arbitrarily lowered Beatles song royalties, but he had stuck his nose into their personal life. This couldn't be tolerated.

There was an internal rage in Paul as Dick James poked his chubby fingers into the Beatles affairs. As James waved his ever present Havana cigar, twitched in his tight shirts and silky suits, he represented everything that was repulsive about the music business. By selling his stock to Sir Lew Grade, James had committed the unpardonable sin---he had ignored the family concept. When he set up Northern Songs, James assured the Beatles that he was acting as a friend. This promise had a hollow ring in early 1969.

When the Beatles announced their intention to fight the sale of Northern songs stock, there was a resurgent unity in the group. Then a bombshell burst. Peter Brown revealed that he had been secretly purchasing Northern Songs stock for McCartney. This was the final breach in the Beatles long standing differences. With Paul holding 751,000 shares of Northern Songs and John only 644,000 there was no chance for Lennon and McCartney to reconcile their differences.

No one knows Paul's motivation for secretly acquiring the stock. Perhaps he feared that John would hire the wrong financial adviser. Those who were close to McCartney suggest that he wanted control of Northern Songs. He couldn't bear to see what had happened and would do anything to regain control.

It was McCartney's secret stock purchases that served as the catalyst for John, George and Ringo hiring Allen Klein to manage their affairs When Klein first approached the Beatles even Paul listened to his management overtures. It was not long before Linda Eastman's family painted a dark picture of Klein's business ethics. As he took over the Beatles legal and financial affairs, Klein's abrasive, obnoxious and threatening personality failed to endear him to the genteel English. Clive Epstein tried to make an appointment with Klein, he was turned away abruptly. Klein was loud, unduly impressed with himself and had what Clive Epstein called "a lack of personal cleanliness."

Allen Klein's rise to prominence in the music business is a strange tale. Early in his life he was hired by an accounting firm who handled some musical acts. Soon Klein immersed himself in the business. He realized that many singers and songwriters didn't understand the mechanical rights, songwriting collection process and music publishing end of the industry. In a year Klein became an authority in this area. Then he looked for an act to establish his reputation as an economic svengali.

Bobby Darin was a well known pop act whom Klein approached concerning unclaimed royalties. Eventually, Klein was able to present Darin with a $100,000 check and this made the young impresario a quick reputation. Soon Klein moved on to help Steve Lawrence and Eydie Gorme and Sam Cooke collect past royalties.

When the Beatles completed their first American tour in

late September, 1964, Klein was in the audience at a farewell benefit concert. On September 20, 1964, the Beatles performed in New York's Paramount Theater in a charity concert for the United Cerebral Palsy of New York City and Retarded Infant Services. The $100 a ticket charity bash attracted the best of New York society and Klein was unable to get near the Beatles. He never forgot the reaction to their music or celebrity status. This was the beginning of an obsession. He was determined to manage the Beatles.

The following year Klein convinced Andrew Logg Oldham to bring him aboard the Rolling Stones' management team. In his capacity with the Stones, Klein helped to negotiate a new contract with Decca. Soon Klein was working with Herman's Hermits, the Animals, the Dave Clark 5 and Donovan among others. He quickly developed a reputation for hard nosed business dealings. It was not long before Klein moved into the mainstream of the Rolling Stones business management, and he replaced Oldham as the driving force behind the Stones. When "Satisfaction" catapulted the Jagger led group to superstardom, Klein basked in the glory.

Since Mick Jagger was a good friend of the Beatles, he bragged about Klein's management and promotional skills. This made the Beatles envious. Even though they were commercially more successful than the Stones, they found it difficult to collect their songwriting and publishing money. After Brian Epstein's death, Klein's name came up repeatedly in Beatles affairs. So when he turned up in London with a plan to manage the Beatles, the boys were prepared to listen.

Only McCartney was suspicious of Klein's intentions. This served to strengthen Lennon, Harrison and Starr in their determination to listen to Klein's offer. Paul helped Klein by opposing him. While the other Beatles spent some time investigating Klein, Paul heard nasty things about the hard nosed American manager from the Eastman family. Despite this Klein was persistent and he hoped to change McCartney's negative opinion.

As early as 1967 Mick Jagger approached Peter Brown and inquired about Klein's services. Brown had his own plan to manage the Beatles. But he decided to listen to Klein's proposal. Clive Epstein went along to the meeting and it was obvious that neither Brown nor Epstein had the power to act for the Beatles. "I found Allen Klein repulsive," Clive Epstein remarked. But Klein was a smart businessman and he took advantage of the chaos reigning in Beatle affairs He did so by drawing up a plan to solve the Beatles' financial problems.

For years there had been rumors of money problems among the Beatles. **Rolling Stone** featured information on the Beatles' money problems in every issue, so Klein didn't need any spies, he realized that the Beatles were in financial trouble from the press. When John Lennon pointed out that the Beatles would be broke in six months, Klein prepared to go to London. When he arrived, three of the Beatles listened intently as Klein explained a lengthy plan to save the Beatles. The crux of Klein's focus was to fire everyone at Apple and start over on the business side.

Initially John, George, and Ringo were intrigued by Klein's proposal. What Klein suggested was that he would work without a contract on the Beatles' business affairs. Since Klein didn't demand a written contract, Paul was willing to sign a letter granting him a small degree of power. McCartney believed that he had nothing to lose. The Eastman's warned him about Klein's manipulative ways.

It was Paul's belief that Klein might be able to help in the campaign to finance the purchase of enough Northern Songs stock to guarantee the Beatles' control of their song publishing empire.

In conversations with the Beatles, Klein pointed out that they already owned 31% of Northern Songs and by offering 2 million pounds for another 20% share they could gain control of the company. It seemed an easy and plausible solution. One question remained. Where would the money come from? The eventual answer to this question created a web of intrigue and betrayal.

The Beatles reasoned that the Apple Corporation could yield part of the money, and they also expected to appropriate funds from two Beatle companies Subafilms and Maclen. Then a merchant banking firm, Henry Ansbacher and Company, pledged 1.25 million pounds to help the Beatles purchase the stock if collateral was furnished through Apple stocks and John Lennon's shares in Northern Songs. Paul refused to jeopardize his Northern Songs holdings by using them as collateral. This caused a deep rift among the two chief Beatles and Lennon reacted by demanding that the Beatles break up.

It became obvious to Paul that Klein couldn't do much to prevent the Beatles' songs from being taken over by ATV. He loathed Klein. The pushy, abrasive, power hungry attitudes which Klein manifested made it difficult for Paul to do business with him. In London good manners, genteel behavior and appropriate language were the keys to business success. McCartney found Klein personally repulsive, and he was amazed how easily the American had influenced the other Beatles.

After presenting a restructuring plan for Apple to the Beatles, Klein waited confidently for their answer. John, George and Ringo let Klein know at once that he would handle their affairs. If management was restructured, Klein argued, the Beatles could make millions.

When Klein told Lennon that Apple was losing 20 thousand pounds a week, he also presented a plan to expunge the waste. The Klein management plan was one in which he made no money until he secured the Beatles new business opportunities. In the areas of songwriting, publishing, mechanical royalties, movies and radio-TV broadcasts, Klein was able to promise new revenues. If he didn't make money it would not cost the Beatles a penny.

After thinking over Klein's proposals, Paul argued that an outsider couldn't accomplish what the Beatles had failed to do. From March to May, 1969, Klein jockeyed for position within the Beatle empire. In May, 1969, he took over John's, George's and Ringo's affairs. It was Klein's Machiavellian struggle for power that brought the Beatles as a musical group to an end.

If the other Beatles wanted Klein to represent them, why did McCartney fail to agree? The reason that Klein was not able to persuade McCartney to represent his interests was a simple one. Paul's father in law, Lee Eastman, was critical of Klein's American career. He neither approved of Klein's tactics nor was impressed with his future plans. As a result, Eastman advised Paul to disassociate himself from Klein and the other Beatles. John Eastman, Linda's brother, also advised Paul to steer clear of Klein. The differences between the Eastman's and Klein resulted from a get together in New York earlier in the year. This meeting at the Claridge Hotel did not go well but neither side made any public statements. Tension between the Eastman's and Klein festered for some months, and these differences prevented the Beatles from uniting under one management operation.

Paul learned to depend upon Lee Eastman's advice. The Eastman reputation for honesty and integrity in the music business was unquestioned. McCartney was impressed by Eastman's list of clients: a diverse lot including artists Willem de Kooning and Robert Motherwell, musicians Tommy Dorsey and Hoagy Carmichael. Eastman also owned the music publishing copyrights on "Never on Sunday" and "Young At Heart." Lee Eastman's accomplishments intrigued McCartney. A well thought of New York lawyer who specialized in music copyrighting, Eastman not only headed a successful law practice, but he led an exciting public life. In his own way Eastman was a celebrity and Paul eagerly peeked into a new and exciting world. Eastman's Park Avenue apartment was a second home to painters, musicians, actors and assorted show business figures.

Lee Eastman, John's son, was a lawyer in his late twenties. He had graduated from Stanford University and the New York University Law School, and young Eastman had established a thriving law practice. A clean cut, Kennedy type, Lee was the perfect person to run the Beatles affairs. At least this was Paul McCartney's assessment.

Once Paul got to know Lee and John Eastman, he realized that they not only possessed style, class and an understated elegance but a clear and tough minded understanding of the music world. McCartney told a Liverpool chum that Klein looked like a fish peddler next to the Eastman's. Bob Wooler remembers seeing Paul some months prior to his marriage and the conversation centered around his future father-in-law. There was no question in Paul's mind that his affairs should be handled by the Eastman's. Unlike Klein, the Eastman's didn't push to take charge of Paul's business interests. They simply allowed Paul a glimpse into their life. It was a vision that excited McCartney. As he sat in the Eastman's Fifth Avenue palatial home in New York ogling the fine furnishings, he felt at home. Yet, he couldn't help but think that his St. John's Wood home paled by comparison.

As the Beatles sorted out their affairs, Eastman wrote to Clive Epstein suggesting that the boys business problems could be worked out. In a carefully worded letter Eastman questioned "the propriety" of some of the business decisions made for the Beatles. This made Clive furious. Not only was Clive Epstein a testy and arrogant individual, he was one who didn't understand the Beatles' business needs. So in a defensive posture, he sent a nasty letter to Eastman demanding an explanation. It was obvious to Eastman that Epstein was in over his head. Not only did Clive not understand the entertainment business, but he had little inkling of the intricacies of the Beatles' affairs. The Eastman's gently pointed out that Clive Epstein was not the man to solve the Beatles' problems.

Because of the Eastman's honest advice there was renewed conflict among the Beatles. When Lee Eastman met John and Yoko he began talking about Franz Kafka's writing and he drew an interesting link between Kafka's writing and the Beatles' life. This infuriated Lennon, who viewed Eastman as a pompous and pretentious intellectual. But John's reaction was only a microcosm of a more serious problem.

From February to May, 1969, the escalating differences between McCartney and the other Beatles created an impasse. It also caused the Beatles to ignore John Eastman's intelligent and business minded advice.

When he arrived in London to talk to the Beatles, John Eastman cut straight to the core of their problems. If the Beatles were to control their own interests they had to purchase NEMS, which was now known as Nemperor Holdings. Clive Epstein had to sell Nemperor Holdings because the British death taxes were due on Brian's estate. Moreover, Eastman pointed out, Nemperor Holdings paid themselves a 25% royalty and would continue to do so for nine more years. Since Nemperor provided little in the way of legitimate services, it was money given away and the Beatles could save this sum by purchasing the company.

Since Clive Epstein's death taxes were due on March 31 1969, he was desperate to sell Nemperor Holdings. The word in the London financial community was that Clive would accept a low offer and he was frantically trying to unload what he called "a musical lemon." Clive's shortsighted view was the result of his discomfort in the music business. Brusque, curt, short with most people, he was known reverently as "Mr. Epstein" in Liverpool. While not a personally nasty man, Clive Epstein simply did not get along well with most people. He hated confrontation, was a highly private man and he carried the burden of Brian's life. So it was not surprising that he wanted nothing more to do with the Beatles.

Allen Klein realized the Eastman's hoped to sign the Beatles to a management agreement. When John Eastman flew to London to make a pitch to handle the Beatles affairs, he found that Allen Klein had beaten him to the punch. So his dad, Lee Eastman, flew into London to convince the Beatles that his law firm could straighten out their affairs.

When Lee Eastman called Peter Brown to set up a meeting with Klein and the other Beatles, he was treated discourteously. The Eastman's weren't prepared for the vitriolic confrontation that ensued over Beatle affairs.

Lee Eastman had not dealt with the volatile rock and roll community. So he was surprised during the meeting when Klein vitriolically referred to Eastman as Epstein. This immature, childish prank caused John Lennon to giggle. Everyone else looked surprised at the use of the name Epstein. After some research Klein had found out that Lee Eastman's real name was Epstein. John Lennon mumbled: "Epstein, Epstein." George and Ringo looked surprised. Paul was furious. This meeting with Klein turned into a shouting match, prompting Paul and Eastman to stomp out of the room. The end was near for the Beatles. There was no doubt in Paul's mind that Klein was a "worthless bastard." At least that's how Clive Epstein recalled Paul's outburst of anger.

As Lee Eastman left London's Claridge Hotel, there was no doubt about his feelings. He advised Paul to disassociate himself from Allen Klein. Not only did Klein lack grace and manners, he displayed an inordinate desire for power. Eastman also mentioned the possibility of the mismanagement of Beatle affairs.

Horrified by this turn of events, Clive Epstein opted to sell his interest in NEMS to Leonard Richberg's Triumph Investment Trust. Because of his loyalty to the boys, Clive graciously offered them a thirty day extension to purchase his stock. Privately Epstein doubted that they could match Triumph's bid. Clive feared that Klein would become embroiled in corporate warfare with Eastman. This is precisely what happened as Klein informed the press that the Eastmans' were blocking the accumulation of the necessary Apple assets necessary to purchase the remainder of the NEMS stock. Privately, Klein boasted that he would force Clive Epstein to give the Beatles stock in exchange for past royalties.

None of Klein's plans worked. NEMS was taken over by the Triumph Investment Trust. But this failed to slow Klein's ambition. Klein urged the Beatles to renegotiate their recording contract with EMI and Capitol. Since Klein didn't yet have a management contract with the Beatles, he had to retreat. The original contract that Klein drew up to represent the Beatles contained a clause which awarded him 20% of all increased revenues. A new recording agreement for the Beatles would make Klein millions. The shrewd, manipulative nature of Klein's proposal angered McCartney.

When Paul approached John Lennon about Klein's malevolent business dealings, John responded: "Anybody that bad can't be all bad." Paul blinked. He couldn't believe what he had heard. When Paul pointed out that Klein had litigated against the **London Sunday Times** for misrepresenting his career, Lennon smiled. He agreed that Paul might have some legitimate concerns, but Lennon loved his style. Paul realized that John was about to sign a contract with Klein out of spite. Could it be true that Lennon's hostility to McCartney was strong enough to bring Klein into the other three Beatles' management fold? It was.

On May 8, 1969, John, Ringo and George signed an agreement appointing Klein the Beatles' business manager. Clive Epstein reacted to the news by vowing to remain in Liverpool. This placed Klein's ABKCO Industries Inc. board in charge of the Beatles and their various Apple enterprises. Immediately, the top Apple officials, Ron Kass, director of Apple Records, Dennis O'Dell, head of Apple Films, Peter Asher, the A and R chief and Brian Lewis, coordinator of contracts, resigned. With characteristic good British manners they refused to attack Klein. Publicity sheets announced they resigned to pursue new business opportunities. The real reason was Allen Klein. He simply dismissed the old employees. Friendship was no longer a concern. An era had come to an end. The Apple family was dismantled.

Klein dismissed one of McCartney's favorite writers. Ken Kesey, the American author of **One Flew Over the Cuckoos Nest,** was fired from his position as house poet. Since Christmas Kesey had been in London preparing a poetry album for Zapple Records. Klein didn't want a man who wrote about crazy people turning out a record. "Who would buy it?" Klein allegedly screamed. The answer that Klein gave to everyone was to dismantle Zapple, Apple Retail, Apple Publishing and the Apple Foundation for the Arts.

On another level there was concern about Klein's company, ABKCO, which was in charge of Beatle affairs. This concern was prompted by Klein's arrogance and lack of respect for others. He also handled some of McCartney's other close friends callously. When Alistair Taylor, Brian Epstein's longtime assistant, was fired, he couldn't reach Paul by telephone. Bitterness swept over Taylor and he vowed never to talk to any of the Beatles.

When Neil Aspinall and Peter Brown resigned from the

Apple Board of Directors, they did so as a courtesy to Allen Klein. They were stunned when they weren't returned to the board. Klein was determined to get rid of all the Beatles old friends. It was a psychological means of reminding the Beatles that their fiscal woes might be due to their old friends. Allen Klein had driven the last nail in the Beatles coffin.

Litigation, hatred, name calling and petty charges ruled the day. Alistair Taylor wept openly at the end of the Beatles career. Others tried to spite Klein. Peter Brown, for example, leased his townhouse to Ron Kass. It was a building that Klein had requested. "I got supreme pleasure in seeing Kass get that town house," Brown remarked. This indicates the petty feelings surrounding the Beatles.

Paul McCartney surveyed the damage. Apple's business future was uncertain. London was a tense place. Girls were constantly standing outside his St. John's Wood home. Old flames were in the shadows. Paranoia, indifference, drug busts, business problems and declining popularity all spelled trouble for the Beatles. These conditions prompted Paul to leave London for his Waterfall home some ninety miles south of London. The pressures from the music business created a great deal of change in McCartney's life. Changes that would support a solo career and end his association with the Beatles.

The hostility that Paul built up during this period continued permanently, and he felt violated by the problems surrounding the Beatles' career. Not even induction into the American Rock and Roll Hall of Fame could persuade Paul to reunite with George and Ringo. The dream was over. It was slain by corporate greed, Machiavellian ambition and personality differences.

Paul McCartney made one last attempt to bring the Beatles back. He broached the subject of live concerts to the group and urged his mates to think about taking the music to the people. Much to Paul's surprise the others were sick of touring, tired of Paul's suggestions and burnt out by the music business. The tragedy was that the most revolutionary rock group of the 1960s ended in acrimony and discord. There would be no reunions.

For the remainder of 1969 Paul urged an economic unity. In an attempt to restore some order, Paul met with John at least a dozen times. Lennon rejected the notion that he was still a Beatle, and he openly proclaimed his hostility to the Beatles concept.

One day outside of Apple Records, Paul was standing with one of the Scruffs. She was talking to McCartney about the **White Album**, she loved it. This Texas lass spent most of her afternoons hanging out at the Beatles' business headquarters, and she was basking in McCartney's attention. Suddenly, she was standing next to his old friend John Lennon. It was a dream come true. The two chief Beatles standing next to her and talking. Then the dream turned to a nightmare. Lennon began violently arguing with McCartney. As she witnessed a shouting match, John walked away. He turned and smiled at McCartney. There was a tense moment of silence.

Then John had the last word, Lennon screamed, "the Beatles are dead."

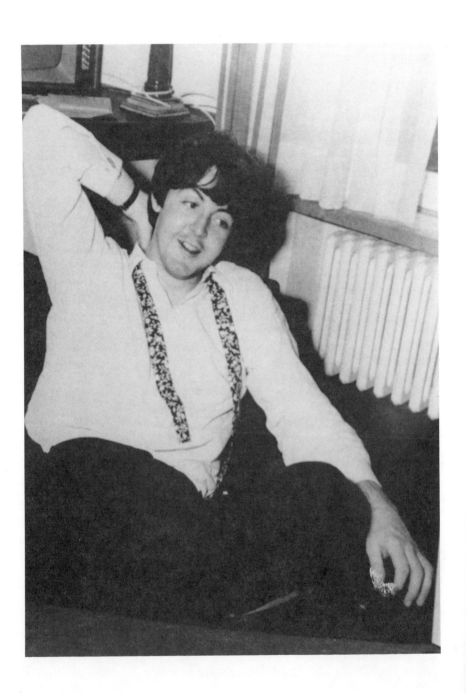

14: EPILOGUE: THE BEATLES, JUNE, 1969

In early June, 1969, Jimmy McCracklin dressed in a new blue suit for an appearance at the Continental Club. McCracklin played at this Oakland, California blues night club regularly. "I was thinking about singing the blues in a blue suit," McCracklin chuckled, "but I was also noticing what the white kids were listening to." For some time McCracklin had observed how British artists covered American blues tunes. "I loved that boy Eric Clapton, he could sure play the blues," McCracklin remarked. Earlier in the day, McCracklin had listened to a new Beatles song. "I couldn't believe how much that song took from my music, those boys must have listened to me." McCracklin was playing the Beatles recently released "Get Back." When Little Joe Blue walked backstage, Blue commented: "Sounds like those boys took one from you." McCracklin responded: "The sound man, listen to that sound," "The black man never gets a nickel of it," Blue concluded. "I'm getting mine," McCracklin remarked.

Earlier in the 1960s McCracklin had written a song entitled "Get Back." It appeared on Premium Records and was distributed by Ralph's Record Sales Company of Gardena, California. The record failed to make a ripple. "I didn't have the distribution the Beatles had," McCracklin remarked, "but I sure as hell made good music. I was happy to influence those boys." McCracklin's gracious comments mask his obvious disappointment. He would love at least creative credit for influencing McCartney's version of "Get Back." But there were not enough similarities in McCracklin's "Get Back" to suggest that the Beatles had copied it. There is no doubt that Paul had heard McCracklin's tune.

"I listened to the Beatles "Get Back" and was amazed at the way Paul McCartney took the chorus from my version of "Get Back" and wrote a whole new song around it," McCracklin remarked. "McCartney can really write a song." The powerfully muscled McCracklin circled the backstage area of the Continental Club, smiled and began to talk. He liked the Beatles music. When he performed in Europe, McCracklin's fans told him the Beatles played his American hit 'The Walk' to warm up in the Abbey Road Studio. "I sure wish those boys would release that short minute version of 'The Walk." A fan played that song for me once from a bootleg record. It's a potentially big hit record," McCracklin said.

Before he went on stage at the Continental Club in the summer of 1969 McCracklin decided to change his song selection. So he gathered his band and worked on a new song. In a playful mood, McCracklin boomed: "Boys we're going to do a Beatle song."

The band screamed "What!" McCracklin laughed and had them play his version of "Get Back." That night in a dank Oakland blues club Jimmy McCracklin played a wry tribute to the Beatles. He sang his song and thought about the rumors that the Beatles had recorded his class hit "The Walk."

In London the Beatles had disintegrated into separate groups. The most famous rock quartet in history was finished. Infighting, personal hatred, media abuse and personal change had taken its toll on the Beatles. They would still make music together, but the Beatles would never be the same again. It was a sad and ignominious period in one of the most fabled careers in rock and roll history. What went wrong? Who was to blame? Why couldn't the Beatles solve their internal problems and end their business differences?

There are no easy answers to these questions. Rock and roll was undergoing a dramatic change. The press had a field day with the death of rock stars like the Rolling Stones' Brian Jones, and the problems with Altamont and Woodstock seemed to signal the end of the rock revolution. In this period of cataclysmic change, no one realized that the Beatles were disintegrating. The Apple Scruffs, who dutifully stood outside the Apple Corporation or the various Beatles' homes, offered a number of important insights into the Fabulous Four as they witnessed the pressure that was placed on the Beatles.

The Beatles' demise was apparent by June, 1969. Although the group didn't formally disband until 1971 there was little doubt about the future. It was a bleak one. There were many issues left unresolved. What about the unreleased songs? These tunes constituted an enormous potential future income. Unhappily, the law suit between McCartney and the other Beatles placed these tunes in limbo. Although Apple was a success, financial problems remained.

On June 1, 1969, John Lennon and Yoko Ono recorded "Give Peace a Chance" at the Hotel la Reine in Montreal, Canada. This peace party dominated the press and took attention away from the more substantial Beatle problems. Paul ignored the press and was busy in the studio producing Jackie Lomax's, "Thumbin' A Ride." Paul also orchestrated the publicity for Mary Hopkins' two week concert series at the Royal Box in the Americana Hotel in New York.

But life was not all work and no play. Linda and Paul were reported by the London press to be looking for a larger home. As Paul and Linda went about their life a number of changes took place at Apple. Peter Asher quietly resigned as A and R manager. No one noticed because there were plans made to celebrate Paul's twenty seventh birthday. Life seemed to go on as usual. People left Apple. People were hired at Apple. Yet, this was an illusion. The Beatles and Apple were finished. They would limp along for another couple of years, but the damage was done. The unity, cooperative musical creativity and the position of the Beatles in the rock music world underwent a dramatic change.

In 1971 a nasty lawsuit would end their social relations. Yet, a strange bond remained. Many problems were left unresolved and the Beatles would not settle their differences for years to come.

McCartney's main concern was the music. Could he continue to make music without John Lennon? The answer was an unqualified yes. He had taken over the Beatles' affairs since 1967, and he was confident of his ability. There was the question of public acceptance. Would one Beatle sell records as well as the group? Again the answer was an unqualified yes.

Paul had a need for creative isolation. He hated the limelight, the false front friends and the hedonistic life that destroyed rock stars. Paul went into creative seclusion. A kind of splendid isolationism that carried his singing-songwriting talents into a new and fruitful direction. He possessed enormous integrity and discipline. The backbiting, the psychophants who lurked on every street corner were left behind as McCartney went off into Scotland to raise a family and continue as one of the worlds most creative musicians.

Perhaps the best compliment that McCartney received during the last stages of the Beatles career was Hunter Davies assessment that Paul hadn't changed since the Liverpool days. In late 1968 Paul and Linda spent some time with Davies' family and he was surprised by McCartney's down to earth nature.

The decision to retire from the public eye and concentrate upon Wings was not due to the Beatles giving up the road. Philip Norman's pathbreaking study, **Shout: The True Story of the Beatles** suggests that by giving up the road the Beatles had given up the faith. Nothing was further from the truth. Paul wanted off the road until the sound systems, the concert schedules and the venues provided the right atmosphere for his sound. As a seasoned and skilled professional musician, McCartney was no longer content to perform anywhere at anytime and under any conditions.

Jimmy McCracklin: An Oakland Blues legend influenced the Beatles.

APPENDIX 1: COLLECTING THE BEATLES ON APPLE: SOME IDEAS

The Beatles released a great deal of music on Apple Records. One of the problems with Apple collectibles is that there are so many of them. In addition the non-Beatle records by Badfinger, Mary Hopkins, Billy Preston and Jackie Lomax among others further confuses the direction of serious collecting. For Beatle collector the following lists are important items that can still be obtained in the world market.

BEATLE APPLE SINGLES: A STARTING POINT FOR COLLECTORS IN THE WORLD MARKET

The best place to begin in collecting Beatle singles is to find two releases from the **White Album**. A Scandinavian issue of "Back in the U.S.S.R." backed with "Don't Pass Me By" (SD 6061) in late 1968 is a rare item. "Ob-La-Di, Ob-La Da" backed with "While My Guitar Gently Weeps" was a February, 1969 release in Brazil, Japan and a number of European nations. In South Africa the single of "Ob-La-Di, Ob-La-Da" was released with a different b side "Oh! Darling" from the **Abbey Road** LP.

In 1970 Apple released "The Long and Winding Road" in Australia, Canada, Scandinavia and America. In 1972 "All Together Now" and "Hey Bulldog" was released from the **Yellow Submarine** LP.

By 1978 Apple issued "Sgt. Pepper's Lonely Hearts Club Band" backed with "With A Little Help From My Friends" in the world market. However, in France and Germany "Sgt. Pepper's Lonely Hearts Club Band" was backed with "Within You, Without You."

One of the rarest collectable Beatle Apple items is the Indian edition of "The Ballad of John and Yoko" backed with "Old Brown Shoe" (R5786). **Record Collector**, the prestigious British magazine, ranked this record among its top 350 rarities. The reason that this record is so collectable is that the A and B sides were reversed. There was similar confusion in 1969 in Canada when "Something" backed with "Come Together" was pressed with "Come Together" as the A side.

During the 1970s Italian jukeboxes featured a white promo Apple record, "Let It Be" backed with "You Know My Name (Look Up My Number)." What makes this record desirable is the white label promo and the fact that it was a jukebox record.

The Italian discs are some of the strangest Apple releases, because many of them weren't Apple records. A reissue of "P.S. I Love You" backed with "I Want To Hold Your Hand," which was the Beatles' third Italian single in 1964, was issued on Apple.

A New Zealand set of twenty two singles in a box set in 1980 is a significant item.

The United States market was flooded with a four inch "Pocket Disc" in 1969. The Apple singles were sold in vending machines and each one had a rec cardboard cover. These records were manufactured under license from Americom and the result was that the "Hey Jude" backed with "Revolution" single was edited down. The four discs only allowed for so much music so the seven minutes and eleven seconds were edited down to three and a half minutes. This helped to make the disc even more desirable.

The American market has three highly sought after items, and they are not coincidentally the Beatles' first four Apple picture sleeve releases-"Get Back" backed with "Don't Let Me Down," "the Ballad of John and Yoko" backed with "Old Brown Shoe," "Let It Be" backed with "You Know My Name (Look Up The Number)," and "The Long and Winding Road" backed with "For You Blue."

Beatle Apple EPs: A Starting Point For Collectors in the World Market

There are only two countries where EPs appeared,.Japan and Mexico.There were twenty four EPs issued in Japan. The first dozen were 1968 repressings of Odeon originals that charted during Beatlemania. This series ends with "Strawberry Fields Forever" and "Penny Lane." There were some strange releases in the Japanese series. The best example of a Japanese oddity is Apple AP 4118 which included "Anna," "Boys," "You Got To Hide Your Love Away" and Sie Liebt Dich" (the German version of "She Loves You)."

In Mexico during the early 1970s. It seems that John Lennon got in touch with a Tijuana bootlegger who helped to put out one of the most interesting collection of Apple Beatle records in the world market. There was an egalitarian tone to the Mexican EPs. John and Paul were on six EPs and the remaining eight contained George and Ringo songs. There were five George Harrison Mexican EPs that exclusively featured his tunes

.All twelve of Ringo Starr's Beatle vocals were released on the Mexican EPs. with three EPs of his own, Ringo was treated royally by the Mexicans. Unfortunately, poorly produced picture sleeves, inferior pressings and a lack of attention to detail make these items inferior in value to most other collectibles.

BEATLE APPLE ALBUMS: A STARTING POINT FOR COLLECTORS IN THE WORLD MARKET

For Beatle aficionados there are a number of Brazilian albums that are sought after by collectors. In 1969 the mono recording process was downgraded because of the rise of technologically sophisticated stereo systems. The last two Beatles albums were not issued in mono. They were available in England on open reel tapes. But in Brazil the two stereo channels were mixed down to mono and two albums **Abbey Road** (BTL 1008) and **Let It Be** (BTL 1013) were issued. The Brazilians also issued two other mono Beatle albums, **Hey Jude** (BTL 1009) and **Beatles Forever** (BTL 1017).

An interesting collectable is the Israeli **White Album**. It was issued in a single sleeve and, as a result, is a much sought after item.

The German white vinyl pressing of the White **Album** was issued in the late 1970s and is an important collectable. The American and Canadian red and blue vinyl editions of **The Beatles, 1962-1966** and **The Beatles, 1966-1970** are interesting items. In France a green vinyl edition of **Abbey Road** drew some interest from collectors.

One of the more interesting album pressings is EMI's 1982 **The Beatles Mono Collection**. This was a limited edition box set of all ten Beatle LPs. There were only 1,000 copies of the set and each one contained a "Certificate of Authenticity." About two hundred of this item were released in red boxes. Although they were not numbered, in the present market they are highly collectable.

In Japan there were two issues of a fourteen LP box set using the Apple logo. This box set was entitled **The Beatles Collection** (EAS 50031-EAS 50044) and the first edition came with a poster while the second pressing included four mirrors. The sets were limited and numbered editions that are highly sought after collectibles.

There are three Japanese albums on red vinyls that collectors prefer, they are **Yellow Submarine** (AP 8610), **Abbey Road** (AP 8815) and **Hey Jude** (AP 8940).

The most valuable Beatle album is **The Beatles Christmas Album** (SBC 100) issued by the Beatles Fan Club. The seven

Christmas messages were originally issued as flexi discs to Beatle Fan Club members in 1970. One simply sent in two dollars and received this collectable in the mail. Thanks to the counterfeiters there are excellent copies of this around.

BOOTLEG RECORDS AND CD'S

A bootleg album **Off White** contains fifteen cuts from the **White Album**. It is a 1988 record released on white vinyl. This LP concentrates upon John Lennon demo versions of tunes from the **White Album**. Most of the tunes are throw always or ones not good enough for the album. Maclen Records, whoever they are, spliced some strange sounds such as jet plane noise into the record. It is a strange LP with only average sound. It was also released on a compact disc with seven extra songs.

A better version of **White Album** songs is **Unsurpassed Demos** issued by the superb Yellow Dog label. This CD contains twenty-two cuts and includes an instrumental version of "Julia."
The sound quality is excellent on this 1991 release due to a digitally re-mastered sound from original demo tapes.

For bootlegs the Melvin Record collection is a legendary one. Melvin Records began in 1974 and issued some of the strangest and most interesting bootlegs. For the Melvin Records story see, "Confessions of a Beatle Bootlegger: The Melvin Records Story," **Beatlefan**, (Vol. 13, no. 6), pp. 29-31. The best Melvin bootleg is **The Beatles Order Lunch** (MM 17) which is a collection of what was once unreleased tracks from the "Get Back" sessions.
Another Yellow Dog CD is the 67 minute **Get Back And 22 Other Songs**. **The 910 Magazine**, arguably one of the finest sources on bootleg CD's writes: "The "Get Back" portion of this CD is undistinguished...." But, as they suggest, the bonus cuts are "Maggie Mae" and "I Lost My Little Girl," and this is reason enough to buy the CD.

APPENDIX II: WHO WROTE THE WHITE ALBUM SONGS?

The following analysis of the **White Album** is an attempt to show how much input Paul McCartney had in crafting the tunes from this revolutionary album. The seminal influence of John Lennon, the emergence of George Harrison as a songwriter and Ringo Starr's increased role in the band is examined. For a full list of Beatle songs complete with writing, production credit see William J. Dowlding, **Beatlesongs** (New York, 1989) and for an indepth look at the recording sessions see the seminal study by Mark Lewisohn, **The Beatles: Recording Sessions** (New York, 1988).

BACK IN THE U.S.S.R.

This song is one hundred percent from the pen of Paul McCartney. As John Lennon remarked in the April, 1972 issue of **Hit Parader**, "Maybe I helped a bit, but I don't think so...." The main influences upon Paul for this tune were the Beach Boys and Chuck Berry. He described "Back In The U.S.S.R." to **Playboy** "as a kind of Beach Boy parody." Chuck Berry's guitar riffs were also an important part of the song.

Ringo quit the group during this session. A few days later when he returned, Mal Evans decorated his drum set with flowers which spelled out the message: WELCOME BACK RINGO. Since Ringo wasn't in the studio a composite drum track was used and rumor has it that John, George and Paul all took turns playing the drums.

"Back In The U.S.S.R." was written for Twiggy. Billy Joel liked the tune and had a chance to include it in his July 1987 Moscow concert.

Recorded: Takes 1-5 were recorded on August 22, 1968 at Abbey Road. The following days overdubs were added to the song. A stereo mixing was completed on October 13 from track 6.

DEAR PRUDENCE

John Lennon wrote "Dear Prudence" and it was inspired by the trip to India. It was about Mia Farrow's sister. John believed that she was a bit eccentric, becuase was never left her bungalow while in India.

Recorded: August 28, 1968 at Trident Studios followed by two days of overdubbing.

GLASS ONION

A tune that John Lennon wrote, and as he suggested in a 1980 **Playboy** interview: "I threw the line in-'The walrus was Paul'-just to confuse everybody a bit more." The result was that in some parts of Scandinavia there was a rumor that Paul was dead. As Lennon suggested the line "was a joke." What John intended in this song was to confuse the pompous critics who were searching for hidden meaning in his songs. "Glass Onion" is replete with references to the Beatles' recent songs, and it also contains an obscure reference to the "Cast Iron Shore." This is a place in Liverpool and was an example of how the Beatles used nostalgic images in their songs. Although the Beatles cut 34 takes, Mark Lewisohn writes: "Glass Onion' was not especially difficult to record.

Recorded: September 11, 1968 at Abbey Road Studio with five subsequent days of overdubbing in September and October.

Ob-LA-DI, OB-LA-DA

This is a Paul McCartney song with a couple of lyrics thrown in by John Lennon. The tune resulted from McCartney watching a band of the same name perform. From all accounts this rock group was awful and Paul wrote the song in a light moment. The Beatles had some trouble recording the song. Richard Lush, the second engineer, commented that McCartney came into Abbey Road stoned and cut a loud and speedy version of "Ob-La-Di, Ob-La-Da," that was used on the **White Album**. The other Beatles were reportedly unhappy with the amount of time McCartney spent on this song. They considered it to be "pop nonsense."

"Ob-La-Di, Ob-La-Da" was not an easy song to record. The original cut and two re-makes were completed during July 1968. The re-makes were different from the way that McCartney had conceived the tune. The Beatles fought in the studio over whether or not take 4 or take 7 was the best cut. McCartney won the argument and take 4 was selected for Paul's lead vocals.

Recorded: July 3, 1968 with another seven days of overdubbing and rerecording.

WILD HONEY PIE

This Paul McCartney tune was the result of a sing-along at the Maharishi's retreat in India. Patti Harrison liked the tune and for this reason it was included on the **White Album**. "This was just a fragment...," Paul remarked, "which we were not sure about...."

This was a spur of the moment song by McCartney, and it captures the spontaneous magic of Paul in the studio.

Recorded: August 20, 1968 at Abby Road. Only Paul McCartney was on the session, no other Beatles performed on it

THE CONTINUING STORY OF BUNGALOW BILL

John Lennon wrote this tune at the Maharishi's retreat and it appears he did so as a joke. The Maharishi, a man of peace, went out to hunt tigers and Lennon couldn't believe it. So he wrote the song as something of a dig at the giggling holy man. "There used to be a character called Jungle Jim," Lennon told **Playboy**, "and I combined him with Buffalo Bill. It's a sort of teenage social-comment song."

The tracks for this song were cut in three takes and then it was filled with overdubs. This spirited song reflected Lennon's happy go lucky attitude in the studio. Yoko Ono was in the studio with John, and she sang one line, Yoko wailed:"not when he looked so fierce." This was the first female vocal on a Beatle record. Lennon played a mandolin-type mellotron, and the atmosphere was described as a happy one.

Recorded: October 9, at Abbey Road Studio. This tune was recorded immediately after the Beatles cut "I'm So Tired."

WHILE MY GUITAR GENTLY WEEPS

This George Harrison tune was based on the **I Ching: Book of Changes**. The spiritual background to the song is, as Harrison explains it, "based on the concept that everything is relative to everything else, as opposed to the Western view that things are merely coincidental." One of the lines for this song occurred when George visited his mom in the north of England. While visiting with his family, he picked up a book and opened it to a page. On the page of this unnamed book was the line "gently weeps." This became the basis for Harrison's song.

"I always had to do about ten of Paul and John's songs before they'd give me the break," George commented. Because of Harrison's obvious frustration, he was allowed to cut five songs for the **White Album**.

The changes in "While My Guitar Gently Weeps" from the initial recording to its final completion were enormous. Despite a beautiful three minute and thirteen second acoustic version of the song, John, Paul and Ringo didn't appear interested in it. The reason was not the song, but the pressures building up over the Apple experiment.

So George persuaded Eric Clapton to come along and add some guitar riffs. The result was one of Harrison's strongest early songs.The publicity over Clapton's addition to the song helped George to launch a solo career.

Recorded: An acoustic version was cut on July 25. On August 16 it was remade with takes that continued until September 6 in an attempt to improve upon the beautiful July 25 acoustic demo version of the song. "While My Guitar Gently Weeps" was a historical turning point because the Beatles, not George Martin, produced the song.

HAPPINESS IS A WARM GUN

This John Lennon song was written after he looked at a gun magazine. The title of one article in this magazine was "Happiness Is A Warm Gun." Rather than reading the article, John wrote a song about it. "It was put together from three different songs and just seemed to run the gamut of many types of rock music," Lennon remarked.

Although not a complicated song, "Happiness Is A Warm Gun" required 65 takes to complete. In America there was a great deal of concern over the tune and its lyrics. The National Rifle Association was critical of Lennon's tune, but the New Left loved its obvious anti-gun implications.

Recorded: The song was cut on September 23, 1968 at Abbey Road. The following day another batch of takes were recorded. Of the sixty-five cuts that Lennon sorted through he used two different takes to splice the song together. It was completed by September 25.

MARTHA MY DEAR

Paul McCartney recorded this song, but he didn't use his sheepdog, Martha, as the central character. Those close to Paul claim it is not about Martha, he simply used the name. "Martha My Dear" is generally believed to be about a broken love affair. No one knows, but it's a nice song.

Mark Lewisohn argues that this tune may have been a one-man recording effort by McCartney. "Contrary to popular opinion," Lewisohn writes, "It was not about Paul's sheepdog."

Recorded: October 4 with overdubs the following day at Trident Studio.

I'M SO TIRED

John Lennon wrote this song while in India. "I couldn't sleep," Lennon remembered. "I'm meditating all day and couldn't sleep at night." This song reflected the stress in his life over his impending divorce from Cynthia. This song is famous because of the "Paul Is Dead" hysteria which resulted from some inane Lennon comments at the end of this track. When these words were played backward, they seemed to say "Paul is dead, man, miss him, miss him." This tune is nothing more than a song about insomnia.

"I'm So Tired" is an example of an instant Lennon song. He wrote it quickly and the 14 takes cut on October 8 essentially finished the tune.

Recorded; October 8 at Abbey Road Studio. On October 15 remixes from cut 14 were completed.

BLACKBIRD

With a small amount of assistance from Lennon, this tune was a 95% McCartney effort. After reading a newspaper article on American race riots during the summer of 1968, Paul quickly penned this song. He used it to express his outrage over the American civil rights mess. What the tune represents is a look into McCartney's highly political life. Although it was a private form of political protest, Paul still was conscious of racial problems.

When Paul recorded this tune he was in Studio 2 and John was next door in Studio 3. George Martin walked between the studios supervising the sessions. After 30 takes 11 of which were complete ones, McCartney finished the song.

Recorded: June 11 at Abbey Road.

PIGGIES

This is a George Harrison song with approximately a ten percent input from John Lennon. There was a spirit of cooperation as all four Beatles were in Abbey Road Studio No. 2 to record this song. As George remarked: "Piggies' is a social comment. I was stuck for one line in the middle until my mother came up with the lyric." The song has nothing to do with the police, it appears that this tune had no real purpose. Yet, it was an example of Harrison's growing maturity as a song stylist. A Beatle insider suggests that "Piggies" was a song about the breakup of the Beatles. This interpretation seems unlikely because of the studio atmosphere.

Prior to this session, George played a rough version of "Something" and he asked Chris Thomas, the producer, his opinion of the new song. When Thomas wanted to record it, Harrison declined. Between takes of "Piggies," Paul practiced a rough version of "Let It Be." Not a bad historical night.

Recorded: September 19 at Abbey Road. The following day "Piggies" was completed.

ROCKY RACCOON

Another Paul McCartney song. This tune had an English musical hall flavor to it. The lyrics, however, have a decided American flavor as Paul crooned: "This hear (sic) is the story of a young boy living in Minnesota...."

Strangely enough this song was written at a time in which Paul was exposed to the exotic teachings of the Maharishi and the mysteries of the Far East. Donovan Leitch and John Lennon were instrumental in helping Paul compose this song. The inspiration for "Rocky Raccoon" took place while Paul, Donovan and John were playing their guitars on the roof of one of the Maharishi's buildings.

During the ten takes of "Rocky Raccoon," George Martin decided to add a honky tonk piano solo. Mark Lewisohn suggests that "Paul was surprisingly uncertain of the lyrics, formulating them as he went along...."

Recorded: August 15 at Abbey Road.

DON'T PASS ME BY

Ringo Starr allegedly wrote this tune. When the Beatles went into Studio 3 At Abbey Road the song was labelled simply "Ringo's Tune." In its various forms this song was entitled: "Some Kind of Friendly" and "This Is Some Friendly."

Those people close to the Beatles speculate that this song created a strong rift between Ringo and Paul. This was because of the persistent rumor that McCartney wrote the song for Ringo to keep him in the group. It was a no. 1 hit in Scandinavia where it was released as a 45 single. The "Paul Is Dead" hysteria continued on this song as the lyrics contained a reference to a car crash which some people interpreted as alluding to a fatal McCartney auto accident.

Recorded: June 5 at Abbey Road with two overdubbing sessions and an edit piece which included a tinkling piano intro which was recorded on July 22.

WHY DON'T WE DO IT IN THE ROAD?

This was a McCartney song. John Lennon called it one of Paul's best. "I was always hurt when Paul would knock something off without involving us," John told **Playboy**. Paul responded: "There's only one incident I can think of which John has publicly mentioned....It was when I went off with Ringo and did 'Why Don't

We Do It In The Road." As McCartney explained: "It wasn't a deliberate thing." McCartney wrote and produced this song, his close friends believe, because of what John did with "Revolution No. 9." Whatever the reason, it indicated that all was not well in the Beatle Kingdom.

McCartney taped this on a four track machine, and it was a marvelous example of his continued ability to make solo music. In an experimental mood, Paul alternated between recording quiet and loud versions of the song.

Recorded: October 9 at Abbey Road with an overdub session the next day.

I WILL

Paul McCartney wrote and recorded this song in a marathon 67 take session during mid-September, 1968. The tune was modeled on "I'll Follow the Sun." The 65th take was the best one recorded and it was used along with overdubbed instruments and vocals to create take 68 or the final cut.

For some reason George Harrison was not in the studio during this recording session. Mark Lewisohn calls this: "A very interesting session."

Recorded: September 16-17 at Abbey Road.

JULIA

Although this is a song that is 75% Lennon and 20% Yoko Ono, it also owed a 5% debt to Kahil Gibran's trendy tome, **The Prophet**. Lennon's mother Julia was the vocal point for this song. It was a sad tune which referred to the pain that Lennon experienced because he never really knew his mother.

When "Julia" was recorded it was intended as the 32nd and last song for the **White Album**. After only three takes, John was reasonably happy with the song. Because it was a plaintive wail about his mother, John cut this tune in a solo effort and in record time.

Recorded: October 13 at Abbey Road.

BIRTHDAY

This tune is 70% McCartney and 30% Lennon. It was written in the studio to fill the **White Album**. Chris Thomas, the producer for this session, remembers that Paul came into the studio and started to fool around with the song. Soon John arrived and helped him complete it. This was the night that the Beatles went to Paul's house to watch the American rock movie,

The Girl Can't Help It, which featured Gene Vincent, Fats Domino and Little Richard among others.

In an unusually productive session, Paul walked into the studio and began harmonizing a rough version of "Birthday." The Beatles finished the song that night

Recorded: September 18 at Abbey Road.

Yer Blues

This quirky John Lennon tune was a critical blast at the British blues scene. Graham Bond was a particularly pompous bluesman that Lennon hated, and he directed this little dirge toward the revisionist blues artists in England.

But Lennon fooled the critics when stated that he wrote the song "trying to reach God and feeling suicidal." This tune was the only Beatles song that John sang at the Toronto Rock and Roll Revival Concert in September, 1969. One of the best versions of this tune is contained in the Rolling Stones' movie **Rock 'n' Roll Circus**.

Recorded: August 13 at Abbey Road.

MOTHER NATURE'S SON

Another song written by Paul while he was at the Maharishi's compound. After the silly little guru lectured the Beatles about nature, Paul was inspired to write this tune. While McCartney was working on the final arrangement with George Martin and the brass players, John and Ringo walked in. Ken Schott, the engineer, describes the studio scene: "...you could cut the atmosphere with a knife. It was like that for ten minutes and then as soon as they left it felt great again. It was very bizarre."

This tune took 25 takes to complete. It was a simple song that once again demonstrated McCartney's remarkable studio skills.

Recorded: August 9 at Abbey Road. On August 20 there was some overdubbing.

EVERYBODY'S GOT SOMETHING TO HIDE EXCEPT ME AND MY MONKEY

Another John Lennon song. It was a interesting phrase that John turned into a **White Album** song.This tune was written to celebrate Lennon's union with Yoko Ono. The lyrics suggest that Lennon was unhappy with the manner in which fans, reporters and the music industry were reacting to Yoko.

Recorded: June 26 at Abbey Road in a rehearsal session and recorded on June 27 with July 1 and 23 overdubbing.

SEXY SADIE

Lennon's tune was the result of the Maharishi's compound. He wrote it as the Beatles prepared to leave India. The Maharishi was mentioned in the song's original lyrics in a pointed and cynical manner. This approach was modified during the recording session.

The 21 takes saw Lennon substitute the word "Sexy Sadie" for the Maharishi. John feared a law suit. When Mark Lewisohn listened to studio tapes of "Sexy Sadie," it revealed Lennon's intense hostility to the giggling Indian Holy Man. A sample line played for Lennon was: "You little, twat, who the fuck do you think you are?" Obviously, John was unhappy.

Recorded: July 19 at Abbey Road with three subsequent remake and overdubbing sessions.

HELTER SKELTER

McCartney wrote this song after he read in **Melody Maker** that the Who's Pete Townshend wrote a loud, raucous and dirty song. Paul decided to compose a Beatle tune with the same intent, it turned out to be "Helter Skelter." This was the tune that California murderer Charles Manson interpreted as an omen for an eventual race war. When Manson and his followers committed their murders the song was used to justify it. Lennon pointed out that Manson's actions had no bearing on the Beatles. After all, in England, helter skelter was a reference to an amusement park slide.

Recorded: July 18 at Abbey Road Studio. The initial version was 25 minutes long, but it didn't appear on the **White Album**. This version still remains an unreleased Beatle masterpiece. An LP cut was recorded on September 10 with overdubs the following day.

LONG, LONG, LONG

Another George Harrison tune. Influenced by Bob Dylan's "Sad Eyed Lady of the Lowlands," Harrison wrote a tune which was one of the weaker cuts on the **White Album**.

Recorded: October 7 at Abbey Road in Studio No. 2.

REVOLUTION 1

The first day that the Beatles began recording the **White**

Album, they cut "Revolution" using the working title "Revolution 1." This was a song written in India and more than a subtle bite to it. It also was recorded three different ways with three working titles. "Revolution 1" and Revolution 9" appeared on the **White Album**, whereas the third version appeared on the b side of the Beatles' hit, "Hey Jude."

As Mark Lewisohn has shown, eighteen takes of "Revolution 1" were cut in an atmosphere of discordant chaos. Yoko Ono reportedly screamed: "you become naked." The eighteen takes of "Revolution" completed during the first day created a backlog of material for the **White Album** as well as a bonanza for the bootleggers. Circulating among collectors is a July 10, 1968, completed version of "Revolution," and this has shown up on **Ultra Rare Trax**, Volume 5 and **Unsurpassed Masters**, Volume 7.

It was take 18 of "Revolution 1" which was a substantially different song. Although it was an excellent tune, it was far too long for commercial release. Eventually, the last six minutes were taken as the foundation for "Revolution 9."

This slow, blues oriented version of "Revolution 1" is a landmark in Beatles' musical history. It reflects their concern with the anti-war movement and the direction of American and British democracy. The Vietnam war was foremost in John's mind when he recorded the various versions of "Revolution."

During this session a young, recently hired, assistant George Thomas was brought into the studio to begin learning record production. The twenty-one year old Thomas was a quick learner, liked by the Beatles and an extremely competent student of the recording process."I wasn't their engineer...I wasn't their producer," Thomas remarked. "I worked on stuff with them...." A modest man, Thomas was a positive force during the production of the **White Album**. For this reason he was given production credit.

On May 31 in an marathon session that ran from two-thirty in the afternoon to about Midnight, the Beatles continued to work on "Revolution 1." By overdubbing two separate Lennon vocals and Paul's bass guitar onto take 18, George Martin produced a tape reduction that turned into take 19. This was followed by more overdubbing of Paul and George's backup vocals.

One of the peculiar byproducts of "Revolution" was the question of whether or not John Lennon wanted in the revolution or out of it. By the time the Beatles released the single version known as "Revolution," John wanted out of it.

The production on this song seemed to go on forever. On Friday, June 21, 1968, a two-thirty to nine o'clock session created a 330 minute remix session for "Revolution 1" and "Revolution 9." Then once again on June 25, Paul improved the "Revolution 9" mix and he also completed "Revolution 1."

Paul was in America when this session took place, and he returned home while it was in progress. George Harrison also missed the session as he was playing on and helping produce Jackie Lomax's, "Sour Milk Sea."

Recorded: May 30-31, June 4 , June 21 at Abbey Road with a number of overdubbing sessions.

HONEY PIE

A McCartney tune that had a snappy jazz and pop orientation. Lennon's brilliant guitar solo on "Honey Pie" had a Django Reinhardt touch to it. The 1920s dance band flavor of Jim Mac's Jazz Band surfaces in this song.

Recorded: October 1 at Trident Studios with two days of overdubbing on October 2 and 4.

SAVOY TRUFFLE

The continued productivity of George Harrison is demonstrated on a song that he had 90% writing credit for and Derek Taylor shared a 10% credit. This whimsical tune was written while George hung out with Eric Clapton. It seems that Clapton needed dental work but couldn't quit eating chocolates. As a result, Harrison memorialized this experience in "Savoy Truffle." Clapton loved to buy Mackintosh's Good News Chocolates and George delighted in the lyrics to this tune.

Recorded: October 3 at Trident Studios with three subsequent overdubbing sessions

CRY BABY CRY

A John Lennon tune that was written from an advertisement that Lennon saw on British television. The first night that this song was recorded there were thirty unnumbered takes. The Lewis Carroll inspired lyrics prompted critics to label this song as a "Beatle nursery rhyme."

Recorded: July 15 at Abbey Road and then rerecorded the following day with overdubbing on July 18.

Revolution 9

John Lennon wrote this tune with Yoko Ono. It was completely different from the "Revolution" single and is more of a musical montage than a song. John Lennon recalled the song: "It was (written) somewhat under Yoko's influence, I suppose. Once I heard her stuff...I thought 'my God,' I got intrigued, so I wanted to do one."

Lennon remarked: "This is the music of the future. You can forget all the rest of the shit we've done...."

Recorded: May 30 at Abbey Road with a least five effects sessions at later dates.

GOOD NIGHT

Another Lennon song which was written for his son Julian. When it came time to record it, John told George Martin to arrange it like a lush and phony Hollywood song. Thus, it was a natural commercial vehicle for the **White Album**. It was also the perfect song to conclude the LP. The first five takes on the night of June 28 took the Beatles from seven at night until almost five in the morning. Although John was the writer, the lead vocals were supplied by Ringo. It was the sad, eerie quality of Starr's voice which made it work on the **White Album**.

Recorded: June 28 at Abbey Road with a July 2 overdubbing and a July 22 remake.

Appendix III: The McCartney File, From the 1950s to The Late 1960s, Facts and Fantasies

The following list of facts, people and events are intended to supplement the book's look at Paul's life. This list provides some material for analyzing the depth of McCartney's involvement in the revolutionary period from 1967 through 1969. Generally, this listing does not include Beatle songs but it does include tribute and novelty tunes associated with McCartney.

Steve Abrams: This American student at Oxford University in 1967 studied the effects of marijuana on people to determine its influence. Although marijuana was illegal in England, Abrams hoped to make a case for its legal use. His Ph.D. studies made Abrams something of a celebrity and he was hired by the **International Times** to cover the Rolling Stones drug bust trial. This put Abrams into contact with McCartney and he approached Paul about supporting a full page ad in the **London Times** which advocated the legalization of marijuana. Paul paid for the ad through the Beatles' advertising account. When the advertisement appeared on July 24, 1967 in the **London Times** it created something of a sensation.

Alfred The Great: This British made film starred David Hemmings and when it opened in London's West End on August 11, 1969, Paul and Linda McCartney attended the screening.

The Algrave: A region of Southern Portugal where Hunter Davies author of **The Beatles: Authorized Biography** traveled and while he was on vacation the McCartney's knocked on his door during the middle of the night. This was in December, 1968 and resulted in some good stories for Davies revised edition of the book.

Aspinall Neil: From the 1950s to the 1990s Aspinall has been a constant factor with the Beatle.s He began as a quasi-road manager in the 1950s and moved into top management. Aspinall is in charge of all Beatle checks in the 1990s. He was a student at the Liverpool Institute where attended Art and English classes with Paul. He was appointed Managing Director inf Apple in 1968 and was an excellent and loyal employee.

Ballad of Paul: This is a novelty record issued by MGM Records (14097) in 1969. The group listed on the disc is the Mystery Tour and the song is "Ballad of Paul (Follow The Bouncing Ball)." It is a very collectible item.

Besame Mucho: This early tune was one selected for the Beatles Decca audition. It was Paul who helped pick it out, because he had the Coasters version of this song in his personal collection.

Black Dyke Mills Band: This is a British brass band of international repute. Paul recorded his song "Thingumybob" with the band and it served as the theme song of London Weekend Televisions comedy series of the same name. On April 30, 1968, Paul recorded the single with Geoffrey Brand conducting the orchestra. When the single was released in England in September, 1968 it failed to chart. The b side was an instrumental version of "Yellow Submarine."

The Bonzo Dog Doo Dah Band: There is no band which highlights the excesses of the late 1960s more than this group. They were an eclectic group of musical eccentrics who had attended art college. They were featured in the Beatle film **Magical Mystery Tour** and they released a famous single, "I'm the Urban Spaceman." This song was written by Neil Innes who went on to fame with Monty Python. On this record Paul played under the name Apollo C. Vermouth. When the record was released in June, 1969, it became a collector curiosity because word leaked out that McCartney played on it.

John Bratby: A London artist who completed three portraits of Paul. The paintings were displayed at Bratby's West End exhibition at the Zwemmer Galley when it opened on November 7, 1967. A price tag of 350 pounds was on each portrait. There is no indication whether or not these were sold to the general public.

Brother Paul: A 45 released in America on Silver Fox 21 in 1969. The "Brother Paul" record is credited to Billy Shears and the ALL-AMERICANS. The flip side was "Message To Seymour." It is a collectors item that vanished quickly from view.

William Campbell: During the "Paul Is Dead" rumors William Campbell was a double who had plastic surgery to look like McCartney. As the tale suggested he would replace Paul for concert tours.

Charity Bubbles: This is a 1969 Scaffold single on which Paul plays guitar.

Christmas Album By McCartney: In 1965 McCartney made a Christmas LP for the other three Beatles. This special Christmas greeting was limited to four pressed vinyl copies, and no one outside of the Beatles is aware of the content.

Corfu: Paul, Linda and daughter Heather vacationed on this Greek island in 1969. They rented a villa and Paul called it a "belated honeymoon."

Curtis, Lee: Stage name of Pete Flannery. He led a group in 1961 known as Lee Curtis and the Detours which his brother Joe managed, and he soon hooked up with Pete Best in Lee Curtis and the All Stars. He was the first Mersey side artist to record a solo song and move to Hamburg where he became a local star. With an excellent voice, great stage presence and sizzling good looks, Lee Curtis appeared destined for stardom. It didn't happen, but his songs recorded at the Star-Club in Hamburg attest to his enormous, if unrecognized, talent.

Davis, Meta: Mrs. Davis is the meter maid who was the inspiration for McCartney's "Lovely Rita" tune. She lives in St. John's Wood and was giving Paul's car a ticket in 1967 when he rushed up and demanded to know her name. They talked and Paul went home to write a song. In Australia the Beatles release of "Lovely Rita" included Meta's name, but this was changed in England and America for legal reasons.

Donovan: This British folk singer convinced McCartney to make a guest appearance on his 1968 album, **Mellow Yellow**. In a fifteen minute recording session Paul allegedly sang the words "Mellow Yellow." An American bootleg record, **No. 3 Abbey Road, NW 8**, has captured this bit of horseplay for posterity. During a studio session Paul and Donovan exchanged songs with Paul singing "Blackbird" and Donovan playing selections from his album **HMS Donovan**.

Do You Want To Know A Secret: In 1963 this demo was prepared for the first Beatles LP. It wasn't used and John and Paul's vocals were shelved. It was eventual sold in an auction for 350 pounds.

Elevator: This was a single by the British psychedelic group Grapefruit. Although Apple discovered Grapefruit and recorded their earliest songs, the group's records were issued on RCA. For their 1968 single "Elevator"McCartney crafted a promotional video. Paul used Hyde Park to film a three minute music clip.

Emmetts Garage: In June, 1969, this 4,600 acre baronial estate was up for sale. Paul and Linda looked at it and decided not to purchase it.

Every Night: This was a song that Paul wrote in 1969 while in Greece for his first solo LP, **McCartney**.

Fascher, Horst: This Hamburg, Germany boxer is usually referred to the as "Beatles Bodyguard." This is an oversimplification. Fascher had a direct hand in Hamburg's music and the Beatles listened to his opinions. He was a former boxer who was heavily involved in the Reeperbahn music scene. Fascher was particularly close to McCartney, and he retains a strong friendship with Paul to this day. For a profile of Fascher see, **The Beatles: Untold Tales**

Felix, Julie: This dark haired American folk singer was Paul's mysterious romance. She was a regular on the David Frost Show and Paul arranged to meet her after watching the program. The British press missed this McCartney romance.

Flannery, Joe: A close friend of Lennon and McCartney. Flannery entered the Liverpool music scene managing his brother, Lee Curtis. He was a boyhood chum of Brian Epstein. A gracious and bright man, Flannery is one of the most knowledgeable people about the Mersey Beat. See **The Beatles: Untold Tales** for a full profile of Flannery.

Garbo, Doug: An albino American living in San Francisco. It was Garbo who was sent by Bill Graham to escort the individual Beatles around San Francisco during their 1960s bay area visits. Garbo promoted his own band while working for Bill Graham Presents.

Gibbs, Russ: A Detroit, Michigan disc jockey who was heard on WKNR. On October 12, 1969, Gibbs broke the story that Paul had died in 1966 in an automobile accident. Gibbs maintained that a double was foisted off on the public. To validate this ludicrous claim, Gibbs suggested that a number of clues on the **Magical Mystery Tour** LP supported his contention.

Heather: Unreleased McCartney song which was written for his stepdaughter. This 1968 record appeared on a number of bootleg LP. My personal choice for a bootleg version of "Heather" is the **Cold Cuts** album.

In Spite Of All The Danger: This mysterious song was recorded in the summer of 1958 at Percy Phillips Liverpool Studio. Some books suggest it was co-written with George Harrison. Mark Lewisohn in his interview with Paul for **The Beatles: Recording Session** prompted McCartney to claim that he had written the song without George's help.

Ivor Novello Award: this is an award named after the Welsh composer Ivor Novello who died in 1951. Paul has won the honor a number of times. In 1967 he was presented this award for the song "Love In The Open Air." This tune appeared in the movie **The Family Way**.

Jefferson Airplane: This San Francisco based rock group met with Paul during an April 4, 1967 rehearsal in San Francisco. After this discussion Grace Slick went to dinner with McCartney at Enrico's on Broadway. After dinner they went to the Condor and saw a topless act. The doorman remarked how much he looked like Paul McCartney.

Kennedy, Paul: This American graduate student in history became the first person to disguise himself as a Beatle and wander into the Abbey Road Studio. Kennedy had a McCartney look and used stage makeup and clothes to make his way into Abbey Road. He was thrown out when the real Paul McCartney showed up.

Lomax, Jackie: He was a vocalist with an early Liverpool band known as the Undertakers. They became one of Liverpool's most important bands and Pye Records signed the group. Despite some excellent sides for Pye, Lomax was not a successful solo artist. In 1968 he signed with Apple and George Harrison produced "Sour Milk Sea." Paul McCartney played bass on the record with Eric Clapton on lead guitar, Nicky Hopkins on piano, Ringo Starr on drums and George Harrison also played some lead guitar. When the single was issue in the U.S., it was expected to hit the charts. This didn't happened and Lomax faded into obscurity. After Allen Klein got his fingers into the Apple mess, Lomax moved to America and recorded two LPs for Warner Brothers. He returned to England in 1974 and joined Badger. Then he returned to America where he currently resides.

The Long And Winding Road: This solo demo by Paul was recorded for the album "Let It Be." It eventually was sold in auction for 400 pounds, and another acetate of the Beatles' performance of the same song sold for 260 pounds. It appears that these versions have not been bootlegged.

McCartney: Mike: Paul's brother was a hairdresser who became a fine photographer for **Mersey Beat**. Eventually, he became a member of the satirical comedy, music and poetry group, The Scaffold. He was a British stage, TV and record personality. He changed his name to McGear so as not to tread upon Paul's fame. In 1964 with poet Roger McGough and humorist John Gorman, Scaffold had a regular spot on the British TV show Gazette. By the 1990s McGear was an established lecturer, author and spoke at the Beatlefests and other fan conventions. Anyone who has seen him realizes that he is an intelligent, talented young man.

McFall, Ray: This former accountant was the Cavern owner from 1959. Along with the bouncer, driver and general handy man, Paddy Delney, they helped to establish the Mersey Beat. When he took over the Cavern on October 1, 1959, McFall had a secret love for rock and roll music. In the summer of 1960 he introduced rock music to the startled jazz fans who frequented the Mathews Street venue. On August 2, 1961, the Beatles began what the locals called a series of "resident nights." Eventually, the Beatles performer 292 times at the Cavern with the last show on August 3, 1963.

McGivern, Maggie: This waitress at London's Revolution Club in Bruton Place went out with Paul a few times after his break with Jane Asher. In 1968 McGivern went on a brief vacation with Paul to Sardinia.

Magpie: This children's' TV series on the ITV network in 1968 screened "A Day In the Life of Mary Hopkins." This short film was shot at the Apple offices and screened shortly thereafter.

Martin, Rose: She was Paul's housekeeper in 1967 and was the inspiration for the album **Red Rose Speedway**.

Money, Zoot: This was the stage name of George Bruno who organized a big band with a rock and roll sound in 1964. By 1967 Zoot Money's band was known as Dantalion's Chariot. He left music and worked with Paul on the **McGough and McGear** album.

My Dark Hour: This single issued by the Steve Miller Band on June 16, 1969 was recorded at AIR Studios in London on February 3. Paul played drums, bass, guitar and sang backing vocals and employed the pseudonym Paul Ramon on the session. This tune was included on the Steve Miller Band's album **Brave New World**. This song suggests how close McCartney was to musicians on the San Francisco scene. He frequently took trips to the city and had a working relationship with the bands.

Newsfront: This is an American television show that McCartney appeared on with John Lennon on May 15, 1968. They discussed the various Apple projects and promoted Beatles records.

Nurk Twins: This was the name that Paul and John used when they performed for friends. In 1960, according to legend, Paul and John used this name in an obscure local performance.

Ob-La-Di, Ob-La-Da: This mysterious raggae band was the inspiration for the **White Album** song of the same name. Paul wanted to release the tune as a single but John and George objected. The Marmalade had a No. 1 British hit that remained on the charts for twenty weeks with the song. The Bedrocks recorded "Ob-La-Di, Ob-La-Da" and it reached No. 20 on the English charts and remained there for seven weeks. Ironically, the Beatles never charted in England with the tune.

On Our Way Home: This Paul McCartney tune was recorded by the obscure New York trio, Mortimer, in April, 1969 for release on Apple. It was shelved and the song re-emerged with the title "Two of Us." This song was performed in the movie **Let It Be** and released on the album.

Paolozzi,Eduardo: This internationally acclaimed Scottish sculptor helped Stu Sutcliffe enter art school in Hamburg. Paul purchased some of his work and used one of the cover of the **Red Rose Speedway** LP.

Parnes, Larry: This British rock promoter began in the 1950s and can be considered one of the Founding Fathers of English rock and roll promotions. He booked the Silver Beatles to back Johnny Gentle on a Scotland tour in 1960, and he hung out at the Jacaranda Club. Parnes was short sighted about the Beatles and he had little sensitivity toward their music.

Penina: This song was written during the Portuguese vacation, and the title is taken from the hotel in which McCartney was staying. Carlos Mendes, a Portuguese singer, heard the tune and released it on July 18, 1969, on Parlophone. The next year the Dutch group Jotte Herre recorded it.

Ramon, Paul: A name that Paul made up while on tour with Johnny Gentle in Scotland. In 1969 Paul used the name once again when he recorded "My Dark Hour" with the Steve Miller Band. The New York based punk rock group The Ramones allegedly used this as the basis for their name.

Rembrandt: This name was given to the house that Paul purchased for his dad for 8,750 pounds. The Baskervyle Road, Heswell, Cheshire residence overlooked the River Dee estuary and is roughly fifteen miles from Liverpool. It has five bedrooms, a wine cellar, and a least 8,000 pounds was spent on central heading. Jim Mac found it difficult to move because of the fans and a midnight move brought the old furniture from the Forthlin Road home.

Rhone, Dorothy: This young lady was Paul's first serious girl. Rumors from those close to Paul suggest that from the late 1950s until the early 1960s they dated. There is a picture of McCartney with Dorothy at the Forthlin road house and another one at Rory

Storm's house. She is reported the inspiration of Paul's "P. S. I Love You."

Schwartz, Francie: This New York girl arrived in London with a script for a screenplay and wound up as McCartney's girl friend. She wrote a kiss and tell book, **Body Count**, which ranks as one of the worst books ever written on rock and roll. Her journalistic piece in the **News of the World** was well written but in poor taste. See chapter 7 for a lengthy description of Schwartz' relationship with McCartney.

Sheridan, Tony: This English musician attended art college and began working at London's 2-Is club in 1958. Soon he found his way to Hamburg where he became the first British rock star to take Germany by storm. For a time he was a member of the Playboys, Vince Taylor's backup group, but he quickly blossomed at Bruno Koschmider's Kaiserkeller Club in Hamburg. When the Beatles came to Hamburg, he was an important influence upon them. For a full sketch of Sheridan see, **the Beatles: Untold Tales**

Storm, Rory and the Hurricanes: This is one of Liverpool's most influential bands. Storm whose real name was Alan Caldwell was a magnificent showman despite a terrible stutter. Ringo Starr was his drummer. In concert, Ringo sang about five number with Storm's band. They were known as the Roving Texans when Ringo joined the group. Although they were an excellent group, Rory Storm and the Hurricanes failed to achieve chart success. Some of their songs are included on **This Is The Mersey Beat** LPs. When they were signed to a Parlophone recording contract, Brian Epstein produced their single of "America" from West Side Story. The group broke up. Later, Storm achieved some success as a disc jockey. Then his life took a bizarre turn. His dad died and he returned home from his job in Amsterdam to console his mother. In 1972 Storm was found dead with his mon. They had committed suicide through pills and alcohol.

Taylor, Alistair: When Taylor was hired to work behind the counter of Brian Epstein's NEMS record depart, he began a lengthy career with the Beatles. He was Brian's first assistant and witnessed the signing of the contract between Epstein and the Beatles. After Epstein's death he was hired in in London to fix problems. He became known as "Mr. Fix-It." there is a poster of Taylor as a one-man band on an Apple poster which was designed to draw new talent. Although he had a long association with the Beatles, he never came back into the fold after Allen Klein fired him. In 1981 he auctioned a number of items from his personal collection at Sotheby's in Belgravia, London. A man of unusual intelligence and integrity, Taylor moved on to other pursuits. He has written an excellent book on his experiences.

Taylor, Kingsize: Edward Taylor was a gargantuan fellow with a marvelous r and b voice. As the lead singer of Kingsize Taylor and the Dominoes, he was a hit in Hamburg. By the 1970s he was a butcher in Southport. With the help of Allan Williams, Kingsize Taylor released an album in 1977 entitled: **The Beatles Live! At the Star Club in Hamburg, Germany: 1962**. It wasn't a hit and demonstrated that Williams had not lost his magic touch. He still couldn't make a profit.

That'll Be The Day: This song was recorded during the summer of 1958 at Percy Phillips Liverpool Studio. This tune surfaced in McCartney's video special "The Real Buddy Holly Story."

Thingumybob: This comedy series starred Stanley Holloway and McCartney wrote the theme song for this TV show. The Black Dyke Mills Band performed the song.

Thumbin' A Ride: This was a b side of a Coasters' record, and it was a part of McCartney's record collection. This July, 1960 song was recorded for ATCO and it was an obscure tune. In 1969 Paul resurrected it for Jackie Lomax. Rumor has it he recorded this song sometime just before his marriage. It was common for Paul to search through his record collection for songs to produce during the Apple era.

Till There Was You: This tune written for the American Broadway musical The Music Man was a favorite of McCartney. It was a staple of the Beatles' early performances. The best studio version was recorded in November, 1963 and was issued on the American **Meet The Beatles** LP.

Vegetable: This is a Beach Boy cut issued on the **Smile Smile** LP. Paul dropped in on a Beach Boy session and some feel that he had a hand in helping produce the song. Mike Love in a **Goldmine** interview stated that Paul sang background on "Vegetable." Love claims that McCartney played "Back In The U.S.S.R." for him in India, and he suggested to Paul that "what you ought to do is to talk about the girls all around Russia, the Ukraine, and Georgia. He was plenty creative not to need any lyrical help from me, but I gave him the idea for that little section." The next day McCartney returned and played bass on an unreleased version of "On Top of Old Smokey."

Vermouth, Apollo C: This was the name McCartney used when he appeared on the Bonzo Dog Doo Dah Band, "I'm The Urban Spaceman." When the single and album was released in America, Paul's name was leaked to the press in an attempt to break the band. They faded into obscurity but a few years later the band and the song were a cult item among collectors.

Webb, Bernard: This pseudonym was used by McCartney when he wrote "Woman" for Peter and Gordon. The song reached no. 21 on the charts and then Paul announced that he had written it. It was important to Paul to have chart songs without his name on them. So he developed a large number of pseudonym's.

We Can Work It Out: This McCartney song was allegedly inspired by his problems with Jane Asher. Those close to Paul dispute this conclusion and suggest that the song had another source. This tune has been recorded by such diverse artists as Johnny Mathis, Deep Purple, Petula Clark and Humble Pie.

Welch, Chris: For many years Welch was a reporter for **Melody Maker**, and he covered the rock music scene. He became a free lance writer and was the author of **Paul McCartney: The Definitive Biography**. "I think I would have enjoyed the book more if I could have been able to deal directly with Paul," Welch told Bill Harry.

Williams, Angela: The young widow who married Jim McCartney in 1964. The press has had a strong interest in the marriage. It appeared he be a happy one, despite Jim Mac being twenty years older than Angela. When Jim Mac McCartney died things got ugly between Paul and Angela. She wrote a series of newspaper stories, ghosted by Tony Barrow, and rumor has it that Paul never spoke to her again. The reported reason for McCartney's anger was that she went into the rock music management business using the McCartney name. Eventually, she left this business and reverted to her surname Williams.

Wooler, Bob: This Liverpool disc jockey, journalist and cartoonist was a driving force behind the Mersey Beat. As a compere, the American equivalent of master of ceremony, he helped to promote the Beatles. A close friend of Allan Williams, Wooler was living with Williams in the 1980s and continued to supply historical knowledge about the Liverpool music scene. He worked at the Cavern and introduced the Beatles more than any other compere. For a full description of Wooler's contributions, see **The Beatles: Untold Tales**

Yesterday: There is a solo demo of Paul's famous song that was auctioned for 520 pounds. It has not appeared in a bootleg fashion.

Sources: Bill Harry, **The McCartney File** (London, 1986) and

Bill Harry, **The Beatles Who's Who** (New York, 1982), **The 910 Magazine, Beatlefan, The Beatles Monthly, The Beatles Book, Goldmine, DISCoveries, Good Day Sunshine, Beatles Now, Melody Maker** and the **New Musical Express.** The selections are arbitrary and hopeful interesting ones. Personal sources include 129 interviews plus the expertise of Steve Marinucci, Lee Cotten, Mike Lefebvre, Fred Worth, David Leaf, Neal F. Skok and Dennis DeWitt.

CHAPTER SOURCES: AN ESSAY

I: PAUL'S YOUTH IN LIVERPOOL: A MUSICAL GENIUS NURTURED, 1942-1959

The material in chapter 1 on Paul McCartney's early life and his relationship to the Beatles was developed in a series of extensive interviews. In Liverpool Bob Wooler, Joe Flannery, and Allan Williams provided information on the early years. The relationship of the Beatles to the musical scene, Brian Epstein and the club appearances were the subject of Clive Epstein's reminiscences. The early concert and small club appearances were detailed by promoters Brian Kelley and Sam Leach. It was Leach who helped me sort through many of the key club dates and suggest which were the most important ones in the rise of McCartney's music. Eddie Hoover was an indefatigable source of anecdotes and conversation on Liverpool. Pete Best and his mother Mona provided some minor insights during a lengthy conversation. A number of hours with Charlie Lennon drinking beer in the Grapes yielded a great many details about John and Paul's relationship. Uncle Charlie also provided a tour of selected sites in Liverpool that John Lennon frequented.

There were a number of American musicians who influenced the Beatles and they provided hours of material. Marshall Lytle, a member of Bill Haley's Comets, talked about his tours with Haley and the success of the Jodimars. Mary Wells reminisced about her tours of Europe and her time in the Cavern relaxing with members of the Motown Review. Melody Jean Vincent recalled her dad Gene's fascination with the Beatles.

At the Los Angeles Beatlefest Billy J. Kramer and Mike McCartney answered questions about the Beatles' early days. A personal interview with Alistair Taylor which lasted for hours at the Beatlefest helped to ferret out much of the early relationship between Paul and the Beatles. In later portions of the book Taylor's reminiscences are examined on the business side. See Alistair Taylor with Martin Roberts, **Yesterday: The Beatles Remembered** (London, 1988).

In Hamburg Tony Sheridan spent a week taking me around the Beatles' haunts and sharing his encyclopedic knowledge of the early Hamburg rock scene. Horst Fascher, who was dubbed the Beatles bodyguard, is another important source in this book. He was able to unlock doors and open up people who had previously refused to talk about the Beatles. Corey at the Blockhutte was once again helpful in recalling Paul's youthful zeal. A brief telephone conversation with the late Bert Kaempfert explained   many of the key problems in recording the early

Beatles. He also explained the difficulty in selling early Beatle recordings.

In Hamburg Joseph Provenzano and David C. Sams helped to recreate the British Sailors Society and its influence upon young McCartney. Tom Shaka, an American entertainer living in Germany, helped in reconstructing this period.

There are a number of important books which contributed to this section. On the Beatles early years see Ray Coleman, **John Winston Lennon: 1940-1966** (London, 1984, Vol. 1) and Ray Coleman, **The Man Who Made The Beatles: An Intimate Biography of Brian Epstein** (N.Y.,1989). Coleman's books are carefully researched, his writing high level and the conclusions offer a great deal of thoughtful historical information.

A very useful work on McCartney's family and early Beatle years is Hunter Davies, **The Beatles** (N.Y.,1985; second revised edition). The Davies study provides in-depth analysis of each Beatle and a great deal of inside information on the growth of the Beatles. The material on Liverpool is also historically very sound and useful.

Although useful for quotes, Peter Brown's, **The Love You Make: An Insider's Story of The Beatles** (N.Y., 1983) is highly unreliable. During my research Clive Epstein and Alistair Taylor complained bitterly about the twisting of facts and misreporting of quotations. It was for this reason that Taylor wrote his memoirs. The English version of Alistair Taylor's reminiscence, differs slightly in format from the American. The American publisher took away the letter or diary aspect of the book and it is an excellent piece of work.

Bill Harry's, **The McCartney File: A Comprehensive Guide To His Life and Career** (London, 1986) is a very important compendium of information. The single most impressive guide to Beatle trivia information is Michael J. Hockinson, **Nothing Is Beatle Proof: Advanced Beatles Trivia For Fab Four Fanciers** (Ann Arbor, 1990).

Bill Harry, **Mersey Beat: The Beginnings of the Beatles** (London,1977) reprints old editions of the Liverpool music newspaper that helped to launch the Fab Four's local career. Also, see, H.V. Fulpen, **The Beatles: An Illustrated Diary** (London, 1983) for a useful compendium of dates, facts and other hidden items on the Beatles.

Johnny Rogan's, **Starmakers and Svengalis: The History of British Pop Management** (London,1988) is a major piece of scholarship which traces the influences of the key business managers in British rock history. It is a pioneering work which goes a long way to explaining the Beatles' successes and Paul McCartney's insecurities. Also, see, Howard A. DeWitt, **The Beatles: Untold Tales** (Fremont, 1985) for information on early English rock and roll history.

George Martin's, **All You Need Is Ears: The Inside,**

Personal Story of the Genius Who Created the Beatles (New York, 1979) is an important book in analyzing the emergence of McCartney and the Beatles. It also attests to Martin's enormous contribution to the Beatles' music.

Mark Lewisohn, **The Beatles: Twenty Five Years In The Life** (London, 1987) saved me from a number of factual errors. Lewisohn's book is a major research addition to Beatle lore. Also see,

Few rock stars possess a brother as talented as Mike McCartney. He is a well known photographer, musician, comedian, Beatlefest speaker and writer. See Mike McCartney, **Thank U Very Much: Mike McCartney's Family Album** (London, 1981) for important insights into the McCartney family.

For Paul's view of his life see, Paul Gambaccini, **Paul McCartney: In His Own Words** (New York, 1976).

For the impact of the Beatles upon 1950s rock stars I depended upon interviews with Chuck Berry and Bo Diddley. Also see, Howard A. DeWitt, **Chuck Berry: Rock N Roll Music** (Ann Arbor, 1985) and Frederic Dannen, **Hit Men: Power Brokers and Fast Money Inside The Music Business** (New York, 1990) for material on how the Beatles altered the business as well as the artistic side of American rock and roll music. The best book on the economics of rock and roll is Marc Eliot, **Rockonomics: The Money Behind the Music** (New York, 1989).

The background of American rock and roll music is important in assessing the British impact. See John A. Jackson, **Big Beat Heat: Alan Freed and the Early Years of Rock and Roll** (New York, 1991) for a pathbreaking book on roots rock music.

2: THE BEATLES' MUSICAL EMERGENCE, 1960-1962

The material in this chapter depends very heavily on than thirty in-depth interviews. On the Beatles early Liverpool years Bob Wooler, Clive Epstein, Joe Flannery, Allan Williams, Alistair Taylor, Mona Best, Pete Best, Sam Leach, Brian Kelley, Eddie Hoover, Willie Woodbine, Charlie Lennon, Eddie Porter, Connie O'Dell and Steve Phillips were of great help.

In Hamburg, German Tony Sheridan, Tom Shaka, Bert Kaempfert, Jurgen Vollmer, Bruno Koschmider, Jim Hawkes, Horst Fascher and Corey were helpful in reliving the early 1960s.

American rock artists Tommy Roe, Mary Wells, Donnie Brooks and Chris Montez recounted their early experiences with Beatlemania.

American rock and blues star Delbert McClinton provided a great deal of information about touring with the Beatles. McClinton was the harmonica player on Bruce Channel's "Hey! Baby," and he toured with the Beatles.

Melody Jean Vincent provided a great deal of information on her dad, Gene Vincent, and she was helpful in clearing up many interpretive problems.

Jimmy McCracklin, Oakland's blues legend, talked at length about how the white British acts helped black music to cross over in America in the early 1960s.

3: PAUL AND THE TWO PHASES OF BEATLEMANIA

The pages of **Melody Maker**, the **New Musical Express**, **Mersey Beat** and **Disc** were important in recreating the English side of Beatlemania. A group of American singers who talked to me over the years were important in this section. They include Tommy Roe, Donnie Brooks and Delbert McClinton.

In San Francisco KYA disc jockey Gene Nelson answered questions about the early impact of the Beatles upon American rock and roll. On the intrusion of the Beatles' into the San Francisco music scene Doug Garbo of Bill Graham Presents granted a lengthy interview as did Larry Catlin. They provided valuable information on local bands and their reaction to the Beatles.

Alistair Taylor provided a great deal of information about the rise of the Beatles and Brian Epstein's role in their affairs. Eric Burdon provided a brief interview while appearing in a Fremont record store in the 1980s.

In Liverpool Bob Wooler, Joe Flannery, Allan Williams, Brian Kelly, Eddie Hoover, Clive Epstein, Charlie Lennon, Mona Best, Pete Best, Willie Woodbine and Sam Leach were helpful. In Hamburg Horst Fascher and Tony Sheridan recalled the early days.

Mark Naftalin, the original keyboardist with the Paul Butterfield Blues band, offered a number of important insights into how the Beatles changed American rock and roll music. Paul Butterfield, Elvin Bishop and Charlie Musselwhite offered ideas on the influence of the Beatles upon the American music scene.

At the Beatlefests held in Los Angeles Billy J. Kramer and Mike McCartney answered questions from the audience that helped in preparing this book.

Alf Bicknell, the Beatles' chauffeur from 1964-1966, provided a wealth of information on the early days. Tim Hudson, the first British disc jockey in Los Angeles, was helpful in recalling the early years. See Hudson's book, **From The Beatles To Botham: And All the B...s... In Between** (London, 1990) for a hilarious look at the rock music industry and the Beatles. This is a gem of a book that has been overlooked because of lack of distribution in the United States.

An interview with Roy Plomley helped to place the Beatles

into the mainstream of British music. Plomley was a British disc jockey who conceived the popular Desert Island Disco program. for forty years this program influenced British musical tastes. It was Plomley who played the music of Gene Vincent, Little Richard, Elvis Presley and other early American rock artists who influenced the Beatles. Paul was the only Beatle to appear on the show. On Saturday, January 30, 1982 Paul selected eight records and in a magnanimous gesture Paul selected John Lennon"s "Beautiful Boy" as the record he would keep. Plomley recalled this story with a tear in his eye.

Bill Osterloh, San Francisco Police Department, provided important insights into the Beatles last concert.

In a lengthy interview at the Great America Amusement Park in 1984, Mary Wells provided over two hours of personal anecdotes about the Beatles. Her comments were amplified by interviews with Martha Reeves.

Michael Braun, **Love Me Do: The Beatles' Progress** (London, 1964) is an extraordinary book by an American sociology student completing graduate work in England. This literate look at the Beatles' early years provides important insights into McCartney's personality.

When the Beatles arrived on the American rock and roll scene it was at an appropriate time. For an analysis of this point see, Charles Shaar Murray, **Crosstown Traffic: Jimi Hendrix and the Rock 'n' Roll Revolution** (New York,1989), pp. 15-22.

A series of lengthy telephone conversations with David Leaf helped to clarify Brian Wilson's role in influenced McCartney's song writing.

Jimmy McCracklin, an Oakland based blues singer, offered his impressions of how the Beatles changed the music business. It is McCracklin's opinion that the Beatles opened up many obscure black artists to white American audiences. The Beatles recorded McCracklin's hit "The Walk" but never released it.

A television clip from the January 3, 1964, "Jack Parr Show" helped evaluate the early American reaction to the Beatles.

4: SGT. PEPPER'S LONELY HEARTS CLUB BAND

Howard A. DeWitt, "Sgt. Pepper-A Turning Point," **DISCoveries**, volume 5, number 1, January, 1992, pp. 22-24 is a condensed version of this chapter.

For help with the American side of the story Doug Garbo of Bill Graham Presents was helpful. A brief telephone interview with Bill graham in 1985 was important to many of the non-Beatle parts of this chapter.

James Sauceda's, **The Literary Lennon** (Ann Arbor,1983)

was useful in analyzing John Lennon's approach to the **Sgt. Pepper's Lonely Hearts Club Band** LP. This book was written by a Ph.D. who possessed literary as well as musical tools in analyzing the Beatles.

Interviews with Clive Epstein, Bob Wooler, Joe Flannery, Alistair Taylor and Tony Sheridan aided in preparing this chapter.

William McCoy and Mitchell McGeary, **Every Little Thing: The Definitive Guide to Beatles Recording Variations, Rare Mixes and Other Musical Oddities, 1958-1986** (Ann Arbor, 1990) was of enormous help in analyzing the **Sgt. Pepper's Lonely Hearts Club Band** LP.

David Leaf helped to explain the influence of Brian Wilson's song writing upon the **Sgt. Pepper** album.

5: A NEW ERA, JANUARY-FEBRUARY, 1968

The lengthy reminiscences of Clive Epstein on business decisions shaped much of this chapter. Bob Wooler filled in details on the personal relationship between Lennon and McCartney. On the Beatles struggle with the **White Album** Joe Flannery contributed some tidbits as did Billy J. Kramer, Eddie Hoover and Tony Sheridan

Tony Barrow, "The Man Behind The Beatles' Empire," **The Beatles Book**, May 1991, pp. 4-8 was important in assessing Brian Epstein as was Ray Coleman, **The Man Who Made The Beatles: An Intimate Biography of Brian Epstein**, chapters 6-9. Also see, Alistair Taylor, **Yesterday: The Beatles Remembered** for an intelligent look at Brian Epstein's virtues and faults.

Richard DiLello, **An Insider's View Of The Beatles: The Longest Cocktail Party** (New York, 1972) is the best book on the Apple experiment. Also valuable is Peter McCabe and Robert D. Schonfeld, **Apple To The Core** (London, 1972).

The **London Daily Mirror** was an important source for intelligent reporting on the Beatles.

Douglas Garbo of Bill Graham Presents was a key source on the San Francisco years.

On McCartney see, "Fab Maca: The Truth" **Melody Maker**, 54, December 1, 1979, p. 10 for a cranky look at the business Beatle. See Geoffrey Giuliano, **Blackbird: The Life and Times of Paul McCartney** (New York, 1991), chapter 6 for a biography that fails to delineate the importance of Apple. Giuliano's shoddy research and ill conceived narrative misses the significance of the Apple business venture. In fact, Giuliano has only four page references to Apple and he describes the incident as an afterthought. For an understanding of Apple within McCartney's life see Chet Flippo, **Yesterday: The Unauthorized Biography of Paul McCartney** (New York,1988), chapter 10. Although devoting only one chapter to the Apple experiment, Flippo's biography treats the business side nicely. Chris Welch, **Paul McCartney: The Definitive Biography** (London, 1984) has very little material on Apple but is a useful biography. Chris Salewicz, **McCartney: The Definitive Biography** (New York, 1986) is an interesting and well written book, but, unfortunately, it has only ten references to Apple. Yet, Salewicz provides important biographical insights into Paul's life.

For the Apple Scruffs contribution see, Carol Bedford, **Waiting For The Beatles: An Apple Scruff's Story** (London,1984).

David Leaf, **The Beach Boys And The California Myth** (New York, 1978) is a brilliant book which suggested what the Beatles and Beach Boys had in common. Peter Brown's, **The Love You Make** provided some of the material for this chapter, but Clive Epstein during a series of interviews in 1983 took exception to the accuracy of the Brown book. Epstein's corrections are included in the context of this chapter.

For an insightful look at the collaboration between the two Chief Beatles see, Deryck Cooke's, "The Lennon-McCartney Songs, in Elizabeth Thomson and David Gutman, editors, **The Lennon Companion: Twenty-five Years of Comment** (New York,1987), pp. 109-113.

6: A PERIOD OF REORGANIZATION

George Harrison, **I Me Mine** (London,1980) provides a wealth of information on the Apple experiment, the relationship between McCartney and the other Beatles, and the general tensions which destroyed the group.

Bob Wooler provided important comments on the differences between the Beatles, Clive Epstein remembered the organizational problems at Apple and Alistair Taylor recalled his role in the early days of corporate reorganization.

Derek Taylor's books, **As Time Goes By** (London, 1974), **Fifty Years Adrift** (London, 1984) and **It Was Twenty Years Ago Today** (New York, 1987) provide insight into the Apple years and the Beatles in general.

McCabe and Schonfeld, **Apple To The Core**, pp. 63-120 was valuable in assessing this period of corporate activity.

A telephone interview with Lillian Roxon established some key facts about McCartney and the Beatles useful to this chapter. Michael Bloomfield during a 1977 interview in Mill Valley talked about his relationship with Linda McCartney and demonstrated surprising knowledge of the Beatles' music. Mark Naftalin offered some insights into the New York rock scene and the influence of blues upon late 1960s rock and roll.

The pages of **Melody Maker, New Musical Express** and **Disc** were helpful in recreating this period.

Joe Flannery provided some insights into the nature of the English music business and Sam Leach recalled the tension that he saw developing within the Beatles' ranks.

7: A GLOBAL AFFAIR, JUNE-JULY, 1968

See the one chapter on McCartney in Francie Schwartz, **Body Count** (San Francisco, 1972). The Francie Schwartz story was developed through interviews with Bob Wooler, Alf Bicknell, a series of Apple scruffs, Alistair Taylor, Clive Epstein and Jeff Simmons of the Frank Zappa band.

Lillian Roxon offered some second hand observations about Francie Schwartz and the staff at Abbey Road Studio kindly shared their private thoughts with me on the matter.

The influence of Bob Dylan was important on the Beatles and during the Francie Schwartz interlude his career seemed to guide Schwartz. For Dylan's importance see, Bob Spitz, **Dylan: A Biography** (New York,1989), pp. 288-289;

The influence of Frank Zappa and Van Morrison is another key part of this period in Beatle history. See Howard A. DeWitt, **Van Morrison: The Mystic's Music** (Fremont, 1983) and Michael Gray, **Mother! Is The Story of Frank Zappa** (New York, 1985). Dylan, Morrison and Zappa's influences are strong in the Francie Schwartz period in that they influenced dress, manners, morals and the approach to rock and roll music. The Beatles, like most everyone, were subject to their trends.

Tommy Roe talked about the New York rock scene as did Clive Epstein. Mark Naftalin recalled his experiences playing at the Fillmore East with the Paul Butterfield Blues band and helped me to set the stage for this chapter. Michael Bloomfield during a 1977 interview in Mill Valley provided the first perspective on the Beatles from a blues musician.

Paul Vincent, formerly a disc jockey at KMEL in San Francisco provided some important insights into Bob Dylan. Vincent played an interview that he had completed with Dylan and provided a great deal of insight into the time period covered in this book. Don West, a San Jose, California disc jockey, provided a great deal of San Francisco rock music history.

8: IN PROGRESS: THE WHITE ALBUM

Clive Epstein discussed the lengthy development of the **White Album**. Equally important is Mark Lewisohn, **The Beatles Recording Sessions** (New York, 1988). Lewisohn's fine book sets straight many of the arguments over the **White Album**. It also contains an extraordinary interview with Paul McCartney which was useful in preparing this book.

Pete Shotton and Nicholas Schaffner, **John Lennon: In**

My Life (New York, 1983) offer some important insights into this album's recording and production. There are also significant comments on the relationship between Paul and John during this time.

Max Weinberg's, **The Big Beat-Conversations With Rock's Great Drummers** (Chicago, 1984) is an important book in analyzing the **White Album.**

For important material relating to the **White Album** see, for example, Charles Avlerson, "The OBE: Lennon's Soul Redeemed," **Rolling Stone**, No. 49, December 27, 1969; Paul Lawrence, "I Am A Very Nervous Character: An Interview With George Martin About Producing the Beatles and Other Things," **Audio**, May, 1978; and Jann Wenner, "Beatles," **Rolling Stone**, No. 24, December 21, 1968.

On the **White Album**, see, for example, "Beatles Record busting LP May Be All-time Biggest," **Rolling Stone**, No. 24, December 21, 1968; Brigitta, "Mother Nature's Synthesizers," **Hit Parader**, July, 1969; Marilyn Doerfler, "Analyzing The Beatles," **Tiger Beat**, April, 1969 and

The London Board of Trade contains annual reports for twelve years for the Maclen (Music) Ltd. Company and these records were useful in the preparation of this book.

On McCartney's legal problems see Flippo, **Yesterday: The Unauthorized Biography of Paul McCartney**, chapter 11; Eliot, **Rockonomics**, chapter 15; George Tremlett, **Rock Gold: The Music Millionaires** (London, 1990 passim and Norman, **Shout: The True Story of the Beatles**, pp. 346-97.

Parts of the Apple Corps. Inc. records from the U.S. Apple Group were available. The U.S. Apple Group is the Apple Corps. Inc., which is a solely owned indirect subsidiary business of the Apple Corps Ltd. and is an intermediate holding company for Apple Records Inc. (California), Apple Records Inc. (New York), Apple Music Publishing Inc. and Apple Films Inc. A small number of documents were available through other sources and contributed greatly to understanding the Apple business mentality.

Willie Woodbine recalled his days with the Beatles from his second hand store in Liverpool. While not as lucid as some, Woodbine did provide some interesting leads.

9:INTENSITY IN THE STUDIO

The business side of the Beatles career was explained by Clive Epstein and Alistair Taylor. Bob Wooler speculated on the in-fighting amongst the boys. Tony Sheridan talked about the visits to Hamburg and how the Beatles reflected on their recording problems.

In Liverpool a bootleg tape of Paul conversing with his lawyers in 1988 explained many of the business and artistic problems which plagued the Beatles. A series of interviews with Clive Epstein in 1983 established that Paul had deep feelings for John but could not work with him. Clive suggested that Lennon's drug abuse bothered McCartney, and he found himself perplexed at making this statement. "I think that John was going over the end is what Paul said to me," Clive remembered. "I never pursued his statement."

The recording logs at Abbey Road Studio for August, 1988 were provided by a sympathetic employee and they were instrumental in writing this chapter.

The London Board of Trade contains annual reports for twelve years for the Maclen (Music) Ltd. Company and these records were useful in the preparation of this book.

Mark Lewisohn's magnificent, **The Beatles: Recording Sessions** took the mystery out of the period of intensity which created **The White Album**. Equally brilliant is the work of L.R.E. King. Not only has King deflated many of the myths surrounding Beatle music, he has also offered an in-depth analysis of bootleg recordings, see L.R.E. King, **Fixing A Hole: A Second Look At The Beatles' Unauthorized Recordings** (Tucson, 1989)

10: PAUL IN CONTROL

Ray Coleman, **The Man Who Made The Beatles: An Intimate Biography of Brian Epstein** contained important insights into Paul's relationship with Epstein and the Beatles. Clive Epstein filled in a number of areas not covered in Coleman's superb biography.

The music press notably **Disc**,. the **New Musical Express** and **Melody Maker** provided some important clues to McCartney's emergence in Beatle affairs. **Rave** and **Nineteen** were magazines which helped to understand this period. The **London Evening News**, the **London Evening Standard**, the **London Daily Mail**, the **London Daily Mirror**, the **London Evening Telegraph** and the **Liverpool Daily Post** were helpful in ferreting out little details. Even the **London Times** had a few tidbits on the Beatles.

Peter Brown's, **The Love You Make**, was important to this chapter despite its bias. For eight years I have benefited from comments made by guests at the Los Angeles Beatlefest. In this chapter some remarks made by Mike McCartney, Billy J. Kramer, Ray Coleman, Alistair Taylor, Sam Leach and Alf Bicknell have answered questions essential in understanding McCartney.

11: THE WHITE ALBUM AND GET BACK

Clive Epstein was an important source for the recordings. Alistair Taylor's comments helped with the general atmosphere.

Mark Lewishon's, **The Beatles Recording Sessions** and George Martin, **All You Need is Ears**, offer a wealth of information on this important transitional point.

A pioneering look at John Lennon's career which was helpful in this chapter was Jon Wiener, **Come Together: John Lennon In His Time** (New York, 1984). Wiener, a political science professor, explains a great deal about the Beatles' cultural and financial differences. Also see, Robert Christgau and John Piccarella, "Portrait of the Artists As A Rock and Roll Star," in Jonathan Cott and Christine Doudna, The **Ballad of John and Yoko** (New York, 1982).

An interview in Seattle with Jeff Simmons formed the basis for the material on Frank Zappa. David Leaf provided important material on the Beach Boys.

For authorship of Beatle songs see, William J. Dowlding, **Beatlesongs** (New York, 1989). Dowlding's valuable book suggests the degree of authorship for each Beatle song and it was a useful tool for this book. A pioneer attempt to analyze the Beatles' songs and still a highly regarded book is Mark Wallgren, **The Beatles On Record** (New York, 1982). Wallgren's book remains a tour de force in analyzing the Beatle sound.

William Mann, "The New Beatles Album," in Thomson and Gutman, editors, **The Lennon Companion**, pp. 152-154.

12: THE FIRST NAIL IN THE BEATLES COFFIN

This chapter depended heavily upon Clive Epstein. He freely talked about the period and elaborated on many key points. Sgt. Bill Osterloh of the San Francisco Police Department was an important source in analyzing the Beatles' last Candlestick Park show. Photographer Jim Marshall talked about taking pictures of the Beatles and he talked at length about the aura surrounding the Beatles.

Jimmy McCracklin, the legendary Oakland blues singer, gave freely of his time and helped me to place the Beatles in another perspective.

George Harrison's **I, Me, Mine** was useful in this chapter as were the Flippo and Welch biographies.

Ray Coleman's, **Lennon** was useful in this chapter. Interviews with Bob Wooler and Joe Flannery helped to flush out key points.

See Paul Gambaccini, **Paul McCartney: In His Own Words** (New York, 1975) for excellent quotes on this period.

Douglas Garbo and Bill Graham contributed non Beatle related material.

13: ANOTHER NAIL IN THE BEATLE COFFIN

For the problems with Northern songs, Allen Klein and business see, for example, "ABKCO, Beatles Widen Battle in U.S.-U.K. courts," **Variety**, No. 273 (November 28, 1973), p. 49; "Beatles' dispute Tying Up $9-Mil; No Reunion Seen," **Variety**, No. 273 (December 12, 1973), p. 47; "Beatles Still Clearing Up $$ Problems, Say Apple Mgr.," **Billboard**, No. 86 (March 16, 1974), p. 52; and "Beatles Still In Stalemate over How to Split Their Partnership Shares," **Variety**, No. 267 (May 24, 1972), p. 51.

Philip Norman, **Elton John** (New York, 1991) contains one of the best explanations of Dick James and his publishing empire. It was very useful in explaining the problems with James, Allen Klein and Apple.

Clive Epstein was the main source for this chapter as he was in the midst of the financial dealings. A brief telephone conversation with Lee Eastman yielded a feeling for the atmosphere surrounding the negotiations over the Beatles' financial difficulties.

The Maclen Music Ltd. Company Files at the London Board of Trade were useful in reconstructing Beatle business problems. A smattering of the New York records of the Apple Company were obtained from a sympathetic employee.

The British Court system has very detailed records of the proceedings over the Apple Music venture, the Beatles other contracts and the various business differences which resulted in this period. See, for example,

While not commenting directly on the law suits, Alistair Taylor provided some important background information for this chapter. The level of hostility and the lack of direction at Apple were amplified in conversations with a dozen former employees who requested anonymity.

George Tremlett, **Rock Gold: The Music Millionaires** is a useful look at the Beatles' fiscal problems.

Irwin and Debbie Unger, **Turning Point: 1968** (New York,1988) is an important source in analyzing non-rock music events.

BIBLIOGRAPHICAL ESSAY: PAUL McCARTNEY

BIOGRAPHICAL STUDIES OF McCARTNEY

Chet Flippo, **Yesterday: The Unauthorized Biography of Paul McCartney** (New York, 1988) is the best biography of Paul to date. Malcolm Doney, **Lennon and McCartney** (London, 1981) is a brief but scholarly work on the two Beatles. Howard Elson, **McCartney: Songwriter** (London,1986) was a useful tome with many insights.

Paul Gambaccini, **Paul McCartney In His Own Words** (London, 1976) collects a great deal of material on McCartney's life through interviews, newspaper articles and off the wall sources. Alan Hamilton, **Paul McCartney** (London, 1983) was brief and vague on important parts of Paul's career.

The strangest biography of McCartney is Chris Welch, **Paul McCartney: The Definitive Biography** (London,1984). The Welch book is well written but highly selective and certainly not definitive. The portions on Apple and the **White Album** were weak and erratic.

Bill Harry, **The McCartney File** (London, 1986) is a collection of facts and trivia useful to any biographical study.

Chris Salewicz, **McCartney** (New York,1986) is a vastly underrated book which provides a terrific view of Paul's career.

The worst McCartney biographies are Geoffrey Giuliano, **Blackbird: The Life and Times of Paul McCartney** (New York, 1991) and the brief volume by George Tremlett, **The Paul McCartney Story** (London,1975). Giuliano's book written with Denny Laine is a woeful tale of excess which bears little resemblance to the truth.

Mike McCartney's books, **Mike Mac's White and Blacks** (London,1986) and **Thank U Very Much: Mike McCartney's Family Album** (Liverpool,1984) are superior books of photography and family history. In fact, Mike McCartney's work is better than most of the biographical tomes.

Paul McCartney, **Paul McCartney: Composer/Artist** (London, 1981) is a useful guide to McCartney's song writing and the manner in which he uses language. A study of the songs was helpful in parts of this book.

For Paul's 1968 trip to Hollywood see, Tony Bramwell, "With Paul To Hollywood,", **The Beatles Book**, no. 61 (August, 1968), pp.7-10.

BEATLE RECORDING AND TOURING BOOKS

Mark Lewisohn's, **The Beatle Recording Sessions** (New York, 1988) was the single most important book in understanding the Beatles studio work. Also see Leiwsohn's excellent, **The Beatles Live!** (New York, 1986) and **The Beatles: 25 Years In The Life** (London, 1987).

H.V. Fulpen, **The Beatles: An Illustrated Diary** (London, 1982) is a generally overlooked book which contains a wealth of information.

In analyzing Beatle tunes see William J. Dowlding, **Beatlesongs** (New York, 1989); Mark Wallgren, **The Beatles On Record** (New York, 1982) and J.P. Russell, **The Beatles On Record** (New York, 1982).

GENERAL STUDIES OF THE BEATLES

Philip Norman, **Shout: The True Story of the Beatles** (London, 1981) remains the best book on the group. Peter Brown and Steven Gaines, **The Love You Make: An Insider's Story of the Beatles** (New York, 1983) is an insipid tome with some good material. Generally, the Brown book fails the clarification test.

Hunter Davies, **The Beatles: The Authorized Biography** (2nd edition, New York, 1985) is a marvelous look at the group.

On John Lennon see an excellent volume by Ray Coleman, **Lennon** (New York, 1984). This marvelous book tells you everything one needs to know about John Lennon. For the book which tells you more than you need to know see Albert Goldman, **The Lives of John Lennon** (New York, 1988). A sophisticated look at Lennon's politics is Jon Wiener, **Come Together: John Lennon In His Time** (New York, 1984).

On the Beatles early years see Howard A. DeWitt, **The Beatles: Untold Tales** (Fremont, 1985): Allan Williams and William Marshall, **The Man Who Gave The Beatles Away** (New York, 1975); Pete Best and Patrick Doncaster, **Beatles: The Pete Best Story** (New York, 1985). An excellent interview with Best is Jeff Tamarkin, "Pete Best: A Beatle Talks," **Goldmine**, 77 (October, 1982, pp. 6-8.

Pete Shotton and Nicholas Schaffner, **John Lennon In My Life** (New York, 1983) is a useful book on the early years.

Michael Braun, **Love Me Do: The Beatles' Progress** (London, 1964) is the work of an American graduate student studying in England. It traces the rise of Beatlemania better than any book on the market and deserves a reprint.

The worst book on the Beatles is Bob Cepican and Ali Waleed, **Yesterday Came Suddenly: The Definitive History of the Beatles** (New York, 1985).

On Brian Epstein see Ray Coleman, **The Man Who Made The Beatles: An Intimate Portrait of Brian Epstein** (New York, 1989). Coleman's marvelous study is light on the Apple years but otherwise is an excellent book. Also see Brian Epstein, **A Cellarful of Noise** (London,1981).

See George Martin, **All You Need Is Ears** (London, 19709) for insights from the Beatles' producer.

Sam Leach, **Follow The Merseybeat Road** (Liverpool,1983) is a fine book by a promoter close to the Beatles.

Tim Hudson, **From The Beatles To Botham, And All The B...S... In Between** (London,1990) is a book by a London DJ who took Los Angeles radio by storm in the 1960s. This is a funny, interesting and insightful book. In the same vein is Alf Bicknell and Garry Marsh, **Baby, You Can Drive My Car** (London, 1989). Bicknell was the Beatles chauffeur from 1964 to 1966, and this book is a delight. It comes with a tape and should be snapped up by collectors in its present limited edition format.

Terence J. O'Grady, **The Beatles: A Musical Evolution** (Boston, 1983) is a serious look at the Beatles music. Particularly useful was O'Grady's analysis of the **Sgt. Pepper** and **White Album**.

An early book by Nicholas Schaffner, **The Beatles Forever** (London,1978) remains one of the strongest studies of the Beatles.

Ray Coleman, "Beatles 65," **Melody Maker**, No. 40 (March 27, 1965), p. 9 is one of the best interviews with Paul McCartney. Also see, Paul Gambaccini, "A Conversation With Paul McCartney," **Rolling Stone**, No. 295 (July 12, 1979), pp. 39-46 and Gambaccini's, "McCartneys Meet Press: Starting All Over Again, **Rolling Stone**, No. 137 (June 21, 1973).

A post script to Paul's Beatle past is "Paul, Beatles' Battles Behind Him, in Control as Biz, Band Blossoms," **Variety**, No. 297 (January 9, 1980), p. 188.

On Beatle differences, see, "Ex-Beatle Paul McCartney Writes To The MM With The Last Word on a Well Worn Subject," **Melody Maker**, No. 45 (August 29, 1970), p 29.

John Gabree, "The Beatles In Perspective," **Down Beat**, No 34 (November 16, 1967), pp 20-22 is useful in analyzing the impact of the Fab. Four in America.

Jeff Greenfield, "They Changes Rock, Which Changed Culture, Which Changed Us," **New York Times Magazine** (February 16, 1975), pp 12-13 is useful in analyzing the Beatles impact. Also see, Fred Kirby, "The Beatles Have Gone, But International Music Hasn't Been Same Since British Wave Hit in the Early '60s," **Variety** (January 3, 1979), p. 167. The same theme on an academic note is examined in Geoffrey Marshalo, "Taking The Beatles Seriously: Problems of Text," **Journal of Popular Culture**, 3 (Summer, 1969), pp. 28-34.

For the Beatles influence upon American intellectuals see, Richard Poirier, "Learning From The Beatles," **Partisan Review**, 34 (Fall, 1967), pp. 526-46.

Tony Barrow, "Money and the Beatles," **The Beatles Book**, No. 152 (December, 1988), 14-16 explains in a cursory fashion why the Beatles never carried any money and points to the general confusion in the Fab Four's finances.

For an interesting examination of people close to the Beatles see, Tony Barrow, "With A Little Help From Their Friends," **The Beatle Book**, No. 66 (October, 1981), pp. iii-viii and pt. 2 No. 67 (November, 1981), pp. vi-viii.

STUDIES OF THE APPLE CORP.

Richard DiLello, **The Longest Cocktail Party** (Chicago, 1972) is an excellent history of Apple by the so called house hippie. He has gone on to a major Hollywood career as a writer and producer, and this book is a marvelous look at the late 1960s. Also see,

Pete McCabe and Robert D. Schonfeld, **Apple To The Core** (New York, 1972) is an important and well written book on the Apple experiment. Also see, J. Sippel, "Apple Sues Capitol For $16 Million," **Billboard**, 91 (June 9, 1979), p. 10 and "Stockholder-- Fans Snag Beatles" Music Company Sale," **Variety**, 257 (February 4, 1970), p. 2.

See Carol Bedford, **Waiting For The Beatles: An Apple Scruffs Story** (London, 1984) for a sensitive and insightful portrayal of the girls attempting to get close to the Beatles. Element of pathos are woven together with sentimental facts in Bedford's excellent book.

Francie Schwartz, **Body Count** (San Francisco, 1972) was the first kiss and tell book. With one chapter on McCartney there is little important information in this self serving volume.

Paul Ackerman, "Beatles Doing Own Things: Paul Quits," **Billboard**, No. 82 (April 18,1970) is important in assessing the post-Beatle McCartney. The hostility to McCartney is examined in a post Apple article by J. Atlas, "Together Again: John, George and Ringo," **Melody Maker**, no. 48 (March 31, 1973), pp. 8-9.

For a post mortem on the Beatles see, "Black Flag Flies at Beatles' Headquarters," **Variety**, no. 260 (August 19,1970), p. 50. Another critical article is Rick Johnson and J. Kordosh, "Who Needs the Beatles," **Creem** (April,1983), pp. 61-65.

TRIVIA BOOKS, GUIDES TO RECORDING RARITIES AND GENERAL INFORMATION STUDIES

The best Beatle trivia book is Michael J. Hockinson, **Nothing Is Beatleproof: Advanced Beatles Trivia For Fab Four Fanciers** (Ann Arbor, 1990). Equally valuable is Tom Schultheiss, **The Beatles: A Day In The Life** (New York, 1981). The Schultheiss volume is an excellent list of Beatle dates.

Bill Harry, **The Beatles Who's Who** (New York,1982). is an important collection of information on people close to the Beatles.

Pioneering works that set a high standard for Beatle discographical information are two books by Harry Castleman and Walter J. Podrazik, **All Together Now: The First Complete Beatles Discography, 1961-1975** (Ann Arbor, 1976) and **The Beatles Again?** (Ann Arbor,1977).

Tim Riley, **Tell Me Why: A Beatles Commentary** (New York,1988) is a fine album by album and song by song analysis of the Fab Four.

On John Lennon's music see John Robertson, **The Art and Music of John Lennon** (New York, 1990).

For a guide to Liverpool see Mike Evans and Ron Jones, **In The Footsteps of the Beatles** (Liverpool,1981). For trivia information on the Beatles that is dated but useful see Goldie Friede, Robin Titone and Sue Weiner, **The Beatles A-Z** (New York, 1980).

Charles Reinhart, **You Can't Do That: Beatle Bootlegs and Novelty Discs** (Ann Arbor, 1981) is an important book in dealing with bootlegs. A more recent volume on bootlegs is the pathbreaking study by L.R.E. King, **Fixing A Hole: A Second Look At The Beatles' Unauthorized Recordings** (Tucson,1989). For rarities, strange mixes and useful oddities see, William McCoy and Mitchell McGeary, **Every Little Thing: The Definitive Guide to Beatles Recording Variations, Rare Mixes and Other Musical Oddities, 1958-1986** (Ann Arbor, 1990).

See Nicholas Schaffner, "Every Little Thing: The Story Behind **Rarities**, The New Beatles LP," **Trouser Press**, 51 (June, 1980), pp. 14-18.

A fascinating book for the audiophile is David Schwartz, **Listening To The Beatles: An Audiophile's Guide to The Sound Of The Fab Four, Volume I, Bootlegs and Singles** (Ann Arbor, 1990).

An interesting guide to collecting Beatle materials is Barbara Fenwick, **Collecting The Beatles: An Introduction and Price Guide To Fab Four Collectibles, Records, and memorabilia** (Ann Arbor,1982). A unique area of Beatle collectibles is described in Richard M. Hochadel, "Yellow Matter Custard: Collecting Beatles Broadcasts," **Goldmine** (October, 1982), pp. 10-15.

Brian Southall, **Abbey Road** (London,1982) is an important book in understanding the Beatles recording studio.

An interesting early article on Beatle recording rarities LPs is Mike Callahan, "The Beatles--Rarities," **Goldmine**, No. 50 (July,1980), pp. 26-27.

Marc A. Catone, editor, **As I Write This Letter: An American Generation Remembers The Beatles** (Ann Arbor, 1982) is an interesting look at the reaction to the Beatles.

Paul McCartney

ACKNOWLEDGMENTS

This book is the result of a great deal of cooperation from those close to Paul McCartney. Among the individuals who helped were Tony Sheridan, Horst Fascher, Bob Wooler, Joe Flannery and most significantly Clive Epstein. Without the late Mr. Epstein's help this book would have been impossible. Alistair Taylor provided key points on Apple as did Mike McGear and Billy J. Kramer at Beatlefest talk sessions. While I didn't interview McGear directly, he answered many questions in casual conversation.

Others in Liverpool who were particularly helpful include Sam Leach, Brian Kelly and Eddie Porter at the Cavern.

My good friend Jimmy McCracklin spent hundreds of hours talking about the blues and rock music. He had more to do with this book than he knows, and I thank him for his friendship and support. Other blues artists who helped were Lowell Fulson, Willie Dixon and Barbara Lynn. They all confirmed the Beatles importance to expanding the music market. Elijah Perkins and Tina Mayfield are good friends who listened to my ideas. Mark Naftalin provided material on the blues and the late Michael Bloomfield spent hours talking about the 1960s.

American performers Mary Wells, Delbert McClinton, Tommy Roe, Jeff Simmons, Chuck Berry, Bo Diddley and Guitar Mac helped with the research.

My good friend Lee Cotten spent hours with me discussing the scope of the book. David Leaf listened to my questions and provided encouragement. Professor B. Lee Cooper of Olivet College was a constant source of information, and his own research aided this study.

Jerry Osborne at **DISCoveries** and Marc Bristol at **Blue Suede News** are owed a debt of gratitude for publishing my earlier efforts and supporting my research.

Mike Lefebvre, Neal Skok and Bruce Wilson criticized my manuscript. The errors are mine, the corrections theirs. Thanks.

The cover was designed by Mick Gray with his usual skill, and Jim McCue provided advice on pictures and typesetting.

The title of the book was supplied by Mark Lapidos. For almost a decade Carol and Mark Lapidos have had me appear as a speaker at the Beatlefest. I appreciate the opportunity. They have had no input into the material in this book and all errors rest with the author, the truth as well.

My wife Carolyn and my children Melanie and Darin listened to endless nights of computer chatter and were strongly supportive of the project.

AUTHOR PROFILE

Howard A. DeWitt is Professor of History at Ohlone College, Fremont, California. His academic specialties are California History, Political Science and the History of Rock and Roll Music. Since the 1970s he has taught a radio course on the history of rock music over KOHL 89.3 FM in the San Francisco area. He is featured regularly on radio and television talk shows.

After receiving a B.A. from Western Washington State University, DeWitt completed an M.A. degree at the University of Oregon and the Ph.D. at the University of Arizona.

Growing up in Seattle he was a concert promoter and presented such legendary locals acts as the Frantics, Ron Holden and the Playboys, Little Bill and the Bluenotes among others in concert at Parker's Ballroom and the Eagles Auditorium.

He is a regular speaker at the Beatlefest and is active in the Popular Culture Association lecturing on the incorporation of rock and roll history into college courses.

Working as a rock and roll journalist DeWitt's articles have appeared in **DISCoveries**, **Blue Suede News** and **Record Profile Magazine**.

The author of fourteen books, including **The Beatles: Untold Tales**, DeWitt is presently working on two new studies: **Del Shannon: Stranger In Town** and **My Search For the Beatles**.
OTHER ROCK AND ROLL BOOKS BY HOWARD A. DEWITT
THE BEATLES: UNTOLD TALES (HORIZON BOOKS, 1985)
BEATLE POEMS (HORIZON BOOKS, 1987)
CHUCK BERRY: ROCK 'N' ROLL MUSIC (POPULAR CULTURE INK., 1985)
JAILHOUSE ROCK: THE BOOTLEG RECORDS OF ELVIS PRESLEY (WITH LEE COTTEN) (POPULAR CULTURE INK., 1983)
SUN ELVIS: ELVIS PRESLEY IN THE 1950S (POPULAR CULTURE INK., 1992)
VAN MORRISON: THE MYSTIC'S MUSIC (HORIZON BOOKS, 1983)

INDEX

Vee Jay Records, 55
Vermouth, Apollo C., 171
Vincent, Gene, 20-22, 26, 31, 168
 W
Warhol, Andy 94
Weberman, A.J., 124
Weiss, Nat, 88, 121-122
Welch, Chris, 144
Wenner, Jann, 89-90
While My Guitar Gently Weeps, foreign sales, 187
White Album
    Chart positions of, 183-184
    Early progress of 137-148
Wilde, Marty,31, 49
Williams, Allan, 7-8, 28, 30-42, 44
Wilson, Brian, 88
Wilson, Prime Minister Harold, 64-65
Winwood, Steve, 120
Wolfe, Tom, 125, 176
Wonderwall (Movie), 95, 105, 183
Woodbine, Willie, 35
Wooler, Bob, 7-9, 15, 22, 27, 29, 42, 44-47, 51, 55-56, 69, 75, 77-80, 152, 174, 191
    Approached To Manage The Beatles, 41
Why Don't We Do It In The Road (song), 170
 Y
Yer Blues, 159-160
 Z
Zappa, Frank, 85, 179-180
Zec, Donald, 59

4 7 0 6